endorsed for BTEC

KU-235-146

BTEC Tech Award

HEALTH AND SOCIAL CARE

Student Book

Brenda Baker
Colette Burgess
Elizabeth Haworth

Pearson

Published by Pearson Education Limited, 80 Strand, London, WC2R 0RL.

www.pearsonschoolsandfecolleges.co.uk

Copies of official specifications for all Pearson qualifications may be found on the website: qualifications.pearson.com

Typeset by Tech-Set Ltd, Gateshead

Picture research by Alison Prior
Cover illustration by Jo Goodberry, NB Illustration

First published 2017

19
10 9 8 7

British Library Cataloguing in Publication Data
A catalogue record for this book is available from the British Library

ISBN 978 1 292 20092 7

Printed in the UK by Bell & Bain Ltd, Glasgow

Acknowledgements
We would like to thank Heather Higgins for her invaluable help in the development of this course.

The publisher would like to thank the following for their kind permission to reproduce their photographs:

(Key: b-bottom; c-centre; l-left; r-right; t-top)

123RF.com: kisiel 171, stockbroker 34, Wavebreakmedia 144; **Alamy Stock Photo**: ALAN EDWARDS 99l, Alex Segre 198, Antony Nettle 150, Art Directors & Trip 173, Asia Imaegs Group Ltd 201, Blend Images 133, David Bagnall 153l, Don Despain 77r, Dwight Cendrowski 89, Homer Sykes 187, Indiapicture 11b, Janine Wiedel Photography Library 147, MBI 61, Nikolaenko Viacheslav 78, Novarc 154, PhotoAlto 44, Rob Bartee 175, Simon Balson 13, Stock Connection Blue 25, Tetra Images 162, ZUMA Press Inc 72**; Fotolia.com**: bokan 191, Dan Kosmayer 179, Gelpi 9r, jlcst 153r, Rawpixel.com 196, Wavebreakmedia 136; Getty Images: Bowdenimages 127, BSIP 105, Jamie Grill 202, Monkey Business Images 3, vm 180; **Pearson Education Ltd**: Jules Selmes 9c, 18, 65, 118; **Photofusion Picture Library**: John Birdsall 98; **Shutterstock.com**: Alexander Raths 58, Anna Lurye 77l, Armi Parikh 11t, Berna Namaglu 106, Blue Earth Planet 167, daeseaford 80, Diego Cervo 69, Dimitry Kalinovsky 94, goodluz 17, Ilike 46, Jessmine 9l, Monkey Business Images 4, 165, pathdoc 117, romevip_md 66, Vladimir Mucibabic 83.

All other images © Pearson Education

The author and publisher would like to thank the following individuals and organisations for permission to reproduce the following materials:

Figure 3.3 Public Health England in association with the Welsh government, Food Standards Scotland and the Food Standards Agency in Northern Ireland; Figure 3.10 reprinted from World Health Organization (WHO) air pollution in cities database 2014; Figure 3.14 *Edexcel GCSE Health and Social Care Evaluation Pack*, Elizabeth Haworth and Andy Ashton © 2009, reprinted and electronically reproduced by permission of Pearson Education Limited; Figure 3.15 and Table 3.7 reprinted from World Health Organization (WHO) BMI classification, retrieved from http://www.assessmentpsychology.com/icbmi.htm; Figure 3.18 Cancer causes: the full list from Cancer Research UK, republished with the permission of Cancer Research UK, retrieved from https://www.theguardian.com/news/datablog/2011/dec/07/cancer-causes-list#data; Figure 3.19 from *'Smoking, drinking and drug use among young people in England in 2010'*, page 85 (July 2012), reproduced with the permission of the Institute of Alcohol Studies.

Contents

About this book

This book is designed to support you when you are taking a BTEC Tech Award in Health and Social Care.

About your BTEC Tech Award

Congratulations on choosing a BTEC Tech Award in Health and Social Care. This exciting and challenging course will introduce you to the health and social care sector. By studying for your Award you will gain the important knowledge, understanding and skills that are the foundations for working in this area. This will include many of the skills that are used by health care professionals on a day-to-day basis, such as assessing people's health and wellbeing and designing individualised health care plans. You will also learn about health care services and the importance of care values, with the opportunity to apply these in realistic scenarios.

How you will be assessed

You will be assessed in two different ways. Components 1 and 2 are assessed through internal assessment. This means that your teacher will give you an assignment brief and indicate to you the deadline for completing it. The assignment will cover what you have been learning about and will be an opportunity to apply your knowledge and skills. You teacher will mark your assignment and award you with a grade. Your third assessment (for Component 3) will be an external assessment. This will be a task that is set and marked by Pearson. You will have a set time in which to complete this task. The task will be an opportunity to bring together what you have learnt in components 1 and 2.

About the authors

Brenda Baker

Brenda worked in the early years and primary sectors before becoming a lecturer in health, care and early years education. She always enjoyed seeing students putting into practice what they had learned in class when she visited and observed them in their work placements. Brenda went on to become Head of School for Health and Social Care in an FE college. She has helped to develop new health and social care courses and has contributed to a number of books, teacher resources and student revision guides.

Colette Burgess trained as a nurse and now works as a college lecturer, supporting young people studying to work in the health and social care sector or applying to take their studies further at university. She also works with apprentices, their assessors and the teacher education and first aid teams at the college. Colette says that the best part of her job is seeing the successes of the young people who work hard and will be the health and social care practitioners of the future. Colette has written many books and other resources for students and teachers of health and social care courses.

Elizabeth Haworth has taught in schools all her working life, starting by teaching physics, then science and maths, and finally health and social care. She is always pleased when she meets ex-pupils who are now successfully working in the health and social care sector. Elizabeth looks for ways to extend her knowledge of the sector through her own life experiences and through volunteering, for example as a member of the advisory board for a group of children's centres and as a primary school governor. Her writing career started in 2000 and she has written many books and teaching resources on health and social care, as well as online resources for careers education, and often visits pupils on work placements in the sector.

How to use this book

The book has been designed in a way that will help you to easily navigate through your course. Each component from the course is covered in a separate chapter that makes clear what you are learning and how this will contribute to your assessment. There are opportunities for you to test your understanding of key areas, as well as activities that will challenge and extend your knowledge and skills. You will get the most from this book if you use each feature as part of your study. The different features will also help you develop the skills that will be important in completing your assignments as well as preparing you for your external assessment.

Features of the book

This book is designed in spreads, which means that each pair of facing pages represents a topic of learning. Each spread is about 1 hour of lesson time. Your teacher may ask you to work through a spread during a lesson or in your own time. Each spread contains a number of features that will help you to check what you are learning and offer opportunities to practise new skills.

Getting started A short activity or discussion that will introduce you to what you will be covering in the lesson.

Activity These will help you learn about the topic. You may be asked to work in pairs, groups or on your own.

Did you know? These include interesting facts that relate to what you're learning about.

Link it up This indicates where what you're learning about is covered in another part of the course.

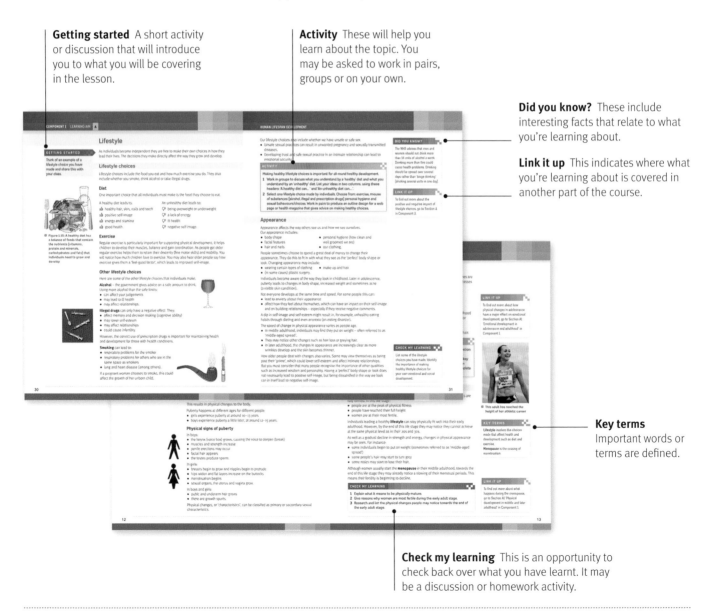

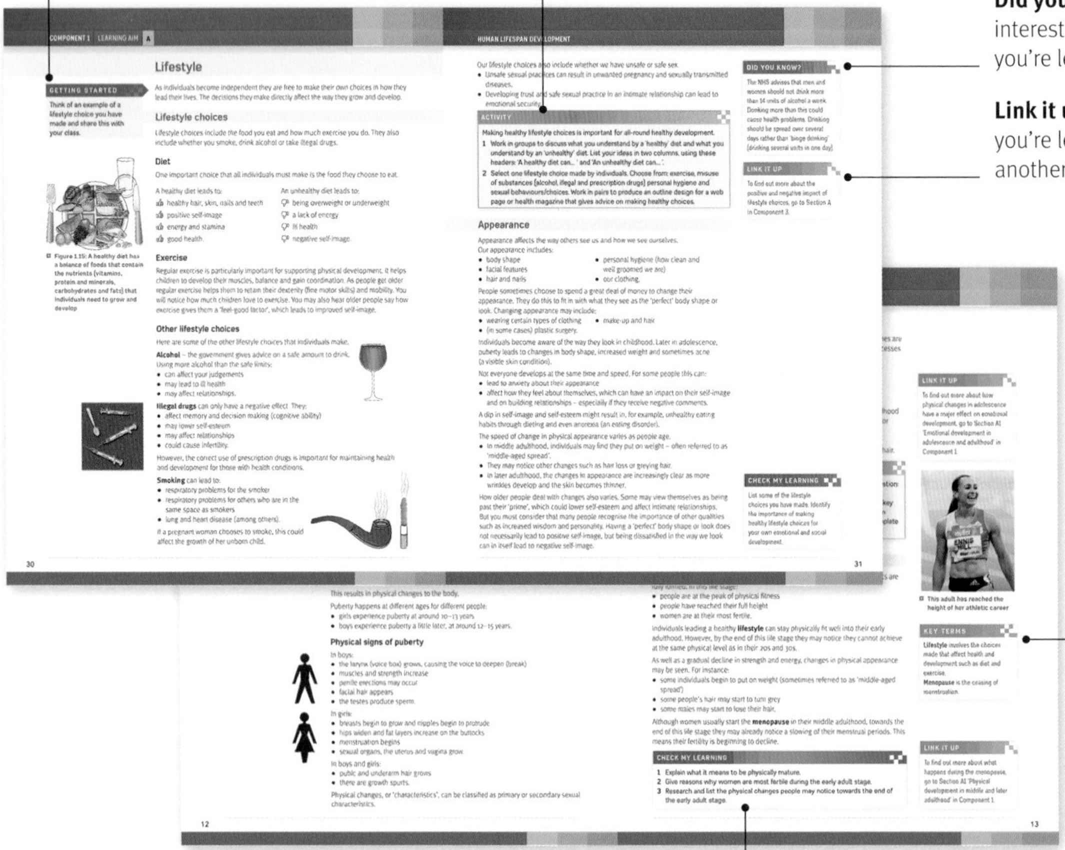

Key terms Important words or terms are defined.

Check my learning This is an opportunity to check back over what you have learnt. It may be a discussion or homework activity.

At the end of each learning aim there is a section that outlines how you will be assessed and provides opportunities for you to build skills for assessment.

Checkpoint This feature is designed to allow you to assess your learning. The 'strengthen' question helps you to check your knowledge and understanding of what you have been studying, while the 'challenge' questions are an opportunity to extend your learning.

Take it further This provides suggestions for what you can do to further the work you've done in the practice assessment.

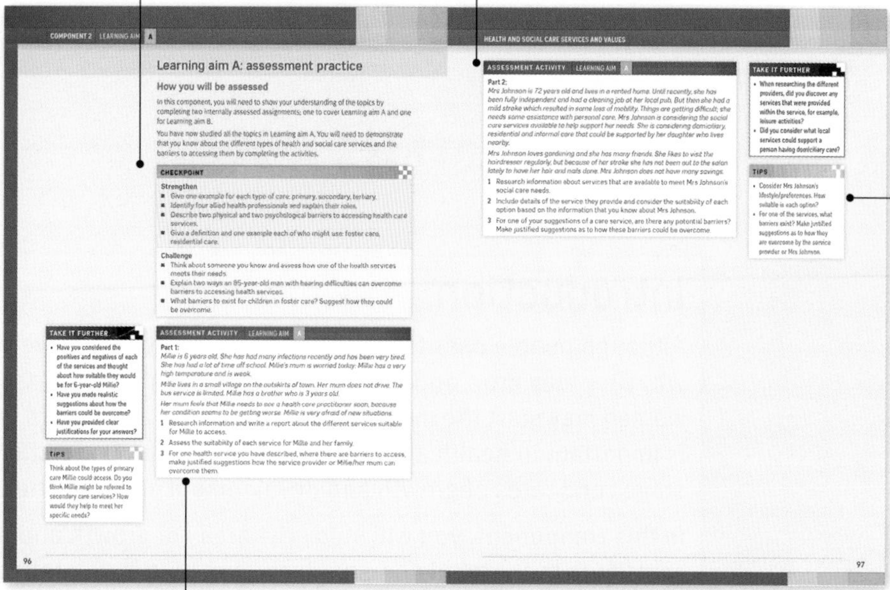

COMPONENT 2 LEARNING AIM A

Learning aim A: assessment practice

How you will be assessed

In this component, you will need to show your understanding of the topics by completing two internally assessed assignments; one to cover Learning aim A and one for Learning aim B.

You have now studied all the topics in Learning aim A. You will need to demonstrate that you know about the different types of health and social care services and the barriers to accessing them by completing the activities.

CHECKPOINT

Strengthen
- Give one example for each type of care: primary, secondary, tertiary.
- Identify four allied health professionals and explain their roles.
- Describe two physical and two psychological barriers to accessing health care services.
- Give a definition and one example each of who might use: foster care, residential care.

Challenge
- Think about someone you know and assess how one of the health services meets their needs.
- Explain two ways an 85-year-old man with hearing difficulties can overcome barriers to accessing health services.
- What barriers to exist for children in foster care? Suggest how they could be overcome.

TAKE IT FURTHER
- Have you considered the positives and negatives of each of the services and thought about how suitable they would be for 6-year-old Millie?
- Have you made realistic suggestions about how the barriers could be overcome?
- Have you provided clear justifications for your answers?

TIPS

Think about the types of primary care Millie could access. Do you think Millie might be referred to secondary care services? How would they help to meet her specific needs?

ASSESSMENT ACTIVITY LEARNING AIM A

Part 1:
Millie is 6 years old. She has had many infections recently and has been very tired. She has had a lot of time off school. Millie's mum is worried today: Millie has a very high temperature and is weak.

Millie lives in a small village on the outskirts of town. Her mum does not drive. The bus service is limited. Millie has a brother who is 3 years old.

Her mum feels that Millie needs to see a health care practitioner soon, because her condition seems to be getting worse. Millie is very afraid of new situations.

1 Research information and write a report about the different services suitable for Millie to access.
2 Assess the suitability of each service for Millie and her family.
3 For one health service you have described, where there are barriers to access, make justified suggestions how the service provider or Millie/her mum can overcome them.

96

HEALTH AND SOCIAL CARE SERVICES AND VALUES

ASSESSMENT ACTIVITY LEARNING AIM A

Part 2:
Mrs Johnson is 72 years old and lives in a rented home. Until recently, she has been fully independent and had a cleaning job at her local pub. But then she had a mild stroke which resulted in some loss of mobility. Things are getting difficult; she needs some assistance with personal care. Mrs Johnson is considering the social care services available to help support her needs. She is considering domiciliary, residential and informal care that could be supported by her daughter who lives nearby.

Mrs Johnson loves gardening and she has many friends. She likes to visit the hairdresser regularly, but because of her stroke she has not been out to the salon lately to have her hair and nails done. Mrs Johnson does not have many savings.

1 Research information about services that are available to meet Mrs Johnson's social care needs.
2 Include details of the service they provide and consider the suitability of each option based on the information that you know about Mrs Johnson.
3 For one of your suggestions of a care service, are there any potential barriers? Make justified suggestions as to how these barriers could be overcome.

TAKE IT FURTHER
- When researching the different providers, did you discover any services that were provided within the service, for example, leisure activities?
- Did you consider what local services could support a person having domiciliary care?

TIPS
- Consider Mrs Johnson's lifestyle/preferences. How suitable is each option?
- For one of the services, what barriers exist? Make justified suggestions as to how they are overcome by the service provider or Mrs Johnson.

97

Tip A hint or tip that will help you with your assessment.

Assessment Activity This is a practice assessment that reflects the style and approach of an assignment brief. In Component 3, tasks in the assessment activity features will be similar to those you should expect in your external assessment.

COMPONENT

01 Human Lifespan Development

Introduction

Although people pass through the same life stages, have you ever wondered why they may grow and develop at different rates? For example, some women may start the menopause in their 40s and others in their mid-50s. It is important in health and social care to have an understanding of the usual stages and rates of growth and development and how they may be affected.

In this component, you will study the areas of growth and development that contribute to the whole person, including physical, intellectual, emotional and social. You will reflect on physical, social and economic factors that are part of everyone's life, such as relationships with family, and consider the ways they may impact on each area of growth and development.

As people progress through their lives they will encounter life events. These events may be expected, such as starting school, and usually result in a positive effect on development. Other events, such as an accident or death, come as a shock and are likely to have a negative effect on development. You will explore the role of different sources of support to help people cope with life events and consider their effectiveness in helping people to adapt.

LEARNING AIMS

In this component you will:

A	Understand human growth and development across life stages and the factors that affect it
B	Investigate how individuals deal with life events.

Main life stages

GETTING STARTED

Alice will be 90 this year. What do you think is the most logical way to break down her life course into six stages of growth and development? Discuss and compare your ideas with a partner.

Life stages are a guide to help you understand the usual patterns of growth and development. There are six stages, and people living to older age pass through each stage.

An older person will pass through each of the six life stages

What happens at each life stage?

KEY TERMS

Characteristic is something that is typical of people at a particular life stage.
Life stages are distinct phases of life that each person passes through.

During the course of a person's life, they will progress through a number of life stages. Looking at development as a number of stages, and understanding their **characteristics**, helps health and social care workers to understand how people usually develop at each life stage and recognise developmental problems or delay.

Think about each life stage for Alice, who will celebrate her 90th birthday this year. She has lived through six **life stages**. Imagine how her growth and development have changed over each of those life stages.

- In her first life stage, Alice would have experienced rapid growth and development. She was totally dependent on her parents for all her needs.
- In her second life stage, Alice developed her physical skills further. This helped her to do things for herself so she became more independent.
- In her third life stage, Alice went through physiological and emotional changes as she progressed towards adulthood.
- In her fourth life stage, Alice reached physical maturity. This was her most fertile stage (when her body was ready to have babies) so it was the time she started a family.
- In her fifth life stage, Alice noticed changes in her body systems and appearance: her hair started to go grey, and her menstrual cycle became less frequent and gradually stopped. Towards the end of this stage she noticed the effects of ageing, her energy levels dropped, her skin became less smooth and she developed wrinkles.
- In her sixth and final life stage, the effects from her fifth life stage have now become more noticeable. Alice experiences more difficulty in carrying out tasks and recalling information.

These six life stages above and in Table 1.1 are a useful guide. However, you need to remember that everyone is unique. They may not show characteristics of the next life stage at exactly the same age.

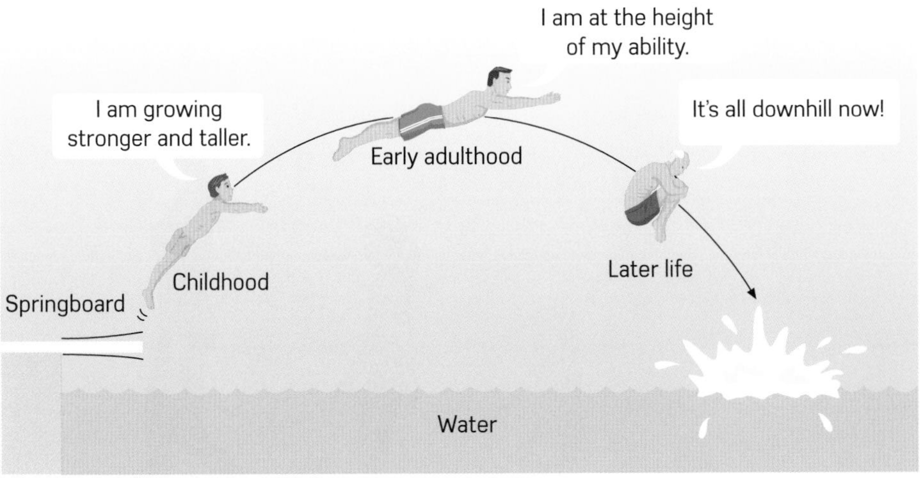

■ **Figure 1.1: Does this model help to explain Alice's life course?**

ACTIVITY

1 Watch a video clip showing how people develop across the course of life and think how this could be separated into six life stages. Label each life stage.

2 Using your knowledge and the video clip, note at least one key characteristic of each life stage.

3 Compare your ideas with others. Give reasons for your decisions about each life stage.

4 Draw a timeline to illustrate your own life. Separate it into the actual life stages you must study in this component. What developmental changes have you experienced so far? What changes do you expect in the future?

DID YOU KNOW?

The oldest person in the UK was Gladys Hooper. She died in 2016, aged 113.

■ **Table 1.1: You will need to learn about development across each of these life stages**

Age group	Life stage	Developmental progress
0–2 years	Infancy	Still dependent on parents but growing quickly and developing physical skills
3–8 years	Early childhood	Becoming increasingly independent, improving thought processes and learning how to develop friendships
9–18 years	Adolescence	Experiencing puberty, which brings physical and emotional changes
19–45 years	Early adulthood	Leaving home, making own choices about a career and may start a family
46–65 years	Middle adulthood	Having more time to travel and take up hobbies as children may be leaving the home; beginning of the ageing process
65+ years	Later adulthood	The ageing process continues, which may affect memory and mobility

CHECK MY LEARNING

1 Watch the video clip again. What other key characteristics at each of the life stages can you identify? Add them to your notes.

Areas of growth and development

GETTING STARTED

Can you identify each area of development?

KEY TERMS

Growth describes increased body size such as height, weight.
Classification involves grouping similar things into a category.
Development involves gaining new skills and abilities such as riding a bike.

Human **growth** is broken into four **classifications**, or areas of **development**. Here you will learn about these areas and how they relate to the life stages.

Growth does not happen smoothly. Infants reach half their adult height at between 2 and 3 years old. Growth continues into adolescence when there are growth spurts. By early adulthood people have reached their full height.

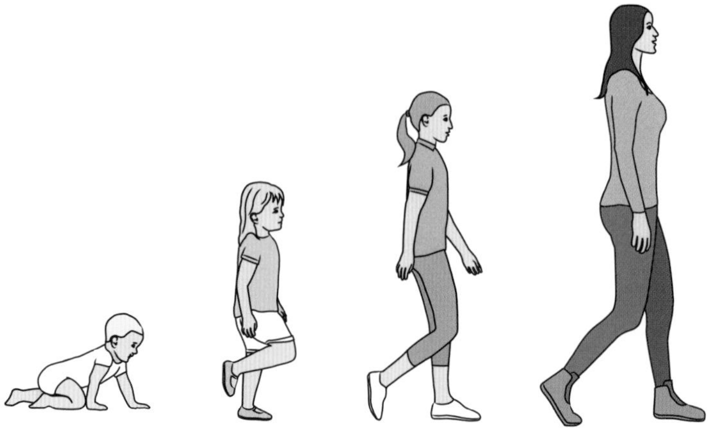

Figure 1.2: Our different stages of growth from infancy to adulthood

DID YOU KNOW?

The word PIES is an acronym for the four areas of development: physical, intellectual, emotional and social. It will help you to remember these classifications.

Development continues throughout life, although in the early stages development is at a faster rate. In later adulthood, development begins to slow down.

Development takes place in each of the following four areas:

- physical
- intellectual
- emotional
- social.

ACTIVITY

1 Write down the four classifications (areas) of development.

2 In groups, discuss what each classification means when describing a person's development. Agree on a definition and share your ideas with the class.

3 Return to the lifeline you drew in the previous lesson. Make links from each of your examples to each area of growth and development.

4 Look at photographs of people of different ages. You can use newspapers or magazines for this. Describe what is happening in each photograph and identify the area of development each photograph illustrates. Can you identify the life stage of each individual?

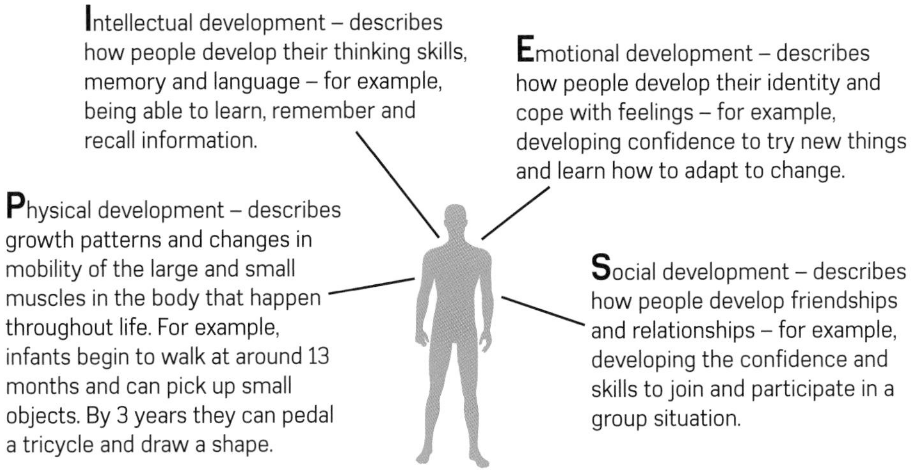

Intellectual development – describes how people develop their thinking skills, memory and language – for example, being able to learn, remember and recall information.
Emotional development – describes how people develop their identity and cope with feelings – for example, developing confidence to try new things and learn how to adapt to change.
Physical development – describes growth patterns and changes in mobility of the large and small muscles in the body that happen throughout life. For example, infants begin to walk at around 13 months and can pick up small objects. By 3 years they can pedal a tricycle and draw a shape.
Social development – describes how people develop friendships and relationships – for example, developing the confidence and skills to join and participate in a group situation.

Figure 1.3: PIES – try to learn what P, I, E and S each stand for

Although you will study each area of development, it is important to remember that these four areas make up the whole person. Development does not happen separately; it is linked across all four areas. For example, without good communication skills (linked to your intellectual development) it is difficult to build friendships (linked to your social development).

CHECK MY LEARNING

1 Draw a large 'pie' shape and divide it into four equal pieces. Write one area of development in each quarter.
2 Identify two or three examples of how a person develops in each area.

DID YOU KNOW?

Intellectual development is sometimes referred to as cognitive development.

Physical development – types

GETTING STARTED

Physical development is classified into two types: gross motor development and fine motor development.

Create a model using pipe cleaners or cut out a paper shape using scissors. Next, use your whole body to jump up and down or step up on a chair. Describe the muscles and skills that you use for each of these activities.

How we develop

Have you ever really concentrated on your physical activity? Have you noticed that sometimes you use different parts of the body – some large movements, and some very small movements? Take a look at Table 1.2, which gives more detail.

Table 1.2: Two types of physical development

Type of development	What it describes
Gross motor development	The skills acquired to control and coordinate large muscles – legs, arms and torso (trunk of body)
Fine motor development	The skills acquired to control and coordinate small muscles – hands, fingers and toes

DID YOU KNOW?

People lose height in later adulthood. By the time they are 80 years old, they may have lost as much as 5 cm. This is because of their change in posture (they may stoop) and compression on their spine.

In later adulthood, our joints become stiffer and our muscles weaker. This results in people becoming less mobile and losing the fine motor control they had in childhood.

ACTIVITY

All the activities you take part in involve your large and/or small muscles. For example, you may manipulate materials using finger muscles in art, but which muscles do you use in sport? Watch a video clip of adults taking part in physical activities.

As you watch, note:

- how each person is using large muscle groups – think about how they balance and how they coordinate movements
- how people use the small muscle groups – think about how they manipulate objects, grip them and use hand-eye coordination.

Early stages of development

Here are three key things to help you understand the early stages of physical development.

1. Top to toe

Development starts from the head down. Infants start by gaining control of their head before their back muscles and legs.

2. Inner to outer

Control starts from the body and moves out to the limbs, toes and fingers. Infants can control movements in their whole arm to reach out before they can use finger muscles to hold an object.

3. Same patterns at different rates

All infants and children pass through the same stages but they may do so at different ages. For example, some infants may walk at 11 months though others might not walk until they are 14 months.

At 3 months old, this infant is controlling their head and neck muscles

At 8 months old, this infant has gained control of their back muscles

At 12 months old, this infant has gained control of the large muscles in their legs

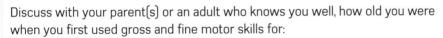

CHECK MY LEARNING

Discuss with your parent(s) or an adult who knows you well, how old you were when you first used gross and fine motor skills for:

- sitting without help
- crawling
- walking
- riding a bike
- controlling a pencil
- building with blocks.

Physical development in infancy and early childhood

GETTING STARTED

Use your 'Check my learning' activity in the previous lesson. Compare with a friend the ages you reached each new physical stage. You may have ridden a two-wheeler bike by the age of 5 but your friend may have been 6.

KEY TERMS

Infancy begins from birth to 2 years.

Infancy is a time of rapid growth and physical development. At birth, infants have little control of movement but by the age of 2 they can walk, run and climb.

Development of physical skills

The development of gross and fine motor skills is essential for infants' and children's health, learning and independence. Knowing the usual pattern of development helps professionals to support development. Take a look at Table 1.3 for some more details.

Table 1.3: Expected development of physical skills from birth up to 3 years

Age	Gross motor skills	Fine motor skills
Birth up to 6 months	Lifts up head and chest when lying on front at around 3 months At 5–6 months will roll over from back onto stomach	At 3 months can hold a rattle for a few moments By 5–6 months will reach out and hold a toy
6 months up to 12 months	Sits without help at around 8 months Can walk holding onto furniture at 11–12 months	At 6 months can grasp and pass an object from one hand to another By 9 months can grasp things between finger and thumb
12 months up to 18 months	Walks at around 13 months Climbs stairs by 18 months	At 12 months can pick up small objects in finger and thumb and hold a crayon to scribble with
18 months up to 2 years	Can kick and throw a large ball Can propel a wheeled toy	Builds a tower with blocks By 18 months can feed self with a spoon
2 years up to 3 years	At 2 years can walk upstairs At 2.5 years will jump off a low step	Draws lines and circles with a crayon Can turn pages of a book

The skills and abilities described at each stage are referred to as milestones. Milestones have been developed by:

- observing a large number of infants and children at different ages
- identifying the stage of development most of the children have reached.

Of course, all children are individual.

- Some do not reach milestones at the suggested ages.
- Others reach them earlier than expected.

ACTIVITY

1 Watch videos of infants at play. Note the physical skills used. Share your notes with a partner, and list all your examples under 'gross motor skills' or 'fine motor skills'. Discuss reasons for your choice.

2 Research gross and fine motor milestones for children aged 3 to 8 years.

- Produce a table with ages 3, 4, 5, 6, 7 and 8 years listed.
- Give at least one example of gross and fine motor skills for each age group.
- You could use examples from a video clip (teacher will advise), information from child development books and examples from this lesson.

Early childhood 3 to 8 years

At this stage children continue to make great progress in their physical skills.

- By the age of 5 years, children will have developed the physical skills needed for everyday activities – for example, dressing, washing and using a knife and fork. This helps them to become independent.
- By the age of 8 years, children will have good control, coordination and balance, which helps them to take part in physical games and sports.

Figures 1.4 and 1.5 give you some examples of physical development milestones in early childhood.

Can ride a tricycle at around 3 years; can ride a two-wheeled bicycle at around 6–7 years.

Can walk backwards and sideways at 3 years; can run on their toes by 5 years; can balance along a thin line by 7 years.

Can catch a large ball with two hands at 3 years; can bounce a ball at 4 years; can catch a small ball with one hand by 7 years.

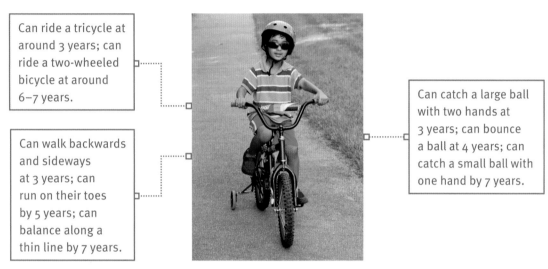

Figure 1.4: At ages 3–7, children generally have these gross motor skills

Can thread small beads at 4 years; can thread and use a needle to sew by 7–8 years.

Can build a short tower with cubes and make detailed models using construction blocks at 5 years.

Can hold a crayon to make circles and lines at 3 years; can copy letter shapes with a pencil by 4 years; can use joined-up writing by 6 years.

Figure 1.5: At ages 3–8, children generally have these fine motor skills

CHECK MY LEARNING

Observe infants and children in your own family or watch video clips (teacher can advise). Can you identify the gross and fine motor skills they are already using? Suggest activities to help them develop these gross and fine motor skills.

Physical development in adolescence and early adulthood

GETTING STARTED

What changes might parents/carers notice when their children move from childhood into adolescence? Think about physical and emotional development.

Adolescence is a time when there can be sudden physical and emotional changes. Parents often complain that their children become difficult and argumentative at this life stage. Why is this?

Adolescence 9 to 18 years

In your school you will have noticed there are sometimes huge differences in heights and builds of young people in the same class and the same age.

Young people notice many physical changes happening over a short period of time. Adolescents may appear not to grow for a while and then grow rapidly. Boys can grow as much as 8 cm each year. You may be tired of older relatives and friends saying, 'Haven't you grown!' There will be a noticeable change in body shape and size. As well as an increase in height:

- boys will become more muscular
- girls will find their hips widen.

This growth is linked to the onset of puberty.

Puberty

Puberty is a process towards sexual maturity, preparing adolescents for reproduction. It starts when hormones are released from the pituitary gland. Hormones send chemical messages to:

- the ovaries in girls
- the testes in boys.

This results in physical changes to the body.

Puberty happens at different ages for different people:

- girls experience puberty at around 10–13 years
- boys experience puberty a little later, at around 12–15 years.

Physical signs of puberty

In boys:

- the larynx (voice box) grows, causing the voice to deepen (break)
- muscles and strength increase
- penile erections may occur
- facial hair appears
- the testes produce sperm.

In girls:

- breasts begin to grow and nipples begin to protrude
- hips widen and fat layers increase on the buttocks
- menstruation begins
- sexual organs, the uterus and vagina grow.

In boys and girls:

- pubic and underarm hair grows
- there are growth spurts.

Physical changes, or 'characteristics', can be classified as primary or secondary sexual characteristics.

Primary sexual characteristics

These characteristics are present from birth but do not mature until sex hormones are released. These characteristics are essential for reproduction. They include processes such as:

- ovulation in girls
- the enlargement of the testicles and the production of sperm in boys.

Secondary sexual characteristics

These are physical characteristics and signs that indicate the change from childhood towards adulthood. They are not a necessary part of the reproductive system. For example:

- one of the first signs for girls is the development of breasts
- one of the first signs for boys is the growth at the base of the penis of pubic hair.

ACTIVITY

1 Carry out research on the physical changes adolescents experience during puberty. Identify the type of change. Is it a primary or a secondary sexual characteristic? Record your information.

2 With a partner, discuss the question: 'Why do athletes peak in early adulthood?' Then research the key physical milestones expected in early adulthood. Produce a template to record your information.

Early adulthood 19 to 45 years

By early adulthood, people are physically mature and their sexual characteristics are fully formed. In this life stage:

- people are at the peak of physical fitness
- people have reached their full height
- women are at their most fertile.

Individuals leading a healthy **lifestyle** can stay physically fit well into their early adulthood. However, by the end of this life stage they may notice they cannot achieve at the same physical level as in their 20s and 30s.

As well as a gradual decline in strength and energy, changes in physical appearance may be seen. For instance:

- some individuals begin to put on weight (sometimes referred to as 'middle-aged spread')
- some people's hair may start to turn grey
- some males may start to lose their hair.

Although women usually start the **menopause** in their middle adulthood, towards the end of this life stage they may already notice a slowing of their menstrual periods. This means their fertility is beginning to decline.

CHECK MY LEARNING

1 Explain what it means to be physically mature.
2 Give reasons why women are most fertile during the early adult stage.
3 Research and list the physical changes people may notice towards the end of the early adult stage.

LINK IT UP

To find out more about how physical changes in adolescence have a major effect on emotional development, go to Section A1 'Emotional development in adolescence and adulthood' in Component 1.

This adult has reached the height of her athletic career

KEY TERMS

Lifestyle involves the choices made that affect health and development such as diet and exercise.

Menopause is the ceasing of menstruation.

LINK IT UP

To find out more about what happens during the menopause, go to Section A1 'Physical development in middle and later adulthood' in Component 1.

Physical development in middle and later adulthood

GETTING STARTED

With a partner, discuss what you have learned about the possible physical changes towards the end of early adulthood. How do you think these changes will progress during middle adulthood?

People reach physical maturity at about age 19, but towards the end of this life stage they may notice the effects of ageing such as less stamina and muscle tone.

Middle adulthood 46 to 65 years

As people move into middle adulthood they begin to notice some effects of ageing even though they may stay active. This can be distressing for some individuals. They sometimes refer to their feelings about these changes as a 'midlife crisis'. Physical changes include greying of hair, and hair loss in men. People may put on weight, particularly if they exercise less but continue to eat and drink the same amount.

One of the main characteristics in middle adulthood for women is menopause – when menstruation ends and they can no longer become pregnant. Men may continue to be fertile throughout life but there is a decrease in sperm production in this life stage.

What happens during menopause

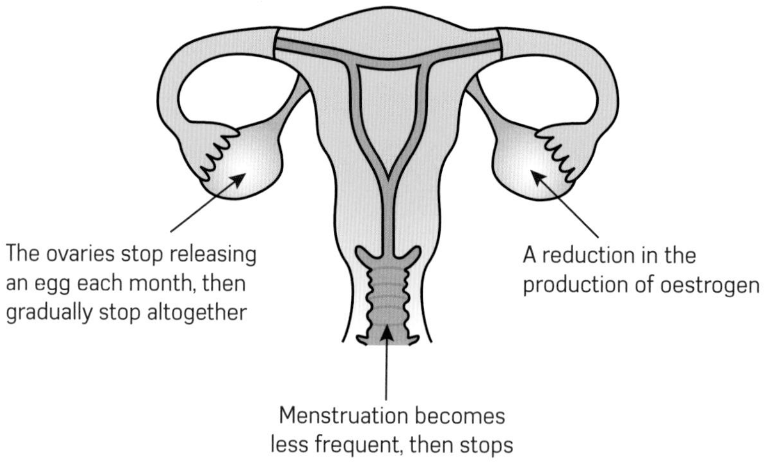
The ovaries stop releasing an egg each month, then gradually stop altogether
A reduction in the production of oestrogen
Menstruation becomes less frequent, then stops

Figure 1.6: Symptoms of menopause can include hot flushes, night sweats and lack of sleep. What effect might this have on a woman's wellbeing?

During menopause, the hormone oestrogen reduces. This causes the ovaries to slow down and gradually stop the release of eggs.

The reduction of oestrogen causes other physical effects such as problems with temperature regulation in the body. Women may notice 'hot flushes' and changes in mood. The health of skin, hair and nails can also be affected.

ACTIVITY

1 In groups, discuss the physical changes that people notice in middle adulthood. Research the process of menopause. At what age does it usually start? Print off or draw a diagram of the female reproductive organs. Use it to label physical changes in the woman's body and list other possible effects she may notice.

2 With a partner, research the possible effects of ageing. You could use health and social care resource books or the internet using sites such as Age UK or the NHS. Record the physical changes older people may notice.

Later adulthood 65+ years

The rate of the ageing process varies but everyone in later adulthood will notice some change in their:

- physical appearance
- physical ability.

Age also brings with it a higher risk of infection, which is likely to have more impact on the body of an older person.

Physical appearance

As well as losing some height with age, people's hair, skin and nails also show effects of ageing:

- women's hair may become thinner; men may lose most of their hair
- skin will lose elasticity and show lines and wrinkles
- nails may become more brittle or harder.

Motor skills

Mobility (the use of gross motor skills) will decline as muscles become weaker and joints become stiffer. People may find it harder to carry out tasks they used to do easily – for example, DIY or gardening.

Dexterity (fine motor skills) will also decline at this life stage. Tasks such as opening packets or changing a plug can gradually become more difficult. This does not mean people give up an active life. Many stay fit and healthy and adapt so they can continue to take part in sports, work or hobbies.

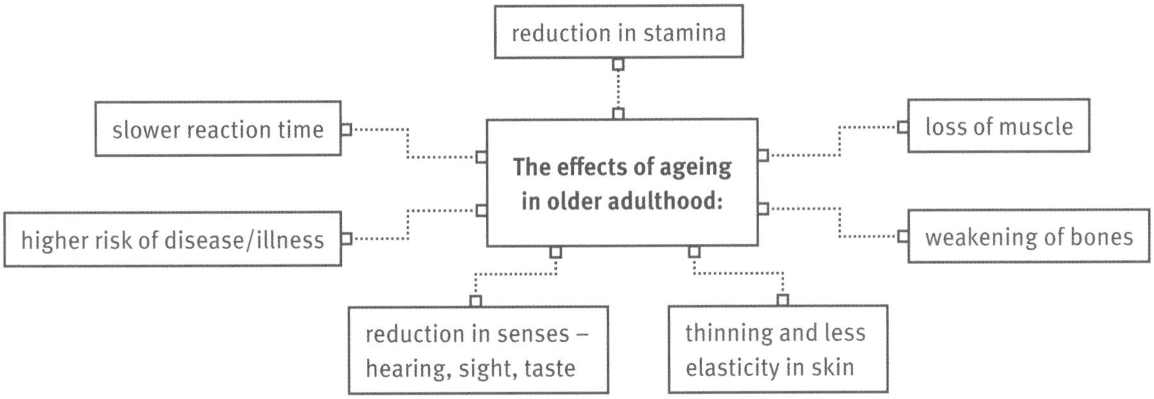

Figure 1.7: Later adulthood may bring new challenges

CHECK MY LEARNING

For homework, interview an older relative on the effects of ageing. Before you start, make a list of open-ended questions you could ask. Check with your teacher that the questions are appropriate.

Intellectual development

GETTING STARTED

When you work out problems in your maths lesson, what intellectual processes are you using? See if you can link the activities to the following terms: 'problem solving', 'abstract thought', 'creative thinking', 'memory' and 'recall'.

When we talk about intellectual development it can involve different aspects of our thought processes. These aspects are sometimes referred to as cognitive development.

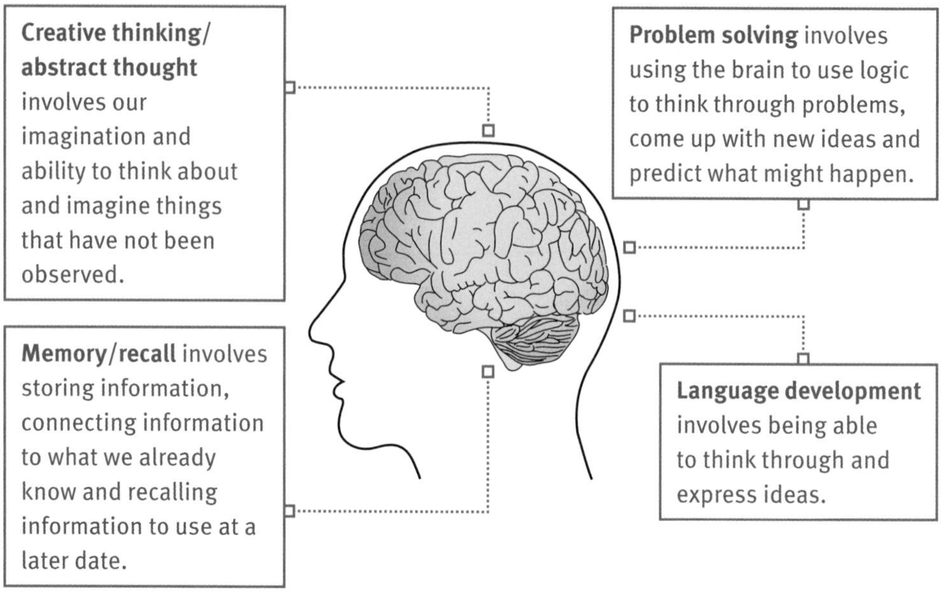

Creative thinking/abstract thought involves our imagination and ability to think about and imagine things that have not been observed.
Problem solving involves using the brain to use logic to think through problems, come up with new ideas and predict what might happen.
Memory/recall involves storing information, connecting information to what we already know and recalling information to use at a later date.
Language development involves being able to think through and express ideas.

Figure 1.8: Aspects of cognitive development

Infancy

At birth, infants' brains are already well developed. Infants use all their senses – touch, smell, taste and hearing – to learn about the world around them. Experiences and interactions with adults help infants to build connections in their brains so that by the time they are 12 months old their brains will have doubled in size.

Infancy is a time of rapid intellectual development.

- At 3 months, infants can remember routines and show excitement – for instance, when they hear the bath being prepared.
- At 9 to 12 months, infants are developing their memory. If you hide a toy under a blanket they will know it is still there and look for it. They will start to remember where things are kept that are important to them (for example, a drinking cup).
- At 12 months to 2 years, infants learn by watching and remembering what things can do. They will press buttons on toys to make them work and will know how to use a toothbrush.

Early childhood

At 3 to 4 years, children are becoming more inquisitive so they enjoy exploring objects and materials.

- They like to find out why things happen and ask lots of questions to satisfy their curiosity.
- They can think through simple problems such as ways to sort objects by colour or size.

From this stage, children learn through 'hands-on' experience. For example, a 5 year old will use apparatus that they can move and count with because they have difficulty working out problems in their head. (By around 7 years they will be able to work out simple 'abstract' mathematical problems without the use of counters.)

By 5 to 6 years, children's memory is becoming well developed which helps them to talk about things that have happened in the past and to anticipate what might happen in the future.

ACTIVITY

Work in your groups to research intellectual development across two life stages. Your teacher may allocate the life stages.

Produce a poster that illustrates development at your chosen stages. Consider development in relation to problem solving, abstract and creative thinking, memory and recall.

If you study the older age group, think about the process of loss of memory and recall.

Adolescence

This is a time when young people are being challenged and exposed to many new ideas and experiences.

Abstract thought is an important intellectual development in adolescence. Instead of the need for hands-on exploration, adolescents can use abstract thought processes to work out problems. By the end of this life stage young people can:

- think logically
- think through quite complex problems and come up with solutions.

In early adolescence, they may still find difficulty understanding the consequences of their actions. But in adolescence, they are able to understand situations from another person's point of view.

Being able to apply abstract thought helps adults to solve complex problems

Early and middle adulthood

By this stage in life, people will have gained a great deal of knowledge. They can use this to help solve new problems they come across in their personal and working life. They use their knowledge and experience to develop new ways of thinking.

Later adulthood

At this life stage, people continue to learn, often taking on new hobbies. Although they retain their level of intelligence, their speed of thinking will decline. This may affect people's ability to:

- think through problems
- make logical decisions.

One effect of ageing is the decline in memory – perhaps in recalling everyday events or names. This can be quite distressing. At this stage, some people can also be affected by dementia, which affects the function of the brain.

CHECK MY LEARNING

Present your posters to the whole group. Invite other students to ask you questions. If you are unsure of the answers you should carry out further research.

Language development

GETTING STARTED

With a partner, discuss ways that infants communicate before they begin to use words.

Language development is an aspect of intellectual development. Expressing your ideas (using language) helps you to develop your thought processes (intellectual development).

How language develops

Even before they can speak, infants are able to communicate their feelings and needs. This happens mainly through sounds and gestures. They will:

- cry when hungry or uncomfortable
- coo when something pleases them.

Age	
0 – 6 months	Makes mouth movements mirroring adults' speech
6 months – 12 months	Coordinates movement of mouth, lips and tongue to copy sounds they hear
12 months – 18 months	Uses speech sounds to say words but understands more words than they can say
18 months – 3 years	Puts words together to make meaningful speech and understands simple requests
3 – 5 years	Organises thoughts to hold conversations and can follow simple instructions
5 years +	Speaks fluently and understands grammar (rules of language) to build more complex sentences

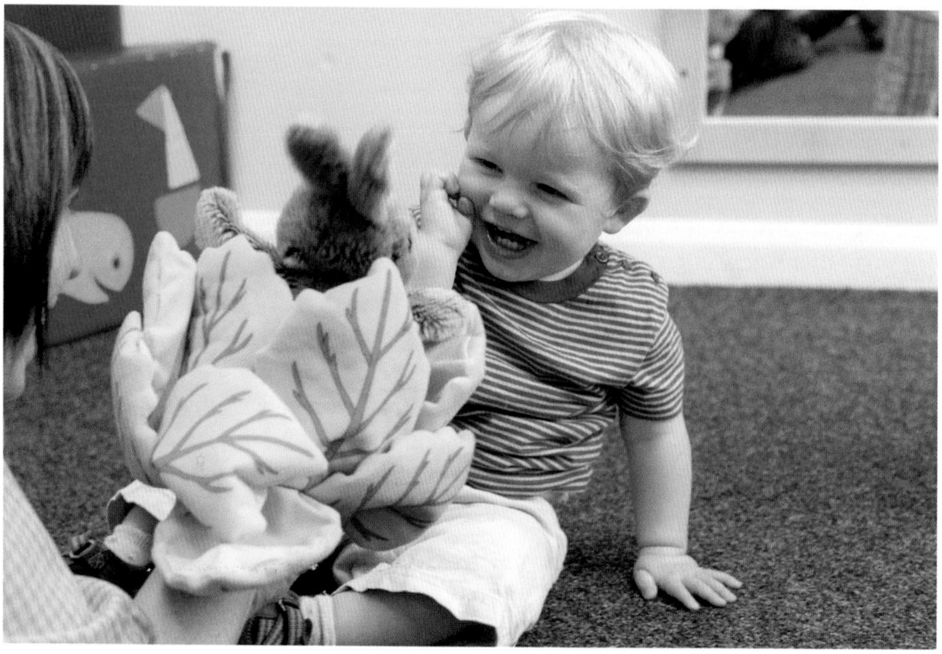

Activities such as nursery/finger rhymes and using puppets are important to support the language development in infants and young children

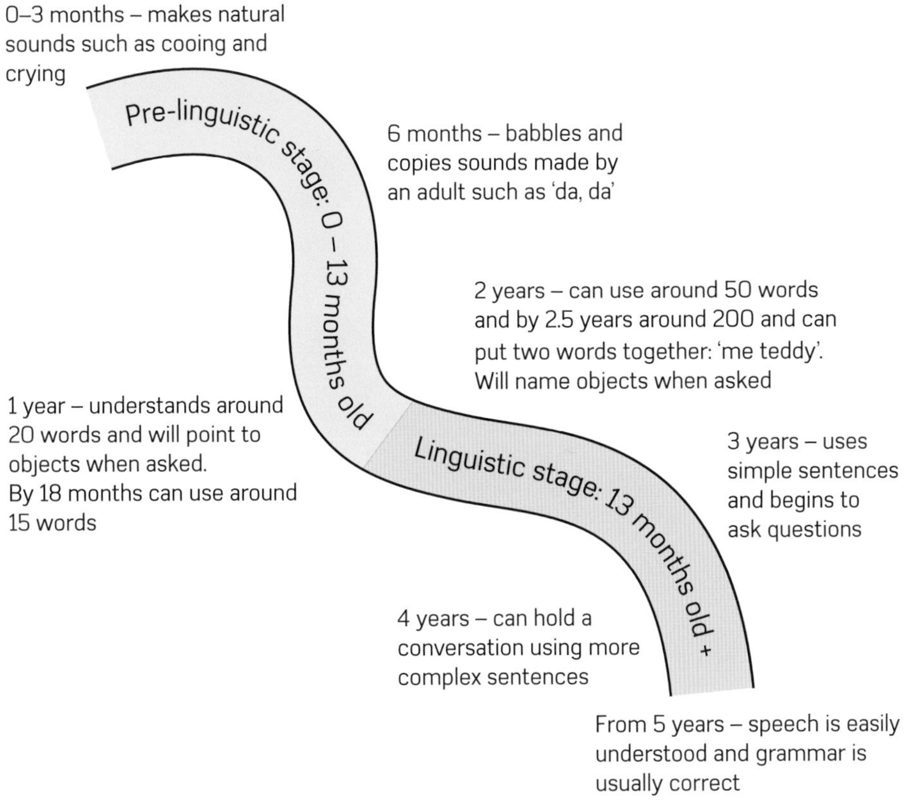

0–3 months – makes natural sounds such as cooing and crying
Pre-linguistic stage: 0 – 13 months old
6 months – babbles and copies sounds made by an adult such as 'da, da'
2 years – can use around 50 words and by 2.5 years around 200 and can put two words together: 'me teddy'. Will name objects when asked
1 year – understands around 20 words and will point to objects when asked. By 18 months can use around 15 words
Linguistic stage: 13 months old +
3 years – uses simple sentences and begins to ask questions
4 years – can hold a conversation using more complex sentences
From 5 years – speech is easily understood and grammar is usually correct

Figure 1.9: How we develop language skills

DID YOU KNOW?

Some theorists suggest that infant's brains are pre-programmed to learn language; others suggest that language is learned through social interactions.

ACTIVITY

Work with a partner to research language development in the three life stages in infancy and early childhood up to adolescence.

Organise your information and produce three PowerPoint® slides (one slide for each life stage) to show how language develops over the three life stages.

CHECK MY LEARNING

Write a few notes for each point you make in your three PowerPoint® slides so that you are prepared to answer questions.

Emotional development in infancy and early childhood

GETTING STARTED

'What do infants need to feel emotionally secure?' Discuss your ideas with others in a small group.

Emotional development refers to how we feel about ourselves and how we cope with life.

Infancy

Infants need consistency in their care if they are to feel safe and emotionally secure. Supporting emotional development requires:

- the provision of sufficient food, warmth and shelter
- being shown love and affection by their carers
- having routines so they know what will happen next.

By the time children are 3 years old, they can more easily cope with their feelings. They are beginning to develop their self-image. Giving them attention and showing interest in everything they do helps to boost their self-esteem.

Bonding and attachment

Bonding and attachment describe the emotional ties an individual forms with others. This process starts in the first year of life when infants form attachments to their parents or main carer. This happens because the main carer fulfils the infant's needs, making them feel safe and secure. It is a process that changes over the infant's life stage.

- At birth up to around 6 months, a child forms attachments with their parent(s) or the main carer but is happy to be looked after by others who provide their care.
- From about 6 months, infants have formed such strong attachments they will be unhappy to go to a stranger. They may cry or not take their feed if cared for by someone they do not really know.
- At around 12 months, infants will be able to form attachments with others. They may get upset when left by their parent(s) or main carer but they can be comforted.

Studies have shown that infants who have been able to form strong attachments in their early lives are more able to form positive attachments with others as they grow.

ACTIVITY

1 Read the scenario and answer the questions.

Callum is 9 months old and lives with his father, Paul. Paul has been offered a new job, which means Callum will be starting nursery next week.

a) How is Callum likely to react when left at the nursery?

b) How might Callum have reacted if he had started nursery at 8 weeks old?

Give reasons for your answers making links to the stages of bonding and attachment in infancy.

2 In your groups, discuss how infants and children are dependent on parents or carers, and how they can be helped to develop independence.

Security

Did you have a favourite toy or blanket when you were an infant? Most infants will have one and continue to take it to bed for a number of years. Comfort toys help infants and young children to feel secure. For infants and young children, security is mainly the feeling of being cared for, being safe and loved and closely linked with attachment.

Contentment

People often talk about **contentment** – for example, how contented a baby looks when settled after a feed. The baby has had enough food, has had love and is clean and dry, so has no other needs.

Independence

Independence is about reaching a stage of development that enables individuals to care for themselves and make their own decisions. Achieving independence is important for our emotional development. Infants are totally dependent on parents and carers for all their needs. Towards the end of this life stage, they will begin to feed and dress themselves.

In early childhood, individuals gradually become more independent. They can now wash and dress themselves, although from the ages of 3 to 5 years they may need some help. From 3 years, children want to make their own decisions about what they eat or what they wear.

CHECK MY LEARNING

What are the emotional development needs of infants' and young children? Note down three emotional development needs.

KEY TERMS

Contentment is an emotional state when infants and children feel happy in their environment and with the way they are being cared for.

Emotional development in adolescence and adulthood

GETTING STARTED

How do you view your own independence? Make a list of three aspects of your life in which you are now independent and another three in which you are still dependent. Think about aspects of personal care, your financial situation and choices you make for yourself.

Emotional development can fluctuate throughout life, particularly in adolescence when young people are coming to terms with their identity. In adulthood, emotions are influenced by levels of independence and contentment.

Independence

Table 1.4 takes a look at three life stages and the levels of independence we may have within those life stages. Do you recognise any of these life stages in yourself or in others you know?

Table 1.4: Three life stages of independence

Life stages	Stages of independence
Adolescence	Still dependent on parents/carers but enjoying more independence and freedom to make own decisions
Early adulthood and middle adulthood	Gaining independence such as living independently and controlling own lifestyle and environment
Later adulthood	A time when individuals may gradually become dependent on others for care

Security

Our security needs will change during the course of our lives. Adolescents, for example, may find that sudden physical change causes them to feel insecure about:

- who they are
- their relationships with others.

This is also a time when they may be making decisions about:

- their education
- a future career.

In early and middle adulthood, an individual's security is linked to:

- relationships
- job security
- income.

Later life brings additional concerns that threaten security such as whether a person is able to stay in their own home and whether they feel safe. A feeling of security helps us to cope better with everyday situations.

Contentment

When people start to feel discontented with aspects of their life – for example, relationships or work – their emotions can be negatively affected.

Self-image and self-esteem

Concerns about **self-image** are heightened during adolescence because individuals are coping with physical change.

- One person may have a positive self-image – for example, they may see themselves as intelligent, successful and/or attractive.

KEY TERMS

Self-image is how individuals see themselves or how they think others see them.

- Another person may only see what they feel to be a negative self-image – for example, feeling overweight, unattractive or a failure at school.

How we see ourselves is based on a number of things, including:

- personal appearance
- what other people say about us
- how we compare ourselves with friends
- how we compare ourselves with people in the media.

Self-esteem is how we value ourselves based on our self-image. Self-esteem can change from day to day. A person may feel confident about their abilities, but if they unexpectedly do badly in a school test or receive unkind comments on social media their self-esteem can dip.

In later adulthood, people's lives are changing. They are no longer working and family members have left home, so they may feel they are not needed. If people feel they do not have a purpose in life it can have a negative impact on self-esteem.

KEY TERMS

Self-esteem is how good or bad an individual feels about themselves and how much they value their abilities.

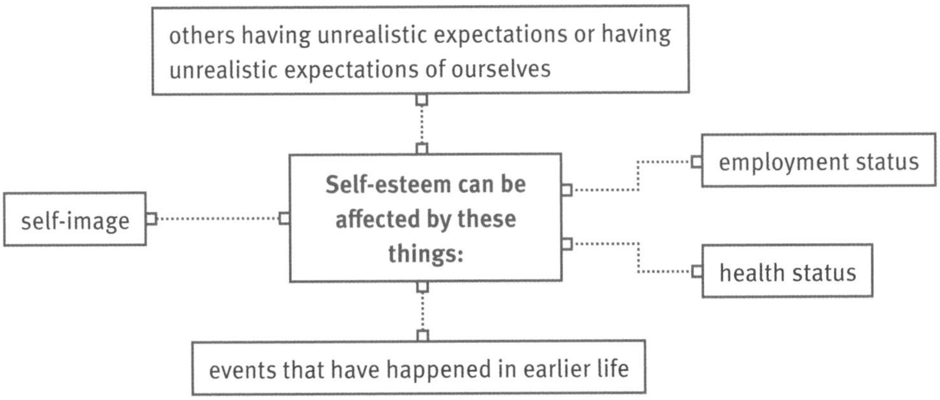

Figure 1.10: A number of factors can affect our self-esteem

High self-esteem can lead to acceptance of ourselves. It can make you confident when coping with difficulties and challenges in life.

Low self-esteem can lead to negative thoughts and problems in coping in difficult situations.

KEY TERMS

Low self-esteem is when you do not feel good about yourself for any reason.

ACTIVITY

1. With teacher guidance, discuss what may make individuals feel secure or insecure, contented or discontented during adolescence and each stage of adulthood. Think about financial, environmental, emotional aspects of life, giving an example for each.
2. With teacher guidance, consider this scenario:

   Nadine, aged 13, is concerned about her body shape compared to that of her friend's.

   How might her worries affect her emotional development? Share your thoughts.
3. Guided by your teacher, discuss:
   - How is self-concept built?
   - How is self-concept destroyed?

   Think about difficult life stages such as self-identity in adolescence and loss of independence in older adulthood.

CHECK MY LEARNING

Discuss the importance of body image for emotional development at the adolescent life stage. You could watch a video clip about body image and discuss the possible effects of wanting to achieve a perfect body image.

Social development in infancy and early childhood

GETTING STARTED

Do you remember having a special friend? What games did you play? In a group, discuss the importance of how play develops during infancy and early childhood.

Social development is a process called socialisation. Socialisation describes how infants and children learn to connect to others, at first through interactions with parents and then gradually through their play.

Forming attachments and friendships

The development of social skills begins in infancy and is very closely linked with emotional development.

- It starts with the formation of attachments with carers.
- It progresses until children begin to develop their skills and abilities to form wider friendships and relationships.

From birth to 2 years, infants are still very dependent on their relationship with their parents and close family members such as grandparents, brothers and sisters. There may be other carers they depend on, too.

By the time children are 3 years of age, they are widening their social circle. If they attend nursery, for example, they will:

- form relationships with other children and new adults
- need to learn how to share and cooperate with others
- start to realise differences in types of relationships between family and those in formal settings such as church or school.

Early childhood is a time when children begin to extend their social development skills. Close friendships start to develop around 3 years of age. By this time they have developed language skills to help them communicate more easily. (By the time they are 8 years old they will have several close friends but are likely to have one person they think of as a special friend.)

Early childhood is also a time when they may go to a nursery, then school. At school, they may take part in after-school activities, which means they will be developing more formal relationships with adults such as teachers, club leaders and sports coaches.

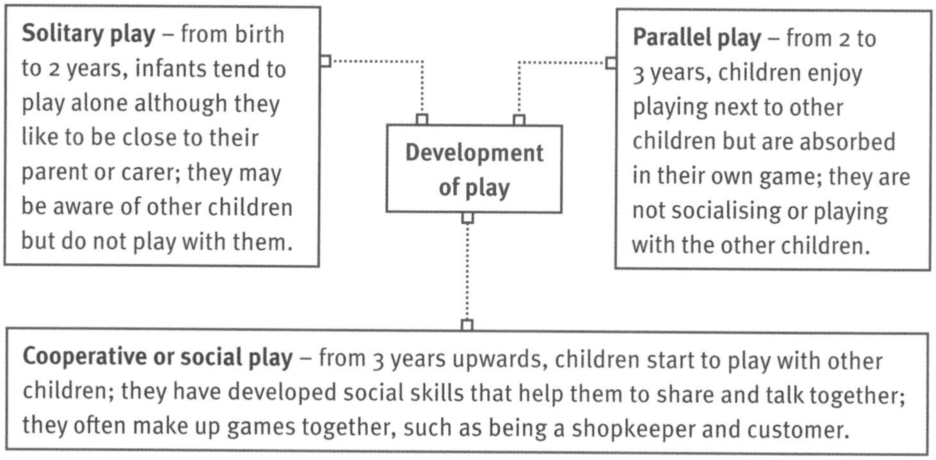

Solitary play – from birth to 2 years, infants tend to play alone although they like to be close to their parent or carer; they may be aware of other children but do not play with them.
Development of play
Parallel play – from 2 to 3 years, children enjoy playing next to other children but are absorbed in their own game; they are not socialising or playing with the other children.
Cooperative or social play – from 3 years upwards, children start to play with other children; they have developed social skills that help them to share and talk together; they often make up games together, such as being a shopkeeper and customer.

Figure 1.11: Play changes with a child's social development

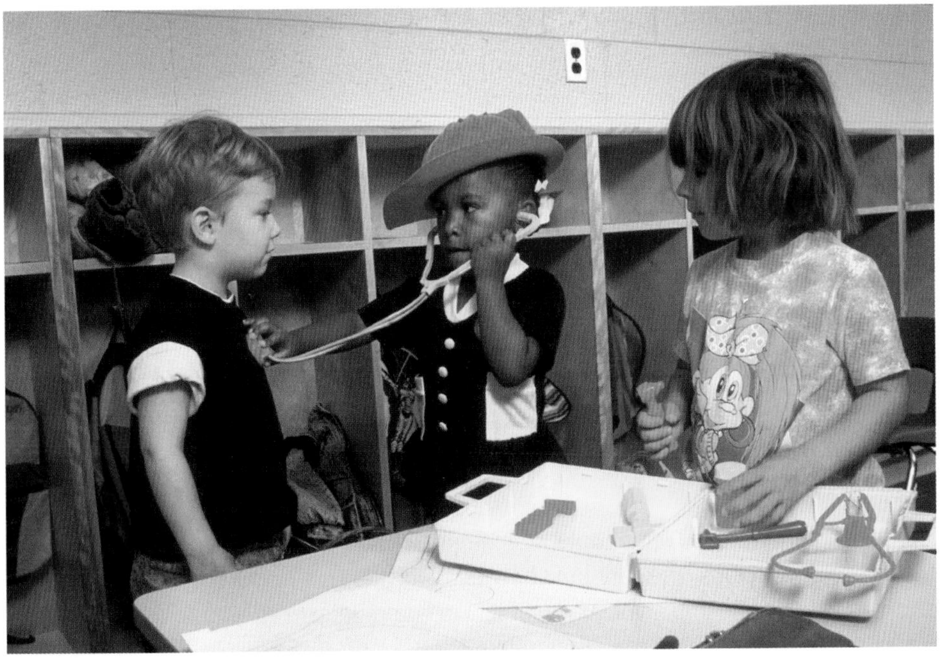

How does this type of play help children's social development?

ACTIVITY

Opportunities for social play are essential for developing social skills.

1 Research how children develop their social play. Share with others in your class your examples of the types of play that help children to socialise.

2 Work with a friend to produce an advice sheet that gives new parents/carers information on the stages of play in infancy and early childhood. You could divide the information into 'solitary', 'parallel' and 'cooperative or social' play.

CHECK MY LEARNING

Make a list of relationships that are formed in infancy and early childhood (remember that initial relationship are formed with parents). At what age do children start to cooperate in play with other children?

Social development in adolescence and adulthood

GETTING STARTED

Identify all the people you have friendships and relationships with. Indicate the friendships and relationships you have had all your life. State your life stage when you made other friends or gained new relatives.

Social development is having skills and abilities to form and maintain friendships and relationships. Socialisation is important for adolescents and adults to be able to live and work alongside others.

Informal relationships

Informal relationships are those formed between family members. These relationships can provide unconditional love and acceptance. They are important for developing positive self-image and self-esteem.

Friendships

Friendships are formed with people we meet in the home or in situations such as schools, work or clubs. They are built between individuals who have common values and interests. Friendship involves the ability to communicate effectively and to adapt behaviour to match that of the other person.

Formal relationships

Formal relationships develop between individuals who are not related or do not have friendships – for example, relationships with teachers or doctors. To develop positive formal relationships, individuals need skills to interact with people in different situations.

Intimate relationships

The first intimate relationships may begin in adolescence. The importance of intimate relationships for positive development continues into later adulthood. Positive relationships are based on trust and respect. They are important for a person's sense of security and positive self-image.

Social development requires individuals to develop a range of skills and abilities.

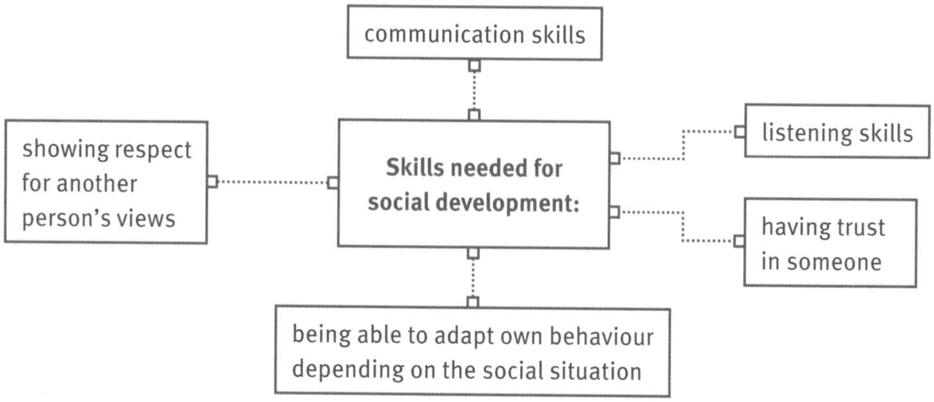

Figure 1.12: Forming positive relationships requires social skills

ACTIVITY

1 Work in a small group to discuss the relationships you have formed in your life. Identify the reasons why you developed those relationships. For instance, was it because of shared interests, a shared problem or because you needed help or advice?

2 Now use two different coloured pens to indicate whether each of these relationships is formal or informal. For example, relationships with a teacher would be formal and relationships with a favourite aunt would be informal.

Table 1.5: Social development at different life stages; which ones do you recognise in yourself and others?

Life stage	Types of relationships and social development
Adolescence	• Individuals become more independent and build more informal and formal relationships. • At this life stage, social development is closely linked to emotions which can fluctuate. • Adolescents are often strongly influenced by their peers, which affects the development of positive friendships. It may result in them acting in a way they would not normally act or in making risky decisions. This is referred to as 'peer group pressure'.
Early adulthood	• Individuals are independent and make their own decisions about informal relationships. • They may have a family of their own; they may be developing emotional and social ties with partners and children of their own. • Social activity is often centred on the family. They are likely to be in work and need to use social skills to build and maintain positive formal relationships.
Middle adulthood	• Middle adulthood is often a time when children have left home. • Individuals are likely to maintain family relationships. • However, they may expand their social circle through travel, spend more time on hobbies or join new groups.
Later adulthood	• Adults are usually retired at this life stage and enjoy their social life with family and friends. • They will continue to socialise with people they have known for some time, but will often join new groups and try new skills. • In the later life stage, social life can change because people may experience the death of partners and friends. • They may also have more difficulty going out and socialising. • These things can cause isolation, which will have a negative effect on all areas of their development.

ACTIVITY

In your group discuss the types of relationships that may develop at each life stage. Produce a table similar to the one below with each life stage listed. Against each stage, identify:

- the social skills required to form relationships – relevant to the life stage
- why relationships are important for development (PIES).

Life stage	Social skills	Importance for development
Infant		
Early childhood		
Adolescence		

CHECK MY LEARNING

You have now completed learning for Learning aim A1. How confident are you? Are there aspects of this topic you need to revise? List the topics you understand and those you need to find out more about.

Physical factors

GETTING STARTED

Work in groups to discuss the factors that could impact on a person's development. Think about things that impact positively *and* negatively.

KEY TERMS

Genetic inheritance is the genes a person inherits from their parents.

There are many factors that influence the way people develop. These factors may relate to a person's physical/personal make-up, social and cultural experiences and economic situation.

Physical factors

Genetic inheritance

Genetic inheritance is the passing of genes from parents to their child. This determines the child's physical features such as height, eye and hair colour. Genetic inheritance can impact on our development because our physical characteristics affect our self-image and self-esteem. It is also argued that genes can determine:

- a person's disposition (that is, their mood, attitude and general nature)
- intelligence
- special skills, such as being good at sport or art.

Genetic disorders

Genetic disorders are health conditions that are passed from parents to children through their genes. Some disorders such as cystic fibrosis have a direct impact on growth and physical development. Conditions such as Edwards' syndrome impact on learning.

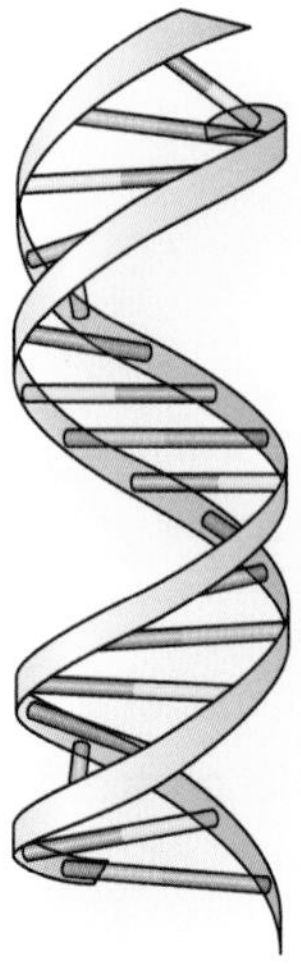

Figure 1.13: A gene can affect us in many ways

Genetic disorders have an impact on these things.

- Emotional development – physical appearance affects how individuals see themselves (self-image), and how others respond to them impacts on their confidence and wellbeing
- Intellectual development – some genetically inherited diseases may result in missed schooling, or have a direct impact on learning.
- Physical development – a person's physical build can affect physical abilities. Inherited diseases may affect strength and the stamina needed to take part in exercise.
- Social development – physical characteristics or disease may affect opportunities or confidence in building friendships and becoming independent.

Disease and illness

Some long-term conditions, whether they are passed on from a parent or not, will have an effect on growth and development. For example, a child who has asthma or an inherited disorder such as cystic fibrosis may miss school, which will impact on their learning.

The impact of disease and illness on growth and development

Physical development
- May affect the rate of growth in infancy and childhood.
- May impact on the process of puberty.
- In later life, illness may cause tiredness and/or mobility problems; this can make it difficult to take part in physical activity; sometimes it may prevent it altogether.

Emotional development
- May cause worry and stress.
- Individuals may develop negative self-esteem.
- Can result in a loss of independence.
- May result in isolation in older adults.

Intellectual development
- Students may miss school.
- Memory and concentration may be affected, which impacts on decision making.

Social development

It can restrict opportunities to:
- socialise with others
- build wider relationships.

Figure 1.14: Effects of long-term health conditions

ACTIVITY

Parents pass characteristics to their children through genes.

1. Discuss with a partner what you understand by the term 'genetic inheritance'. Think about characteristics that can be inherited by individuals. List each idea under: 'Physical characteristics', 'Disposition, skills and abilities' and 'Medical conditions'.
2. Work in a small group to discuss these questions:
   - How do inherited physical characteristics affect growth and emotional development?
   - Do individuals inherit their disposition, skills and abilities or are these learned?
   - How do genes determine social and emotional development?
   - Which medical conditions are inherited?
3. Make notes and share your ideas with the whole group.

CHECK MY LEARNING

Jermaine is 16 years old. He has an inherited condition called sickle cell anaemia. This means his blood vessels sometimes become blocked, causing severe pain. In your groups, discuss the areas of development that may be affected by Jermaine's condition.

LINK IT UP

To find out more about the types of genetic disorders, go to Section A in Component 3.

Lifestyle

GETTING STARTED

Think of an example of a lifestyle choice you have made and share this with your class.

As individuals become independent they are free to make their own choices in how they lead their lives. The decisions they make directly affect the way they grow and develop.

Lifestyle choices

Lifestyle choices include the food you eat and how much exercise you do. They also include whether you smoke, drink alcohol or take illegal drugs.

Figure 1.15: A healthy diet has a balance of foods that contain the nutrients (vitamins, protein and minerals, carbohydrates and fats) that individuals need to grow and develop

Diet

One important choice that all individuals must make is the food they choose to eat.

A healthy diet leads to:

- healthy hair, skin, nails and teeth
- positive self-image
- energy and stamina
- good health.

An unhealthy diet leads to:

- being overweight or underweight
- a lack of energy
- ill health
- negative self-image.

Exercise

Regular exercise is particularly important for supporting physical development. It helps children to develop their muscles, balance and gain coordination. As people get older regular exercise helps them to retain their dexterity (fine motor skills) and mobility. You will notice how much children love to exercise. You may also hear older people say how exercise gives them a 'feel-good factor', which leads to improved self-image.

Other lifestyle choices

Here are some of the other lifestyle choices that individuals make.

Alcohol – the government gives advice on a safe amount to drink. Using more alcohol than the safe limits:

- can affect your judgements
- may lead to ill health
- may affect relationships.

Illegal drugs can only have a negative effect. They:

- affect memory and decision making (cognitive ability)
- may lower self-esteem
- may affect relationships
- could cause infertility.

However, the correct use of prescription drugs is important for maintaining health and development for those with health conditions.

Smoking can lead to:

- respiratory problems for the smoker
- respiratory problems for others who are in the same space as smokers
- lung and heart disease (among others).

If a pregnant woman chooses to smoke, this could affect the growth of her unborn child.

Our lifestyle choices also include whether we have unsafe or safe sex.

- Unsafe sexual practices can result in unwanted pregnancy and sexually transmitted diseases.
- Developing trust and safe sexual practice in an intimate relationship can lead to emotional security.

ACTIVITY

Making healthy lifestyle choices is important for all-round healthy development.

1 Work in groups to discuss what you understand by a 'healthy' diet and what you understand by an 'unhealthy' diet. List your ideas in two columns, using these headers: 'A healthy diet can... ' and 'An unhealthy diet can... '.

2 Select one lifestyle choice made by individuals. Choose from: exercise, misuse of substances (alcohol, illegal and prescription drugs) personal hygiene and sexual behaviours/choices. Work in pairs to produce an outline design for a web page or health magazine that gives advice on making healthy choices.

DID YOU KNOW?

The NHS advises that men and women should not drink more than 14 units of alcohol a week. Drinking more than this could cause health problems. Drinking should be spread over several days rather than 'binge drinking' (drinking several units in one day).

LINK IT UP

To find out more about the positive and negative impact of lifestyle choices, go to Section A in Component 3.

Appearance

Appearance affects the way others see us and how we see ourselves.
Our appearance includes:

- body shape
- facial features
- hair and nails
- personal hygiene (how clean and well groomed we are)
- our clothing.

People sometimes choose to spend a great deal of money to change their appearance. They do this to fit in with what they see as the 'perfect' body shape or look. Changing appearance may include:

- wearing certain types of clothing
- make-up and hair
- (in some cases) plastic surgery.

Individuals become aware of the way they look in childhood. Later in adolescence, puberty leads to changes in body shape, increased weight and sometimes acne (a visible skin condition).

Not everyone develops at the same time and speed. For some people this can:

- lead to anxiety about their appearance
- affect how they feel about themselves, which can have an impact on their self-image and on building relationships – especially if they receive negative comments.

A dip in self-image and self-esteem might result in, for example, unhealthy eating habits through dieting and even anorexia (an eating disorder).

The speed of change in physical appearance varies as people age.

- In middle adulthood, individuals may find they put on weight – often referred to as 'middle-aged spread'.
- They may notice other changes such as hair loss or greying hair.
- In later adulthood, the changes in appearance are increasingly clear as more wrinkles develop and the skin becomes thinner.

How older people deal with changes also varies. Some may view themselves as being past their 'prime', which could lower self-esteem and affect intimate relationships. But you must consider that many people recognise the importance of other qualities such as increased wisdom and personality. Having a 'perfect' body shape or look does not necessarily lead to positive self-image, but being dissatisfied in the way we look can in itself lead to negative self-image.

CHECK MY LEARNING

List some of the lifestyle choices you have made. Identify the importance of making healthy lifestyle choices for your own emotional and social development.

Social and cultural factors

GETTING STARTED

Why is it important that individuals have social interaction? What do we mean by community and how can it help to support an individual's development?

How people develop depends on the opportunities and experiences they have and the cultural, religious or community groups they belong to.

The influence of culture and religion

Development can be influenced by a person's culture and/or religion because it affects:
- their values – how they behave
- lifestyle choices – diet, appearance.

Positive effects of a person's culture or religion include:
- a feeling of security from sharing the same values and beliefs with others
- good self-image through feeling accepted and valued by others.

Negative effects of a person's culture or religion may include:
- feeling discriminated against (treated negatively) by people who do not share their culture/religion, leading to negative self-image
- feeling excluded and isolated because their needs such as diet are not catered for.

Community involvement

Communities are important for people to meet and interact with each other. Community can mean different things to different people:
- it may refer to the local area where the person lives
- it could be their school
- it could be the religious or cultural group to which they belong.

What is common in communities is that they have shared values and common goals.

The feeling of belonging to a group or community brings a sense of belonging essential for wellbeing (emotional development) and for building and maintaining relationships (social development). People who are not part of a community may have minimal contact with others, resulting in isolation. The impact on development may include:
- anxiety, which may lead to depression
- making negative lifestyle choices such as poor diet or using illegal drugs or alcohol
- feeling less secure
- difficulty in building relationships.

ACTIVITY

1 In your groups, discuss the ways in which culture and religion may affect lifestyle. Think about diet, values, marriage, family roles and involvement of communities. Share your ideas with another group.

2 In your groups, discuss the differences in expectations of boys and girls. Why might this be? Think about the impact on gender roles, opportunities, access to services and effects on growth and development.

3 Read the following statement: *Education helps to shape an individual's identity.* Is this true? In your groups, discuss and note the possible positive and negative effects of a person's education on their development.

Gender roles

Traditionally men were expected to go out to work to provide for the family while women took care of the children and home. In recent times **gender roles** and expectations have changed; men now share more responsibilities in the home. Some types of work still attract people of a specific gender. For example, more men work as engineers and more women work as nurses. However, there are still differences in expectations of men and women, which can impact on their development.

- Women are often thought of as more caring and able to express their emotions.
- Men are often thought of as more 'macho' (tougher) and not expected to show their emotions.

Children learn gender roles from around the age of 3. These may be reinforced if girls are given dolls to play with and boys are given trucks or construction tasks. Children may also see pictures of people in traditional 'male' roles or 'female' roles. This affects their self-image, impacting on their social and emotional development.

Despite UK equality laws, some people still face discrimination because of their gender. Discrimination may also lead to a feeling of isolation and low self-esteem.

What happens when people face discrimination because of gender?

- they may be excluded from a group
- they may be expected to carry out a particular role
- they may be refused promotion
- they may be paid less

Figure 1.16: Some effects of discrimination

KEY TERMS

Gender role is the role and responsibilities determined by a person's gender.

Educational experiences

The government has introduced free early education for 3 years olds. These early experiences are thought to give children a good start in life by supporting intellectual, social and physical development that contributes to better outcomes for them in later life.

Research has shown that higher levels of education result in:

- better employment prospects
- improved levels of pay
- less likelihood of becoming unemployed.

Higher levels of education have also been associated with improved health and life expectancy.

CHECK MY LEARNING

Talk with a family member or friend about the impact of each social and cultural factor on their development. Ask them to indicate the level of impact, from 1 (least) to 10 (highest) and record them in a table.

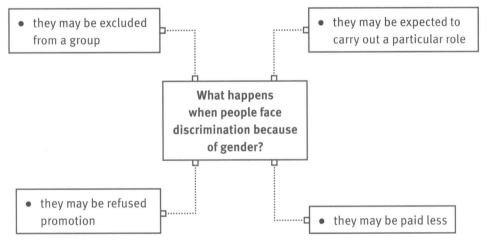

Relationships and isolation

GETTING STARTED

In pairs, discuss how important your personal relationships are to you. Think about the positive effects on each area of your development and how you might feel if your relationships were to break down.

Have you heard the old saying, 'No man is an island'? It means we are all reliant (dependent) on others for our growth and development, and it is still true today.

Personal relationships

Personal relationships are those you form with parents/carers, family and friends. You may have a friend you have known since you were very young – perhaps a friendship you formed at nursery or at your infant school? You may have formed later friendships when you started secondary school.

As children widen their friendship circle they become more confident and independent. When they reach adolescence they are often greatly influenced by their friends' opinions of them. These opinions can affect self-image – positively *and* negatively. Intimate relationships may start in the adolescent life stage and continue into later adulthood. They are important for providing contentment, a sense of security and positive self-image.

Relationships can support you, whatever your age

Family relationships start with attachments in infancy with parents/carers and extend to wider family members and other important people. Relationships with family change over time – for example:

- in adolescence, young people often argue with parents because they are trying to become independent and make their own decisions
- later in life, older people may need to rely on their children for support.

Relationships are important at all stages of life as they provide emotional security, contentment and positive self-esteem.

Personal relationships are very important. The breakdown of a personal relationship can have a major impact on an individual's development. Breakdowns can happen in families if, for example:

- parents do not meet the needs of their children
- there is sibling rivalry.

Breakdowns in relationships may also happen between friends or partners when there is a breakdown of trust. The outcome may be:

- a lowering in self-esteem
- loss of confidence
- stress.

These outcomes may also lead to mental health problems.

Social isolation

Social isolation can happen when individuals do not have the opportunity of regular contact with others. This is more common for older people (although it can happen to anyone) and may happen because:

- they live alone
- are unemployed/retired
- are discriminated against (treated negatively)
- have an illness or disability.

People who experience social isolation have no one to share their thoughts and worries with. This may result in them feeling insecure and anxious.

Role models

Role models are those people others look up to as an example. Others may wish to be like them either now or in the future. Infants and young children learn by copying others or modelling their behaviour on others. Their role models are often a parent, an important other adult or a sibling.

In adolescence, role models become important as individuals explore and develop their identity. Role models may be people who are personally known or those in the media such as athletes or celebrities. They can influence:

- how people see themselves compared to others
- lifestyle choices.

The influence may be positive or negative – depending on the role model.

KEY TERMS

Role model is someone a person admires and strives to be like.

ACTIVITY

1 In a group, discuss and give reasons for your own 'role models'. Then read each scenario.
   - Tom, aged 14, loves spending time with his cousin Niall, aged 17. But Niall has recently been in trouble with the police for using drugs.
   - Claire enjoys gymnastics. She admires Ellie Downie, a medal-winning gymnast.
   - How might Tom and Claire's development be affected by their role models?

2 Choose a soap character or someone in the news. Describe factors that may have affected their life. Suggest how those factors may continue to affect their growth and development over their next two life stages.

CHECK MY LEARNING

Watch a video clip of an older person talking about their life course. You could search a website such as Age UK.

Discuss the lifestyle, social, cultural and economic factors that may have affected the person's development. Make notes for your next lesson.

Economic factors

GETTING STARTED

People often say, 'money can't buy happiness'. What do you think they mean? Is it true? If so, how does it affect development?

KEY TERMS

Material possessions are things owned by an individual.

LINK IT UP

To remind yourself about the requirements for positive emotional development, go to Section A1 'Emotional development in infancy and early childhood' in Component 1.

Economic factors relate to a person's wealth and include their income, wealth and their **material possessions**.

Income and wealth

Income is mainly dependent on the type of work a person does. Receiving a wage from work helps individuals to pay for the things they, or their family, need to keep healthy. Having enough money also gives individuals and their families:

- a feeling of contentment and security
- independence, because they can make decisions about the lifestyle they wish to lead.

When individuals have a low wage or are unemployed it can mean that they, and any children they may have, are living in relative poverty. Without enough income, individuals struggle to provide those basic needs for themselves and for their family. This may have an impact on the development of children.

Many older people rely on the state pension to buy the things they need. Some people have additional private pensions. Without sufficient money, older people may have to cut down on:

- fuel use
- shopping (particularly healthy foods)
- travel or social activities that cost money.

This may speed the ageing process and could lead to a decline in health.

The impact of income and wealth

One aspect of life that is affected by income and wealth is housing. Where an individual lives may impact their health as well as their emotional development.

Living in good housing with open spaces means that individuals may:

- feel good about themselves
- be more likely to stay healthy
- more easily access open spaces to take exercise
- feel safe and secure.

Poor housing with cramped and damp conditions means that individuals may:

- have low self-image and self-esteem
- be more likely to experience ill health
- be less likely to take exercise
- be more anxious and stressed.

Material possessions

How important are material possessions to you? You probably have a smartphone and perhaps a computer. These are not basic needs as described earlier. So are they really important for healthy growth and development? You could argue that a computer helps individuals to develop their intelligence, but if children are often ignored by their parents, and instead just play on their tablets, their language developement could be delayed. Material possessions may affect development negatively or positively but this depends on the individual person and their reasons for having them.

Sociologists argue that material possessions can actually harm our development. As wealth increases, so does the amount of material possessions we own. Advertising has increased so much that some things that were once luxuries are now thought of as essential. Some people argue that an expensive car gives them a positive self-image. Do you think this is true, or might they buy an expensive car because they have low self-esteem?

ACTIVITY

1 In groups, discuss how each individual's economic situation may affect their growth and development:
- a child, aged 3, living in poverty
- an adult, aged 40, who was earning a high salary but has been made redundant
- an adult, aged 75, with their own home and a high income.

2 As a class, debate: '*The impact of material possessions on development*'. One half of the class should argue the negative impact and the other half the positive impact. Take 10 minutes to plan and then take turns to put forward your argument. Your teacher or another student may act as 'chair'.

DID YOU KNOW?

According to the children's charity Barnardo's, in 2016 a quarter of all children were living in poverty.

CHECK MY LEARNING

You have now completed Learning Aim A2. Which of the factors affecting growth and development are you confident about and which ones do you need to revise?

- Physical:
  - genetic inheritance
  - illness and disease
  - diet and lifestyle choices
  - appearance
- Social and cultural:
  - culture
  - educational experience
  - influence of role models
  - social isolation
  - personal relationships
- Economic
  - income and wealth
  - material possessions

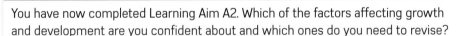

Learning aim A: assessment practice

How you will be assessed

Now that you have studied the topics in Learning aim A, you will need to show that you understand the different aspects of growth and development across the life stages and the factors that may impact on growth and development. Your information will focus on a specific person chosen by you or a person described in a real-life case study. You will need to carry out research to be able to compare the factors that may have affected their growth and development over three life stages and make a judgement about their impact.

CHECKPOINT

Strengthen

- Identify the four areas of development.
- What is the age group for each life stage?
- Give an example of at least one physical, one social/cultural and one economic factor that could impact on development.

Challenge

- Why might an adolescent find difficulty in dealing with their emotions?
- Give justified reasons why illness may impact on a child's intellectual and physical development.
- Explain two ways that a person's culture may impact on their emotional and social development.

TIPS

It is not always possible to know how factors have affected a person or might affect them in a future life stage. Instead, consider what is likely to happen.

TAKE IT FURTHER

Check through your responses and see if you can recognise how factors may impact on growth and development differently at different life stages. For example, the influence of role models is likely to impact more on an adolescent because they are coming to terms with their own identity.

ASSESSMENT ACTIVITY LEARNING AIM **A**

Ask a family member or friend for permission to write about their development. (Alternatively, you may choose another person that you know about.)

- Give an account of each area of your chosen person's growth and development over three life stages.
- Give reasons why different types of factor may have affected their growth and development.
- Compare each of the factors to identify the level of impact each has on the person's growth and development at each life stage.
- Make a judgement about the possible impact of different factors on the person's growth and development at each life stage.

In your response, you should include at least two examples of physical factors and social/cultural factors and at least one example of an economic factor.

Life events

GETTING STARTED

How did you feel on your first day at your new secondary school? Note down words that express those feelings.

KEY TERMS

Life events are expected or unexpected events that can affect development.

Expected is a belief that something is likely to happen.

Unexpected is not thought of as likely to happen.

Life events can have an important impact on growth and development. Some events, such as starting nursery, may seem ordinary but can change many aspects of a young child's life.

The impact of life events

Transferring to a new school is one life event that will have happened to you. This was an **expected** event in your life.

- You probably visited the school beforehand, which would have helped you cope.
- You may have felt confident about this life event.
- You would have had opportunities to make friends with new people and take part in many new activities.
- You may have compared yourself favourably with others in the group, which would have helped your self-image.

These are all positive effects.

However excited you may have been, the change will also have brought some level of anxiety about:

- facing new routines
- meeting new people
- the expectations those people may have of you.

The change may have meant the end of your 'old' routines that you were comfortable with and perhaps the loss of some friendships. For some young people, the change could lead to negative effects. They may worry so much that it could lower their self-esteem and prevent them from building new friendships.

As well as starting school, you will already have experienced a number of other life events. Some you will have expected and some may have been **unexpected** – a complete surprise to you. Examples could include changes to:

- health and physical development (both for you or those close to you)
- relationship changes (perhaps within the family)
- changes in life circumstances.

Figure 1.17: Here are some life events that a person may have to cope with

ACTIVITY

1 In your groups, discuss the positive and negative effects of transferring to secondary school. Think about the impact on emotional and social development.

2 Produce a personal timeline on the course of your life from birth to older age. Note the life events that have already happened and those you expect to happen.

Then:

- identify life events that are expected at a particular life stage (for example, starting school) and expected life events that may happen at different life stages (for example, marriage)
- nominate one person from your group who could join another group to compare the information.

LINK IT UP

To find out more about each type of life event: physical events, relationship changes and life circumstances, continue to work through Section B1 in Component 1.

Expected or unexpected?

As we have already seen, expected life events are those that happen to most people. Other life events such as marriage or parenthood will happen to many people but not everyone. Some life events that are expected happen much later in life – for example, retirement.

Expected life events can usually be predicted and often happen at particular life stages. For example, most children start school at age 4. Settling down with a partner, or getting married and starting a family, usually happen in the early adult life stage. In later adulthood, individuals expect to retire.

Unexpected life events may be more difficult for individuals to cope with.

- Some life events, such as accidents, can happen without warning, so people cannot prepare themselves.
- Other life events may be expected at some time in a person's life, such as **bereavement**, but no one knows exactly when they are going to happen.

KEY TERMS

Bereavement is the process of coming to terms with the death of someone close.

CHECK MY LEARNING

Add any further expected life events to your life course and then list possible unexpected life events that might happen to an individual.

Physical events

GETTING STARTED

Discuss the types of life event with a partner and identify one example for each type of life event.

KEY TERMS

Physical events make changes to your body, physical health or mobility.

Relationship changes impact on informal and intimate relationships.

Life circumstances impacts on day-to-day life and the choices you make.

Life events are grouped under the headings **physical events**, **relationship changes** and **life circumstances** because they have similar characteristics.

ACTIVITY

Use the list of life events suggested by everyone in your class. Identify whether they may have been expected or unexpected. Are there some you are not sure of? If so, give your reasons why.

Physical events

Ill health

We all feel ill from time to time with headaches or colds. These are minor illnesses that are unlikely to affect our development because they occur for a short time. However, when people suffer more serious or long-term illness it can have a major impact on their growth and development. Most illness will be unexpected, although inherited illnesses may be expected and prepared for. Some health conditions can be chronic, lasting throughout a person's life.

The effect of illness throughout life

In infancy – this is a time of rapid growth, so illness in the early years can affect the rate of growth and development of physical skills, such as delaying crawling and walking.

In childhood – chronic illness such as diabetes or asthma may require children to attend hospital regularly. This can have a serious impact on their learning. They miss out on social activities and their ability to take part in physical activities will be restricted.

In adolescence – this is a time when young people are already experiencing physical change, so illness may have a considerable effect on how they feel about themselves and how well they cope with puberty.

In adulthood – illness may result in time away from work, or not being able to work, to take part in sport or to attend social events. It is likely to affect a person's self-esteem, their income and lifestyle. Illness of parents can impact on the whole family.

In later adulthood – illness affects a person's mobility and independence. Older people may need to leave their home and move to residential care (where they are professionally looked after), which can be upsetting for many people.

Figure 1.18: The impact of chronic ill health

Accident and injury

Accidents always happen unexpectedly. Accidents will affect a person's mobility and often impact on their independence in the short or longer term. Some accidents may have a life-long impact on a person's mobility and appearance. This can have a devastating effect on individuals as they learn how to cope with their life change.

After an accident, it is likely that individuals will have to miss time from school or work. For children and adolescents, there will be a direct impact on learning which may affect future prospects. For adults, missing work can mean lost earnings and affect any promotion and career prospects.

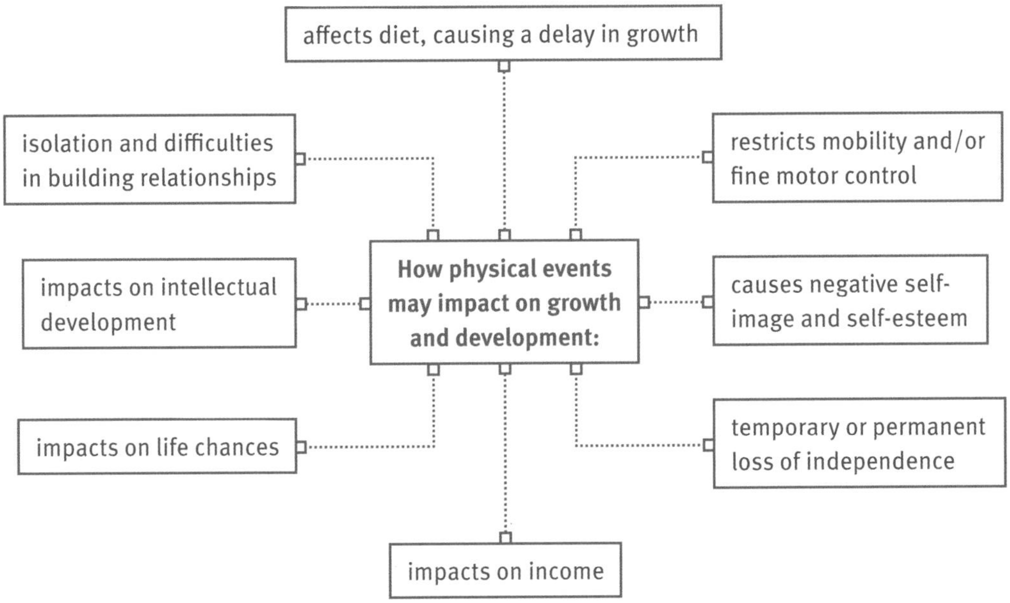

Figure 1.19: The impacts of injury

ACTIVITY

1. In your groups, discuss the types of physical events that could happen to an individual and how they may change that person's life. You might share experiences from your own family, but remember to respect confidentiality.
2. Research news reports to identify a real person who has had a life-changing illness or injury. Examples might include: a teenager injured on a ride at a well-known theme park in 2015, or Simon Weston, who was badly burned during the Falklands War.
3. Discuss the possible effects on areas of their development.

CHECK MY LEARNING

In your own time, interview a family member or friend who has experienced accident/injury or ill health. Discuss ways they were affected (remember to be sensitive). See if you can link effects to areas of their development.

Relationship changes

GETTING STARTED

Make a list of the changes in relationships that might happen during a person's life course.

Relationships can be viewed as important for many individuals. But if relationships with others change or break down, they may have an impact on emotional and social development.

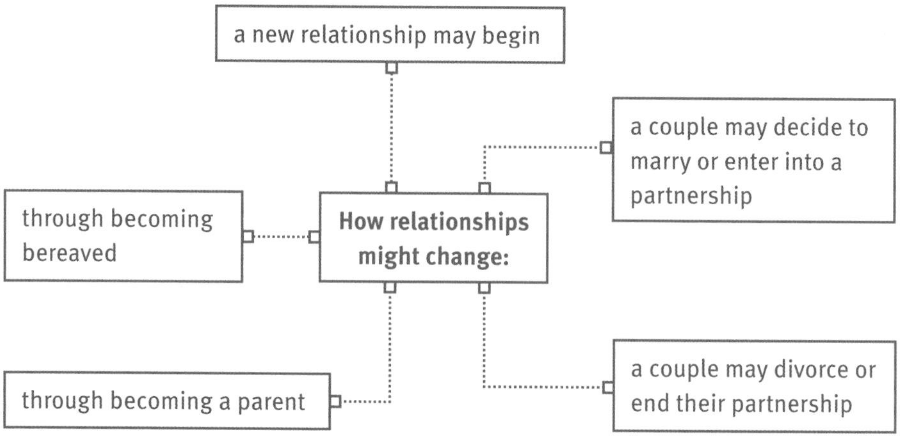
a new relationship may begin
a couple may decide to marry or enter into a partnership
through becoming bereaved
How relationships might change:
through becoming a parent
a couple may divorce or end their partnership

Figure 1.20: Relationships are rarely static

Bereavement

One of the most difficult events a person has to cope with in life is the death of someone close. People deal with their grief in their own way but it will have a considerable impact on their emotional development for some time. Some deaths may be expected – for example, when a person has been ill for some time. In these circumstances, others close to them may find it easier to come to terms with the death because they are prepared. If the death happens unexpectedly through illness or accident, then coming to terms with it could take longer.

New relationships

New relationships are part of our emotional and social development

Relationships are really important for our emotional and social development. People form new relationships at every life stage. In early childhood, children tend to make friends with those they see regularly and have the same interests. From adolescence, people begin to widen their social circles. They tend to form close friendships and intimate relationships with others who have similar values and interests.

Building a new relationship that is based on a mutual understanding, trust and loyalty can result in positive self-image and high self-esteem. Friends are important. They allow us to share social interests such as hobbies, sports and travel. A close or intimate friendship means that individuals have someone to:

- share worries with
- help provide practical and emotional support.

Marriage

Marriage is a major change in anyone's life. It means:

- adapting to life as a couple
- changing lifestyle (to an extent).

Marriage, or commitment to a long-term partnership, can:

- be positive and improve a person's self-esteem
- provide a feeling of safety and security
- provide sexual intimacy.

These things are all essential for emotional development.

Divorce

Research shows that after the death of a spouse or long-term partner, divorce comes second in the level of impact on a person's emotional development. Strong family ties provide the stability and security needed for positive growth and development. A breakdown in a relationship can lead to insecurity for the people involved, the couple and their children. Lack of security and poor self-image can lead to ill health, affecting emotional and intellectual development. It can affect social development, as there is a loss of friendships and wider family networks.

Parenthood

Parenthood generally brings positive emotions of great joy and fulfilment. However, for some it may also have a negative impact.

- Parents change their whole lifestyle and routines.
- New responsibilities for another person can create anxiety, especially if the parent is single and has no one to share their worries.
- It also means they have less time for themselves to pursue their interests and meet with friends.
- There are added pressures if parents work (perhaps around childcare).
- Lack of sleep can put pressure on a partnership or marriage, affecting emotional development.

ACTIVITY

In groups, discuss the possible impact of relationship changes on the emotional and social development of these individuals.

1 Meena, aged 27, dated Tariq for three years and Tariq has proposed marriage. How might marriage affect Meena's development?
2 Sean, aged 45, and Graham, aged 48, have been in a partnership for four years. Graham has decided to leave as they are not getting on. How might the breakdown of the partnership affect Sean's development?
3 Sarah is aged 69. She and her husband Alan were married for 37 years but recently Alan died. How might bereavement affect Sarah's development?

CHECK MY LEARNING

Share your responses to each of the scenarios with others in your class. Identify possible positive and negative effects.

Life circumstances

GETTING STARTED

Did you ever move house or do you know someone who did? What were the effects on your or their development?

Life circumstances may be expected or unexpected.

Circumstances such as redundancy (losing a job) are often unexpected and can be quite a shock to an individual.

- The person's lifestyle will change abruptly, which may affect their emotions.
- Even if there are good reasons, they are likely to feel unwanted. This may have a considerable impact on a person's self-image.
- They may also lose friendships and relationships they have built at work.

In the long term there may be positive effects if the person is able to find new work opportunities.

In contrast, moving house may be expected or unexpected. The impact of moving house will depend on reasons for the move.

- A planned move through choice to a better house and neighbourhood is more likely to be a positive experience for individuals.
- Having to move because a person cannot afford to live there anymore will cause a great deal of emotional stress.

Exclusion: a case study

Meet AJ. He started at New Road Academy just over a year ago. AJ's mother is worried that he goes around with the 'wrong crowd', who have used peer pressure to get him to do things such as stealing and causing fights.

AJ has been disruptive in class for several months now. He has had several warnings for bullying and last week he hurt another student so badly they had to go to hospital. AJ has now been excluded from school. AJ's mother is worried about the effect exclusion will have on his development. She is concerned that it may affect his:

- learning and prospects for going to college or career
- self-image lowering his self-esteem
- his social development, if he is excluded from friendship groups
- his physical development without opportunities for sport in school.

ACTIVITY

1 In groups, discuss the effects of exclusion on development. Think of any positive effects.

2 Carry out a 'hot-seating' activity. Take turns to play a character experiencing a life event. Others in the group will ask questions about the effects on their development.
- Select a life circumstance and an individual from a relevant life stage.
- In your character, answer questions from other students about the effects life circumstances have had on areas of your development.

3 Watch a video clip about an individual coping with redundancy. Discuss in your group. Make notes about how redundancy has affected the individual.

Life circumstances that are particularly difficult will have negative effects on development but as people come to terms with the event they may also have some positive effects, as Table 1.6 shows.

Table 1.6: The positive and negative effects of some life circumstances

Life circumstances	Possible positive effects	Possible negative effects
Moving house	Excitement because of new experiences, opportunities to meet new people and discover new areas	• Anxiety and stress at the physical and mental pressures of moving • Possible loss of close friends/neighbours
Starting or moving school	Opportunities to build new friendships and relationships and learn new things	• Anxiety about learning new routines and building relationships • Young children may feel insecure when leaving parents for the first time
Exclusion from education	May remove the stress that caused the exclusion	• Can lower self-image and self-esteem • Missed schooling may affect learning and loss of friendships
Redundancy	Opportunities to take on new/different challenges or career	• Can lower self-image and self-esteem • Loss of earning may impact on diet/lifestyle choices, ability to socialise
Imprisonment	May provide opportunities for: • learning • developing new skills • making different life choices.	• Can lower self-image and self-esteem • Loss of independence • Loss of social contact
Retirement	• Reduced stress • More time to spend with family • More time to take on new interests and hobbies	• Loss of relationships with colleagues • Loss of self-image if people lack purpose in life • Fewer opportunities for intellectual challenge

CHECK MY LEARNING

Make links from your notes on the impact of redundancy on the individual to physical, intellectual, emotional and social development.

Dealing with life events

GETTING STARTED

Reflect on your discussions about how your friends reacted to starting your new secondary school. Were there any differences? Why do you think change might have affected people in different ways?

Reactions to life events can vary between individuals. The effects depend on how individuals deal with the loss of a previous routine or lifestyle and take on a new situation.

Reacting to life events

You may have found that some friends react to life events such as changing school by isolating themselves because:

- they miss old friends
- they are worried about meeting new friends.

Others may have:

- welcomed the opportunity to meet new people
- quickly formed relationships.

These differences may be because of their disposition (their mood, attitude and general nature). Some people may be shy and withdrawn, while others may be outgoing.

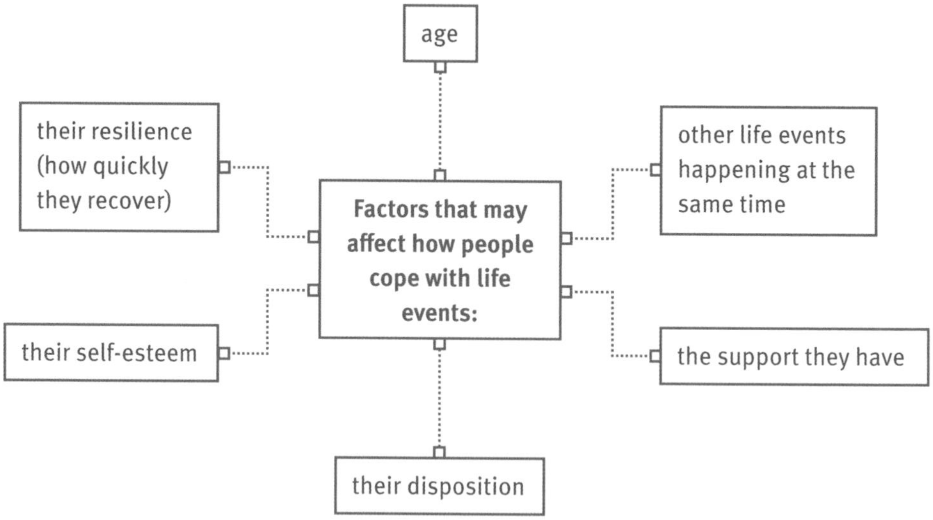

Figure 1.21: People cope with change in different ways

LINK IT UP

To find out more about resilience during change, go to Section B2 'Adapting to change' in Component 1.

ACTIVITY

1 Read the scenario:

Both Joe, aged 22, and Adam, aged 19, have recently split up with their long-term partners. The split affected them both greatly. Two months on, Joe does not socialise and has started to drink heavily. Adam has joined a sports club and met new people.

Why might Joe and Adam have reacted differently?

2 In groups, produce a scenario (a life event and description of an individual). Discuss different ways the individual may react to the event, giving reasons. Suggest factors that could help the individual to cope positively with the life event. Swap scenarios with another group.

People often find change difficult – even positive events such as starting college or getting married. Although change is the start of something new and exciting, it also means the loss of someone's old life. How well individuals cope depends on how well they adapt to their new situation. Table 1.7 gives examples of positive and negative events, and how someone may deal with them.

Table 1.7: Examples of positive and negative events

Event	Why someone may find this difficult
Accident	• May feel a loss of old self (self-image) • May feel a loss of skills and abilities
Redundancy	• May feel a loss of routine, colleagues and friends • May feel a loss of earnings
Moving house	• May feel a loss of neighbours and friends • May feel anxious because of a change of environment
Starting a family	• May feel a loss of independence • May miss old lifestyle

CHECK MY LEARNING

Carry out interviews with your family members and others you know well, to see how they reacted to the same event. Examples could include starting school, starting a new job or retirement. Consider why they may have different experiences.

Adapting to change

GETTING STARTED

At the end of the previous lesson you carried out interviews on how individuals you know coped with change. With a partner, discuss what or who helped them adapt. Remember not to share people's names, so the information stays confidential.

KEY TERMS

Adapt is to adjust to new conditions or circumstances.

Expected or unexpected life events can often force people to make changes to their lives. Individuals must find their own way to **adapt** to the changes that life throws at them.

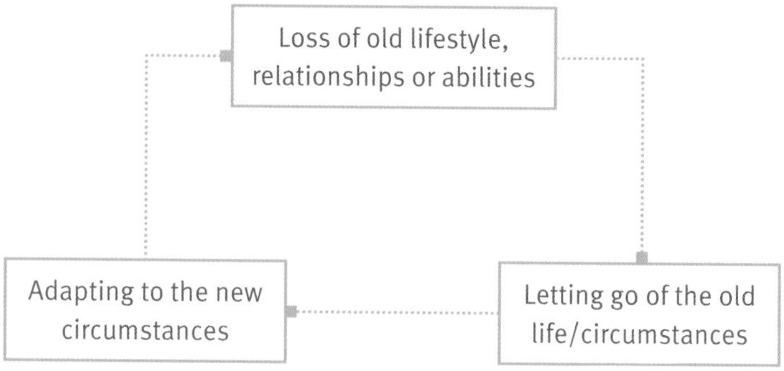

Figure 1.22: Moving through change

Moving through change: a case study

Consider a life event experienced by Alex. When Alex retired in her 60s, she isolated herself for some time. She had been used to getting up at 7.30 a.m. every morning to go to her job as the manager of a garden centre. She felt she had no purpose in life because she had suddenly found she had lost the relationships she had with colleagues and her status as a manager, which affected her self-image.

Alex gradually came to terms with this loss and began to find new hobbies. She had more time to be with her grandchildren and began to travel to see places she had always wanted to see, building new friendships. Her self-image improved greatly and she now feels more contented than when she was working.

Resilience

Resilience is a person's ability to come to terms with, and adapt to, events that happen in life. Resilience can help people to overcome the worst effects on their development. It is stronger in people who:

- have a positive outlook on life
- are able to accept that change will happen
- belong to a close family and community network
- plan for expected life events.

Understanding change

Change happens throughout life, but many people may still find it frightening. Those who try to understand that change can happen at some point can prepare by thinking about:

- how it will affect them
- how they can adapt.

Change that suddenly happens, such as an accident affecting mobility or losing a job, is more difficult because a person has less control over what is happening.

Accepting change

It is impossible for a person to adapt to change unless they can accept what has happened. They may try to hang on to the past and keep thinking about what their life was like. They may see change as a bad thing rather than looking forward to the opportunities it could present. For example, a person who loses their job (made redundant) may accept what has happened and train for a new career that they enjoy more.

Giving time

People may need a long time to adapt. Change following bereavement or a divorce is particularly difficult. These losses can never be replaced and many people can find it difficult to move on. It is difficult to accept that someone who has been close has gone. It can impact on a person's development for some time.

However, with help and time, people do find ways of accepting their loss and adapting to their new life. They may also go on to build new intimate relationships that impact positively on their development.

ACTIVITY

Consider this case study:

Norman is aged 52 and recently had a heart attack. He has now been discharged from hospital and is back at home. His doctor has told him that he must take it easy from now on. He has been told that he will have to give up his job as a bus driver.

1 Suggest how Norman may have reacted following the life event.

2 What might help Norman to adapt to the change in his circumstances?

3 How might the life event affect Norman's future development?

CHECK MY LEARNING

Find out what support is available to help younger students settle into your school. Think about when people transfer together at the start of the year. Then think about the support available for someone starting by themselves (a house move).

Types of support

GETTING STARTED

With a partner, discuss the support available to students in your own school and contribute information to a class list. Sort the examples of support under the headings 'Emotional support', 'Information and advice' or 'Practical help'.

Some people may find it difficult to adapt to change unless given support. It is important that the support they receive is suitable to meet the needs of the individual.

Effective support

If a life event is expected – for example, a transfer to a new school – support can be given before the event. This helps individuals to prepare for change, which can minimise the effect. For example, a primary school may organise for new pupils to visit in advance, so they can become familiar with their classroom and meet their new teacher.

If the life event is unexpected support is given in response to the event.

Effective support is not about making decisions for people. It is about giving them the confidence they need to adapt.

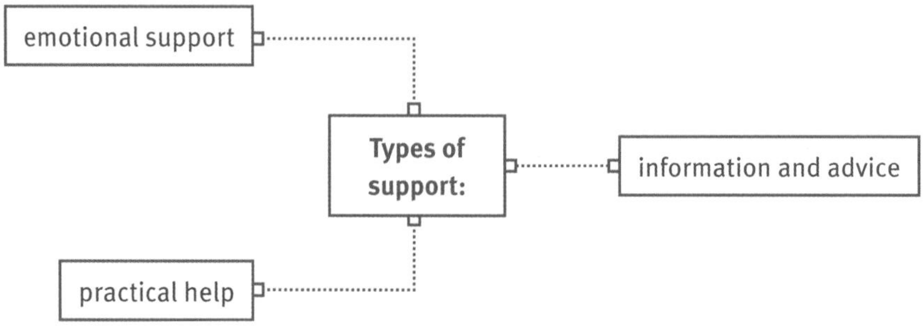

Figure 1.23: Support for change

Emotional support

Emotional support is essential to help individuals cope with all life events. Having someone to talk to helps people feel secure and come to terms with and adapt to change. Emotional support may be given by close friends and family, but some people may need professionals to help them to deal with more upsetting life events.

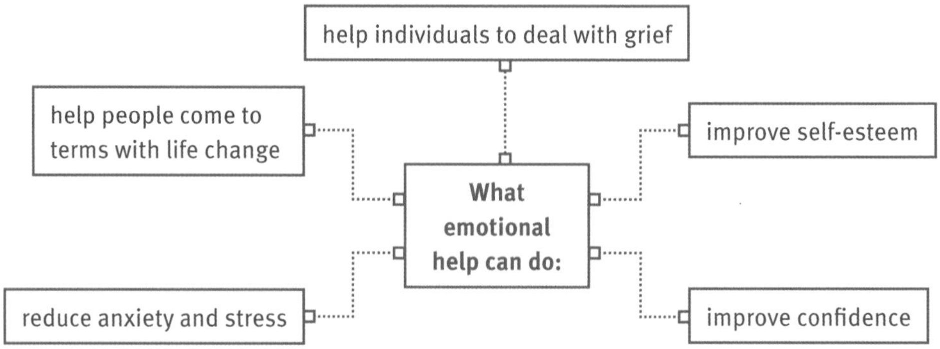

Figure 1.24: The benefits of emotional support

Information and advice

When life events happen people often feel they do not know what to do. Information and advice is important because it helps people to understand:

- where to go for help
- the choices available to them
- how to make healthy choices.

Practical help

Even if people feel able to adapt to their new situation, they may still need practical help. Practical help can include financial help, childcare and transport.

Financial help

Some people may need money to help them adapt to changes.

- An individual with a change in physical condition might need financial assistance to adapt their home to make it easier for them to move around. (This could include an older person who can no longer climb stairs, for example.)
- Someone who has lost their job and is unable to provide for their family may need financial assistance to help them through their crisis.

Childcare

Childcare may be needed to support parents who have a child with a long-term health condition or is disabled. It can also support, for example, a lone parent after a divorce, or provide **respite care** for children who need 24-hour care.

Transport

Transport can support people who have mobility problems. A car, for example, could be specifically adapted to support a person who is unable to walk after an accident.

Types of support

Types of support may come from different sources. Some support may be formal, some may be informal and some may be voluntary.

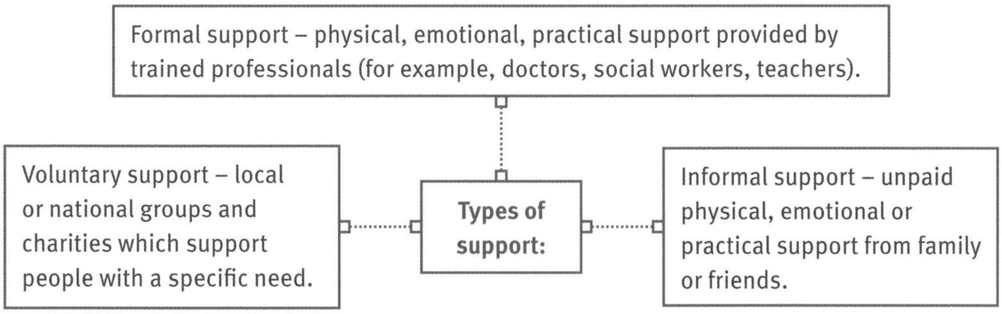

Formal support – physical, emotional, practical support provided by trained professionals (for example, doctors, social workers, teachers).
Voluntary support – local or national groups and charities which support people with a specific need.
Types of support:
Informal support – unpaid physical, emotional or practical support from family or friends.

Figure 1.25: Source of support

KEY TERMS

Respite care involves temporary care of an individual with ill health to provide relief for their parent(s) or usual carer.

ACTIVITY

1. In your previous lesson, you discussed a case study. In groups, identify the types of support that might be provided to support the person to adapt. Include emotional support, information and advice, practical help and add any other type of support you think would be helpful. Give reasons for each of your suggestions.
2. In pairs, research one practical support available to people at different life stages, ensuring different types are covered. This should include financial support (government benefits), childcare (settings and home support) and transport (for example, to take someone to hospital or a day care centre).

LINK IT UP

To find out more about voluntary support, go to Section B2 'Voluntary sources of support' in Component 1.

CHECK MY LEARNING

Identify three sources of information and advice for parents to support their child's development.

Informal support

GETTING STARTED

Discuss the support provided by your family and friends in your everyday life. How important is this for you?

Support given by partners, family and friends is often the first level of support that a person receives. Informal support is usually given alongside formal support.

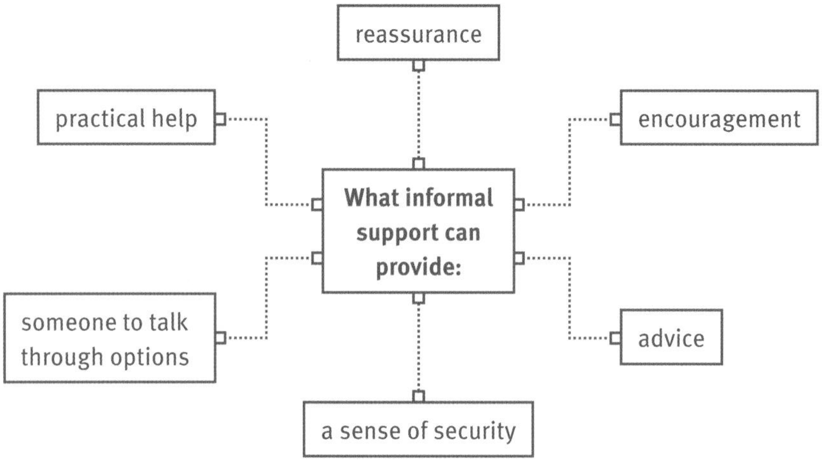

Figure 1.26: The nature of informal support

Reassurance

When life changes, people are unsure of how that change will affect them. A friend or family member with more life experience can help by reassuring another person that they will be able to cope with their new life. This can give them confidence. For example:

- a person who has been made redundant can have their self-image boosted by being reassured that they have the skills and abilities to find a new job
- a child can be reassured that they will enjoy new experiences at their new school.

Encouragement

People are often reluctant to change. But if they have someone who believes in them, they are more likely to accept and adapt. For example, a person with a life-changing injury can be helped to overcome their disability through encouragement to develop new skills and abilities.

Advice

Friends and family are generally the people who know an individual best. They are a good source of advice because they will:

- know the person's background
- understand the person's needs
- recognise when the person is not coping
- suggest ways to overcome difficulties
- suggest when the person would benefit from formal help.

Security

Partners, family and friends provide individuals with a sense of security. Support from people who are trusted is more likely to give individuals the strength to cope with life-changing events.

Someone to talk to

Often, partners, friends and family are there to talk to. Talking is important, as it helps people to express their emotions. Talking through worries helps people to:

- come to terms with events
- find ways to cope.

Practical help

Some life events may mean that individuals cannot continue with their usual way of life. Help may be given through:

- supporting everyday tasks
- providing childcare
- helping with transport.

Practical help is important to help people overcome difficulties. But, if individuals are to come to terms with change, it is also important that they are encouraged to:

- do as much for themselves as possible
- make their own decisions.

New baby: a case study

Misha and Sahil have recently had a baby girl, Siya. It has taken time for them to adapt to their new life. Misha is still feeling anxious about caring for Siya and sometimes feels she cannot cope. Family and friends have been a great help. Here are some ways they have been given informal support.

- Misha's mum gave her practical advice on bathing and feeding her baby.
- Misha's sister babysat while Misha and Sahil went out for a meal.
- Sahil's best friend listened to his concerns.
- Misha's friend reassured her that she was giving Siya excellent care.

ACTIVITY

Select a person from the media or a fictional character (perhaps from a soap opera) and a life event they have experienced.

1 Write a brief description of them and their life event.
2 Swap your description with a friend in your class.
3 Suggest ways the person might be supported by their partner, family and/or friends.

CHECK MY LEARNING

Carry out interviews with family and friends to find out the types of support they have been given at different life stages.

Professional sources of support (1)

GETTING STARTED

With a partner make a list of the types of statutory health and social care that might support people experiencing life events.

KEY TERMS

Professional describes a member of a profession who is trained and skilled in their area of work.

In some situations people may need formal support. This is provided by **professionals** who have the skills and experience to understand and support each person's needs.

Who provides formal support?

Formal support may be provided by:
- statutory care services – provided by the state
- private care services – privately funded
- charitable organisations – non-profit making.

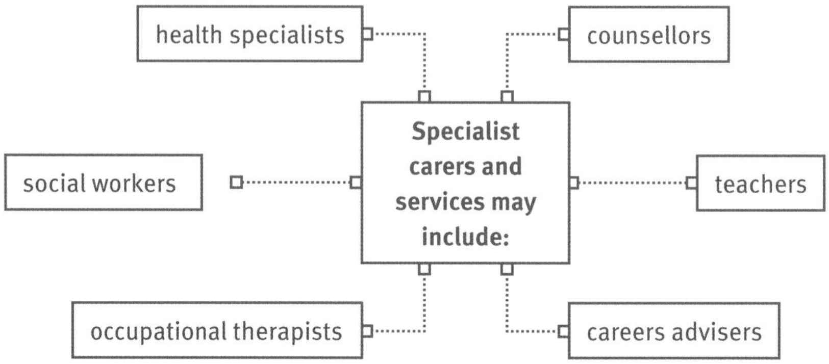

Figure 1.27: Sources of specialist support

People may need to access professional services to support them when they experience expected or unexpected life events. When expected life events happen, individuals may need support and advice to prepare for, and understand, what may happen during the life event.

When unexpected life events happen, people need access to physical or emotional support to help them to cope and adapt to their situation. Often support is needed from more than one carer or professional.

Professional support from carers or services can help people to:
- maintain or improve a health condition
- regain mobility and fine motor movements
- come to terms with life changes
- understand own emotions
- get advice and information
- change their lifestyle.

Professional support for life events

Physical events

It is likely that people will need specialist support following ill health, an accident or injury. People may need the services of specialist doctors and nurses to provide treatment when the illness or injury first happens and for ongoing treatment.

Specialists can answer questions on how the illness or injury might impact on the person's life. They can also help the person to find the best treatment to maintain or improve their health. Depending on the impact on a person's health, a physical mobility specialist such as a physiotherapist or occupational therapist can help them to:
- come to terms with any loss of movement
- adapt to their new situation.

It is likely that a person's emotional development will also be affected. Counsellors provide a 'listening ear' so that people say how they feel about changes to their physical abilities and/or their relationships.

An accident that causes injury is always unexpected. It will require different types of support, as shown below.

When a person experiences an accident and injury they may need:

a trained surgeon and/or medical team to treat the initial injury

↓

a professional counsellor to talk through what has happened and help them deal with their emotions

↓

a physiotherapist to support the person to regain or improve mobility

↓

occupational therapy to help the person to regain independence.

Figure 1.28: How professional support can help

If a person needs to change their career as a result of their life event, a careers adviser can provide information on retraining and job opportunities.

Relationship changes

Relationship changes can affect a person's emotional and social development.

- Bereavement and divorce are the two life events that can have the greatest impact on individuals. When someone dies or their relationship breaks down they feel a sense of loss, which can take time to overcome. Although people often have family to talk to and support them, they may need the support of a professional counsellor to help them through the process.
- Parenthood can lead to anxiety about the new role. New parents often seek professional support to help them come to terms with this major change in life.

ACTIVITY

1 Work with another student to research one source of professional support, a carer or a service. (Your teacher may allocate a carer or service to you.) Think about:
   - how the carer/service is accessed
   - the type of support they provide
   - individuals/circumstances when support would be given.

2 Produce one or two PowerPoint® slides with information on your selected professional carer or service.

CHECK MY LEARNING

Imagine a visiting speaker will talk to your class about formal sources of support. Prepare questions for them. Your teacher will be able to help with these.

DID YOU KNOW?

Counsellors help people to explore feelings and emotions relating to loss. This helps the individual to understand and accept what has happened and cope with change. Counsellors do not give advice but talk through the changes, supporting positive development.

DID YOU KNOW?

Services that can help parents to adapt are: children's centres – offering childcare services and help and advice; health visitors – who work with families to give advice on health and care.

DID YOU KNOW?

Some charities also provide professional carers or services – for example, the Cystic Fibrosis Trust.

Professional sources of support (2)

There are circumstances that occur during the course of a person's life when they need additional support from a professional to help them to cope.

Life circumstances

Even when circumstances are expected such as starting school or moving house, individuals may still find it difficult to cope. For example, teachers often work closely with students to prepare them for transferring to a new school. If they find students are not coping well in the new school, they may need to arrange continued support to help them to settle in.

Some life circumstances may come as a complete surprise. If so, they can have a bigger impact on a person's development. Table 1.8 gives some examples and the specialist services that can help to reduce the impact on development and support individuals through these difficult life circumstances.

Table 1.8: Life circumstances and professional support

Life circumstance	Professional support
Exclusion from education	• Behaviour support teams – teachers' specialist knowledge of social, emotional and behavioural difficulties. • Educational psychologists – provide support for behavioural problems. • Department for Education – provides guidance on the exclusion processes and support to get back into education.
Imprisonment	• Probation service – supervises offenders when they leave prison and provides support such as directing them to training and a place to live. • Children's social services – provides support to families of prisoners. • Counsellors or cognitive therapists – provide support to people with drug or alcohol problems.
Redundancy	• Careers advice services – provide advice on training or job opportunities. • Counsellors - help people come to terms with life change.

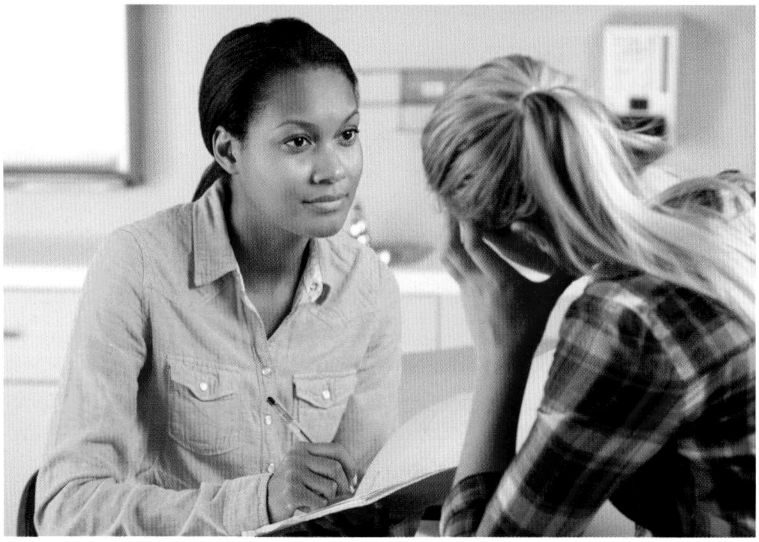

Advice and support following redundancy can help to build a person's self-esteem

ACTIVITY

In your previous lesson you produced PowerPoint® slides giving information about one professional carer or service.

1. Produce notes for your slides so that you are able to answer any questions and present this to your class. Make notes as other students present their own slides on different professional carers or services.
2. Your teacher may organise a talk to your class by a health and social care professional. Note three questions you could ask them about the types of support they provide.

CHECK MY LEARNING

Visit or research online a local organisation such as a children's centre or residential home. What support does the organisation provide? Who could benefit? Make notes on ways the organisation helps people to prepare for and cope with life events.

Voluntary sources of support

GETTING STARTED

Can you think of another voluntary support service? What type of support does the service provide? Share your support service with others in your class.

Organisations offering voluntary support are charities, communities and religious groups. They are funded by donations from individuals and sometimes local authorities or central government. They do not make a profit.

Volunteers

At voluntary support services, many staff are volunteers (they work for free). Voluntary organisations also employ qualified people who are paid from donations (given to the organisation). Voluntary sources of support often work alongside:

- informal support given by families
- formal support given by trained professionals.

ACTIVITY

1. Think of a voluntary source of support. Write it on a sticky note or list so it forms a whole-class list. Is your source of support national or local? Is it a charity, community group or religious group?
2. In your groups, rearrange each example under an appropriate heading.
3. Work with a partner to research one charity, community or faith-based source of support.

Present your information to the whole group using, for example, PowerPoint®, a poster or a handout.

Remember to include the people the support aims to help – for example, gender, life stage, life event.

The purpose of voluntary organisations is to support people experiencing particular difficulties or life events. There are many that you could research online but a few examples are shown in Table 1.9.

Table 1.9: Voluntary organisations and how they support people

Organisation	What it does	Life event	Who it supports
Prince's Trust (www.princes-trust.org.uk/)	Provides advice, support and help with education and training to get a job	Imprisonment	Adolescents and young adults who are disadvantaged
Home-Start (www.home-start.org.uk/)	Carries out home visits or organises groups so that new parents can talk and share their worries; refers parents to other services if there are concerns	Parenthood	Parents with young children
Royal National Institute of Blind People (www.rnib.org.uk/)	Gives help and practical advice on sight loss; supports training, education and work; campaigns for better services	Accident/ill health	People with loss of sight
Cruse Bereavement Care (www.cruse.org.uk)	Provides support, information and advice to people when someone close to them dies. This may be face to face or via email or telephone	Bereavement	People of all ages who have been bereaved
Relate (www.relate.org.uk)	Offers face-to-face counselling, workshops and online chat lines	Divorce	People who are experiencing problems and breakdown in relationships/marriage

Community support

Many voluntary sources of support such as those listed in Table 1.9 are national organisations. Some national charities also provide services within the local community. Community organisations are non-profit making and work at a local level to support the particular needs of people living in the same neighbourhood. Volunteers in community support have often experienced similar life events as the people they support. This helps them to understand their reactions.

Community support may include groups such as the ones below.

Community support:

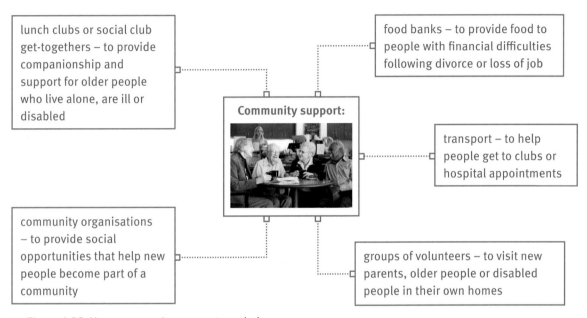

- lunch clubs or social club get-togethers – to provide companionship and support for older people who live alone, are ill or disabled
- food banks – to provide food to people with financial difficulties following divorce or loss of job
- transport – to help people get to clubs or hospital appointments
- community organisations – to provide social opportunities that help new people become part of a community
- groups of volunteers – to visit new parents, older people or disabled people in their own homes

Figure 1.29: How community support can help

Faith-based organisations

Faith-based organisations are formed by groups of individuals who share religious or spiritual beliefs. Faith-based organisations have traditionally supported people in their spiritual and cultural needs. These days, faith groups:

- take on wider responsibilities of community groups
- support people's emotional, social and physical needs.

CHECK MY LEARNING

You have now completed Learning Aim B2. Which of the topics are you confident about and which ones do you need to revise?

- How individuals adapt to changes caused by life events
- Sources of support:
  - family, friends, partners
  - professional carers and services
  - community groups, voluntary and faith-based organisations
- Types of support:
  - emotional
  - information and advice
  - practical help, e.g. financial assistance, childcare, transport

Learning aim B: assessment practice

How you will be assessed

Now that you have studied the topics in Learning aim B, you must show that you understand how individuals adapt differently when they experience the same life event. You must explore the impact that the selected life event has had on each individual, the ways they have adapted and the support they received.

Your information will be on a life event experienced by two people known to you. You will need their consent and to respect their confidentiality. (Alternatively, choose two people from real-life case studies.)

Write a list of suitable questions to ask. Check questions with your teacher before you interview.

CHECKPOINT

Strengthen

- Identify one expected life event that might happen in childhood and one that might happen in later adulthood.
- Give an example of the support a person with an illness may need from their family.
- Give an example of how a charity can support individuals experiencing bereavement.

Challenge

- Explain why divorce may impact on a person's self-esteem.
- Give justified reasons why some individuals may find transferring to a new school difficult.
- Identify and explain the difference between three types of support.

TIPS

To refresh your understanding of 'loss of old life', 'accepting the life event' and 'adapting to new life circumstances', look back at Section B2 'Adapting to change' in Component 1.

TAKE IT FURTHER

Look for similarities as well as differences in the reactions of each person. Then, you must justify your reasons on whether, and how well, each person adapted. Suggest the importance of different types of support considering the extent to which each type of support helped them to adapt.

ASSESSMENT ACTIVITY LEARNING AIM B

Choose a life event from one of the three types of life events (physical events, relationship changes or life circumstances) you have studied in Component 1.

Identify two people who have experienced the life event. Ask their permission to write about how the life event has impacted on them and the types of support they have received.

Give examples of the impact of the life event on each individual and ways they adapted, with reference to growth and development (PIES).

Show similarities and differences in how:

- each individual adapted to the life event, giving reasons for your ideas and making links to areas of development (PIES)
- the types of support given have helped each individual or if little support, give ways it may have helped them.

Give supported evidence on how well each individual adapted to the life event and the importance of the support they received in helping them to adapt.

You may choose to select real case studies. These can be found on websites such as www.womeninprison.org.uk (look for 'Services' and then 'Case studies') or www.redundancyexpert.co.uk (look for 'Case studies').

COMPONENT

02 Health and Social Care Services and Values

Introduction

Have you ever looked after an older relative or a young child? Did they want to be looked after? Or were they trying to prove they would be fine on their own? How did you communicate with them to 'win them over'? Did you feel that you did a responsible job caring for them?

Care professionals from various settings (including hospitals and social care) look after people. They have learned from experience how to deal with the questions above. But it is not only how to do the medical or practical things. They need to understand the people they are looking after: being aware of their circumstances, fears and anxieties and treating them with respect, care and understanding.

In this component, you will learn about the range of health and social care services (primary, secondary, tertiary), any barriers individuals face accessing them and how they may be overcome.

Individuals accessing health and social care services are often vulnerable, for example, children or people with physical disabilities. For this reason, a set of values exists. You will learn how to adopt caring behaviours and practise demonstrating care values. You will also learn how to review your own practice and improve it.

LEARNING AIMS

In this component you will:

A	Understand the different types of health and social care services and barriers to accessing them
B	Demonstrate care values and review own practice.

Primary care

GETTING STARTED

You may go to see your doctor (also known as a general practitioner, or GP) for many reasons. For example, you may have a painful ear. Give five more examples of why you may visit your doctor.

LINK IT UP

To find out more about how primary care services provide for individuals at all life stages, go to Section A1 in Component 1.

Primary care services are the first point of contact you are likely to have with the National Health Service (NHS), for example, when you go to the doctor or dentist.

Primary care providers

When you are unwell or need health care advice, it is important to know where to go and who to see. Primary care providers (often the first point of contact for an individual) will see individuals of all ages for both mental and physical health needs. You can get to know who your primary care providers are by looking at Table 2.1.

Table 2.1: Some common primary care providers and the services they offer

Primary care provider	Location and services they provide
Pharmacist	Available in pharmacies on the high street. Will give advice on minor conditions. They can recommend medication that might help and will also dispense prescriptions.
Registered GP/doctor	Usually based within a local health centre. Will treat patients for a range of medical conditions and refer to specialist services if necessary.
Walk-in centre	Your local walk-in centre can be found via the NHS main website. It provides routine and urgent treatment for minor injuries such as sprains, simple fractures, cuts, abdominal pain and emergency contraceptive advice. An appointment is not needed.
Out-of-hours GP/doctor	Phone your GP surgery; you will be redirected to a doctor who will see you urgently if your surgery is closed. This service is for urgent attention outside of general surgery hours.
Accident and emergency department	Main hospital accident and emergency departments. They provide attention for critical life-threatening conditions – e.g. if a person is unconscious, has breathing difficulties or is bleeding severely.
Dentist	You can find a dental practice via the NHS website. Dentists are doctors who look after the health of the mouth. They provide preventative care as well as treatment for problems in the mouth and teeth.
Optician/Optometrist	You can find an optician via the NHS website. Opticians/optometrists are practitioners who look after eye health. They can also dispense spectacles and other optical aids.

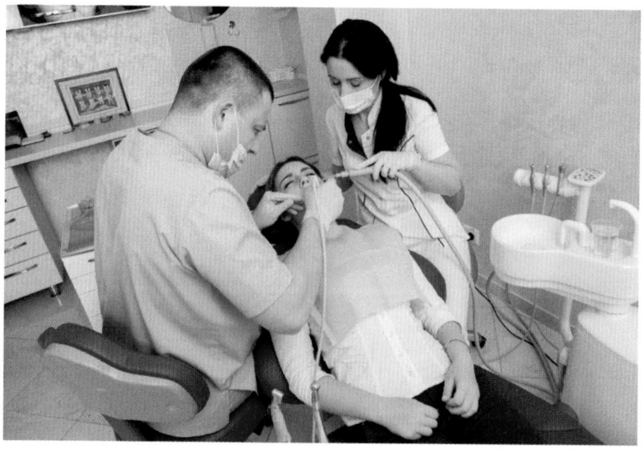

Your dentist is a primary care provider. What other primary care providers can you remember?

DID YOU KNOW?

NHS Choices provides a wide range of information and guidance about primary care service providers. You can access the website at www.nhs.uk/pages/home.aspx

ACTIVITY

1 In your group, research a local primary care service and find out:
   (a) the aim of the service
   (b) who it provides for
   (c) how it provides the service.
2 Create a scenario about an individual who has used this service. Include details of the person's age, the reason they used the service, how the service helped the individual and what the outcome was.
3 Produce a PowerPoint® presentation to share your findings with the class. You may even like to act out the scenario as role play.

Accessing health care online

Did you know you can register to use an online system to book appointments at your GP surgery? The system is secure and password controlled, so only you can view the information. You can:

- book or cancel appointments with your GP or nurse
- order a repeat prescription
- view parts of your health records – for example, information about allergies, test results and medication.

Online contact is designed to be as user-friendly as possible. It can also save time and the need to contact a surgery by phone or in person. However, some people may feel left behind by an online system and may need help with some basic computer training, or might not have access to a computer at all.

CHECK MY LEARNING

It is likely that you will have accessed primary care services yourself.

1 Make a list of the primary care services that you or someone you know has accessed.
2 Describe the care provided by the service.

DID YOU KNOW?

The NHS was launched in 1948. It aimed to ensure that good health care would be available for everyone regardless of how much money they had. These aims remain at the heart of the NHS today.

Secondary and tertiary care

GETTING STARTED

With your partner, discuss what kind of specialist you would need to consult for conditions relating to: the heart; joints and bones; eyes; and mental health issues. Search the NHS website if you need help for your answers.

KEY TERMS

Secondary care is specialist treatment or care such as psychiatry usually given in a hospital or clinic referred from a primary care service provider.

Tertiary care is advanced specialist treatment or care given in hospital such as cancer treatment referred from a secondary care service provider.

You may need more care than a primary service can offer. For example, seeing a specialist for treatment. This is known as **secondary care**; further advanced treatment is **tertiary care**.

Secondary care

If a primary care provider (for example, a GP/doctor) feels a patient would benefit from further advice, tests or treatment, they will refer the patient to a specialist in secondary care. There are a number of specialist areas and departments in secondary care that can support diagnosis and treatment. Take a look at the list of secondary health care specialities below:

- cardiology (heart)
- gynaecology (female reproduction)
- endocrinology (endocrine glands and hormones)
- urology (male and female urinary tract and male reproductive organs)
- paediatrics (children)
- opthalmology (eyes)
- obstetrics (childbirth and midwifery)
- psychiatry (mental health)
- respiratory (breathing)
- neurology (brain, spinal cord and nerves)
- gastroenterology (digestive system)
- haematology (blood)
- orthopaedics (bones, joints and soft tissues)
- dermatology (skin).

Tertiary care

Sometimes, a patient needs more than secondary care can offer. If this is the case, they will be referred to a tertiary care service. For example, a person who has long-term (chronic) pain as a result of arthritis (a disease of the joints that causes swelling and stiffness) may be referred on for specialist pain management. Table 2.2 gives some more examples.

Table 2.2: Examples of tertiary care

Specialist area	Services that may be provided
Spinal	Complex spinal surgery and specialist rehabilitation services
Cardiac	Medical, surgery and rehabilitation programmes
Cancer care	Expert support for those with incurable diseases; palliative and end-of-life care
Chronic pain	Specialist pain management
Burns	Medical, surgery and rehabilitation
Neonatal	Specialist care for premature (early) and sick newborn babies

Rehabilitation

Rehabilitation is a service that:

- helps individuals to recover from illness or injury
- restores the person back to their original state.

For example, a person who has had a stroke may have **physiotherapy** to help them regain mobility and movement.

Palliative and end-of-life care

If a person has an illness or a disease that has no cure, they can be supported by a palliative care team. This kind of support is often carried out in hospital or hospice settings or at home. The aims of both the care and the team are to:

- manage an individual's pain
- manage the physical symptoms of the disease
- improve an individual's quality of life throughout the rest of their life
- offer emotional and spiritual support to the individual, their family and any others affected.

Some people who need care are very ill and close to death. This end-of-life care is an important part of palliative care. Generally, it:

- covers the last year of a person's life (although this cannot be predicted – sometimes it can be just days)
- supports individuals as they plan for their death and offers help with legal matters
- aims to ensure the individual dies with dignity and respect.

Hospice at Home

Hospice at Home is a service that provides expert care and support for people who have advanced illnesses who wish to stay in their own homes. Support is given by nurses and carers who work closely with the GP/doctor and community team – as well as others who are involved.

Primary, secondary and tertiary services working together

Here is an example of how primary, secondary and tertiary services work together:

Mr Lee is having problems with going to the toilet to pass urine, so he goes to see his GP (primary care provider). The GP makes a note of Mr Lee's symptoms and carries out basic urine tests and an examination. The GP suspects Mr Lee has a problem with his bladder, so he is referred to a urology consultant at the local hospital. Mr Lee undergoes further tests. It appears he has cancer of the bladder. Mr Lee is referred on to the cancer care oncology specialist (tertiary care), who manages his radiotherapy and other cancer treatment.

ACTIVITY

1. Imagine as a class, you are going to design a hospital with a range of departments. In a small group, you will research one speciality area/team to contribute to the hospital from: cardiology; dermatology; neurology; orthopaedics; palliative care or psychiatry.
2. You should find out and produce information about: (a) what service your speciality area/team provides; and (b) how they support patients.
3. Use the internet to support your research and keep your notes organised. The work you do on your area will contribute to the overall hospital design, so you will be sharing your work with the class.

KEY TERMS

Physiotherapy involves massages, exercises and other treatments to help people gain physical health.

DID YOU KNOW?

Hospices have been used since the 11th century as safe and caring places for people (of all ages) who are very sick and close to dying.

Why do you think hospices and the Hospice at Home services are important?

CHECK MY LEARNING

Think of three further examples of secondary and tertiary services.

1. With a partner, make a list and explain the services that they provide.
2. Compare your findings with the services that your local area provides.

Allied health professionals

GETTING STARTED

When you think of who works in a hospital, doctors and nurses might come to mind. However, others support patients during their care. Create a mind map that includes other professionals. (If you know their role, note it down.)

Have you ever heard of a 'paramedic'? A paramedic is a good example of an allied health professional. They support patients through all stages of care – from diagnosis to recovery.

Allied health professional roles

Allied health professionals work in a range of specialities. They support individuals who are experiencing both mental and physical health problems. Look at Table 2.3, which gives examples of allied health professional roles.

Table 2.3: Allied health professionals and what they do

Allied health professional	Role
Art therapist	Helps people who have behavioural and emotional problems by using drawing, painting and other art
Operating department practitioner	Contributes to the assessment of the patient; participates in their care before, during and after surgery
Dietician	Uses their expert knowledge about the science of food to advise and support individuals in their dietary needs
Paramedic	Responds to individuals' emergency health needs; highly trained to assess, diagnose and provide emergency treatment
Physiotherapist	Treat people who have mobility, breathing and **neurological** problems
Occupational therapist	Supports people who have difficulties in carrying out essential daily activities
Speech and language therapist	Provides support and treatment for adults and children who have difficulties with speech, communication and swallowing
Podiatrist	Provides essential foot care for individuals with diabetes, circulatory and nerve damage
Radiographer	Produces images to diagnose injury and disease; assesses, plans and delivers vital cancer treatment in the form of radiotherapy
Orthoptist	Works with adults and children who have eye disorders

KEY TERMS

Neurological problems relate to the brain, spinal cord and nerves; for example a brain injury, stroke or multiple sclerosis.

Allied health professional qualifications

The professionals listed in Table 2.3 are all qualified practitioners. To work with the public they must register with the Health and Care Professions Council (HCPC).

- The HCPC keeps a list of who is registered.
- The HCPC has codes of behaviour that allied health professional workers must stick to, to help everyone do their job properly.
- An allied health professional must prove that they regularly update their knowledge and skills.
- An allied health professional can be removed from the register and not allowed to work in that role if they do not work correctly.

Clinical support staff

Allied health professionals are often helped in their work by clinical support staff. They work within a range of settings and departments under the guidance of the allied health professionals. They have training to make sure they are competent, but they are not registered with the HCPC. The diagram on the next page looks at some of the roles of clinical support staff.

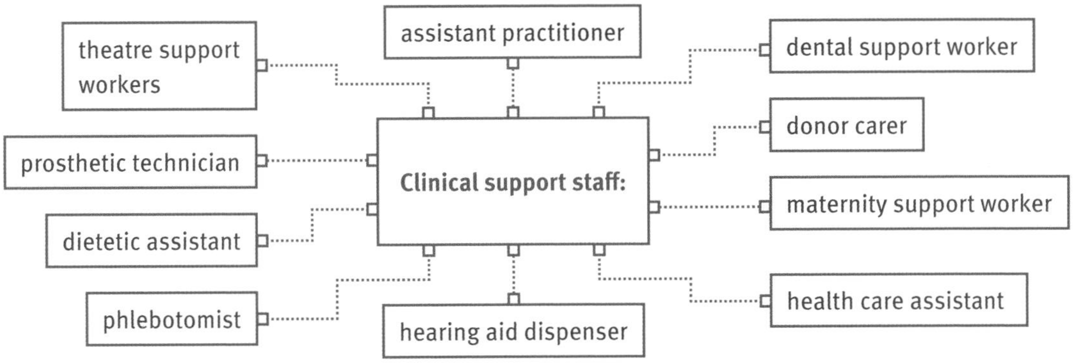

Figure 2.1: Support staff in clinical settings

Clinical support roles explained

Clinical support staff take on a wide range of tasks, as these examples show.

- An assistant practitioner supports qualified health care professionals.
- A dental support worker carries out duties under the supervision of a dentist or dental nurse.
- A donor carer works with individuals who wish to donate blood. They make sure the person is well enough and that their blood is suitable.
- A maternity support worker helps midwives to support women through all stages of pregnancy, childbirth and the early days afterwards.
- A health care assistant works in a range of settings such as a hospital, GP surgeries and the community. They support the registered professional.
- A hearing aid dispenser assesses hearing and provides care for hearing aids.
- A phlebotomist collects blood samples from patients.
- A dietetic assistant works with qualified dieticians. They can advise on food choice and how to use equipment such as feeding tubes.
- A prosthetic technician constructs artificial replacements for limbs.
- A theatre support worker is part of the surgical team in the operating theatre. They help to reassure patients and prepare equipment.

ACTIVITY

Allied health professionals play a key role in the health sector. They are highly trained and work with patients at all stages of their care. They are specialists involved in diagnosis, treatment, recovery and rehabilitation.

1. Choose one allied health professional from the list in Table 2.3 and research their role.
2. Write an account of your chosen allied health professional, titled: 'A day in the life of...'.
3. Create a scenario to give an example of an individual your allied health professional has supported.
4. Attach your work to the hospital plan created in your last lesson.

LINK IT UP

To find out more about how allied health professionals support the care of individuals of all ages and how they play a vital role in health and wellbeing, see Component 3.

CHECK MY LEARNING

Your local hospital is recruiting allied health professionals and would like your help encouraging people to apply.

1. Write a short statement to be included in an advert encouraging individuals to apply.
2. Attach your statement to the class hospital design.

DID YOU KNOW?

Allied health professionals make up 6 per cent of the NHS workforce and are the third largest professional group (source: The King's Fund).

Services for children and young people

GETTING STARTED

Children and young people may sometimes need support from a social care worker. What do you think would make a good social care worker for this age group? Create a mind map showing the qualities you think are important.

Imagine having a big change in your life and people you live with cannot provide support. You might need help from social care workers or leave home for a while.

Reasons for needing support

Some children or young people may need care and support on a temporary or permanent basis. This could be because:

- their parent or carer is ill
- there are family-related problems such as a relationship breakdown
- the child may have behavioural issues or profound additional needs.

Types of support

Foster care can provide a stable home for a short period of time

There are three main types of support that children and young people can access: foster care; residential care; and youth support.

Foster care

When children and young people cannot live with their family, they may live with a foster carer. Foster care provides a stable family life in a safe environment. It may be just for a short while until they are able to return home. Or they may move to longer-term support such as adoption, a residential care home or independent living.

Foster carers support young people through difficult times in their life. They are given training and support through the process.

Residential care

Residential care homes can provide a high quality of care. This kind of care can often be best for some children and young adults because:

- they have more complex needs
- they will be supported by trained carers and educational staff to achieve positive outcomes.

Those staying in residential care often tend to be older.

Youth work

Youth work is a service that aims to support young people aged between 11 and 25 years. The service can help with someone's personal and social development. It can also help them to feel positive about their future. Young people build skills such as:

- exploring their **identity**
- decision making
- problem solving
- building confidence
- better communication.

Youth work creates informal personal and learning opportunities. It can take place wherever young people are – for example, schools, colleges and community areas (such as libraries, shopping precincts or parks).

KEY TERMS

Identity is how you describe or define yourself.

ACTIVITY

With your partner, read one of the scenarios below. Then think about the following.

1. What are the positive aspects of the service that the individual is accessing? Use the internet to find out more information.
2. What difficulties might the individual face when accessing the service?
3. Role play the scenario – one of you is the worker and the other the service user.

Scenario 1: Amir, 10 years old and in foster care

I am living with Mandy, my foster carer. My mum and my stepdad have split up. It was horrible when they argued and fought. Sometimes it would go on into the middle of the night. My mum wasn't coping and got in touch with Children's Services, who found me a place with Mandy.

Mandy and her family are kind. The house is quiet and I sleep better. Sometimes though I get upset and lash out. Mandy listens to me. I like being with Mandy but look forward to when I can go and live with mum again.

Scenario 2: Connor, 15 years old and in residential care

I have lived here for 9 months, I like living here. Most of the staff are good. I like having people around especially when I am feeling worried. I like having my own room. It's better here than when I lived at home. I was always getting into trouble and argued with my mum. Some things I find difficult are the rules and bedtimes and not being able to go out when I like. I never had rules at home.

Scenario 3: Sadie, 16 years old and attends a youth group

I hardly ever went to school; couldn't see the point so started messing about. I used to meet up with mates in the park, drink, smoke and do drugs. There was nothing else for us to do.

A group of adults, 6 months ago, got together and opened a community centre next to the park. We weren't sure at first – I didn't trust them, couldn't make out why they did it. Anyway, it was raining one day so we gave it a go and went in. They turned out to be really good. They seemed really interested in us. It's a good place to go; there are rules, but it's ok.

Tom, one of the youth workers, is great, I love talking with him. He has given me confidence and he believes in me. He is helping me to get work experience. I never thought I would make anything of my life, but I really want to work and do well now. I want to feel proud of myself.

Support workers

Someone who supports and works with children and young people will need to be able to communicate well with the person they are supporting. As you read in the activity scenarios, each person liked those who were supporting them. The diagram below lists some skills and qualities support workers need. Can you think of any others?

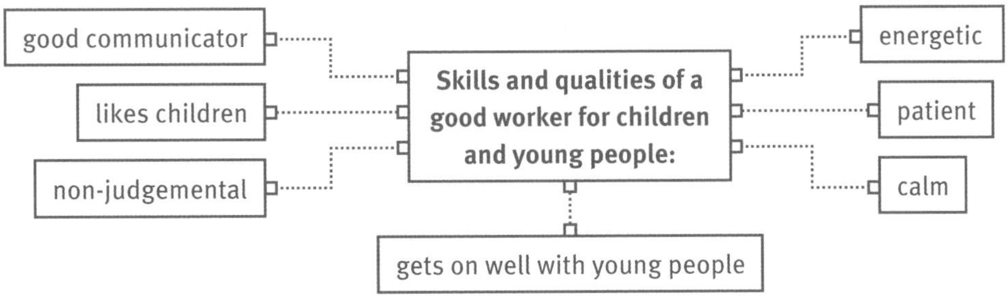

Figure 2.2: Some attributes required by support workers

CHECK MY LEARNING

You focused on one scenario from the Activity box above and answered three questions. Now focus on the other two scenarios. For each one, answer the same three questions.

Services for adults or children with specific needs

GETTING STARTED

Write down one example of a learning disability, one example of a sensory disability (or impairment) and one example of a long-term health issue that can affect adults or children.

Some people have specific needs. But have you ever thought about who supports those individuals or the services available to them?

How specific needs are supported

Specific needs can affect children and adults. They can include:

- learning disabilities
- sensory impairments (perhaps sight or hearing)
- long-term health issues.

However, a range of services is available to support both the individual and their family or carers, as you will find out later.

Learning disabilities

A person who has a learning disability finds it hard to learn things; they may struggle with day-to-day activities such as personal care, household tasks and managing money. A person with mild learning disabilities may successfully live on their own, while others with more severe disabilities may need more intense support 24 hours a day.

KEY TERMS

Sensory impairment is a weakness or difficulty that prevents a person from doing something.

Respite care provides temporary care for an individual, which will give the usual carer a short break.

Domiciliary care is care and support given at home by a care worker to help a person with their daily life.

Sensory impairments

Sensory impairment is a problem that affects the senses, for example vision or hearing. Someone with a sensory impairment may be born with the disorder or it may have developed throughout their life. The ageing process as well as other physical conditions such as diabetes can affect sight. Hearing can also deteriorate with age; some individuals have dual sensory loss and are deafblind.

Long-term health issues

Long-term health issues can affect people in many ways and may include learning, physical or mental health difficulties.

- Some people may be born with conditions such as cerebral palsy or asthma.
- Others may develop disorders such as dementia during their life.

Types of care

Different types of care are available for individuals with specific needs – for example, residential care, **respite care** and **domiciliary care**. Care providers are inspected to make sure the service meets the specific needs of the individuals who are using it.

DID YOU KNOW?

The Care Quality Commission regulates health and social care in England. All care providers in England are monitored, regulated and inspected by the Care Quality Commission to ensure adequate standards of quality and safety are maintained.

Residential care

Residential care can be short or long term. The individual lives in the setting instead of their own home. Accommodation, laundry and meals are provided. Residential care homes need to state which type of care they provide – for example, to support children or adults who have learning, sensory or long-term disabilities. Staff in residential homes are trained to support individuals with specific needs and support is available 24 hours a day.

Respite care

Families often provide care themselves for relatives who need it. But caring for individuals who have disabilities can be demanding and tiring for the family. Respite care provides support (in the form of trained carers) for those families. This gives them relief for a short period of time. Respite care can be provided:

- at the person's home, so that the usual carers can have a break away from home
- in a residential care home, so that the usual carers can relax in their own home for a few days without the pressure of looking after someone.

Domiciliary care

Domiciliary care means that care workers visit the individual in their own home to help with personal care and other daily activities. Some individuals require specialised treatments such as feeding via a tube, which can still be carried out in the person's home if the care worker is trained in its management.

Table 2.4 looks at the other services that are available to support individuals with specific needs.

Table 2.4: Other services to support individuals

Service	How they meet users' needs
Supported living scheme	Accommodation within the community enables a person to live independently with extra support available if needed. A care coordinator will make sure the level of support is right for the individual – for example, a weekly drop-in or more intensive daily visits.
Day centre	Staff are on site to provide services such as bathing, hair care and chiropody as well as run social and leisure activities. Day centres will vary in the services that they provide.
Nursing care home	This is like a residential care home but with registered nurses supporting those with more complex needs.

Changing needs of the individual

As we know, situations and circumstances can change what we need. This is also true for people with disabilities or illnesses. For example, a child with learning difficulties may be supported by parents. But as they move into adulthood they may wish to become more independent. A supported living scheme could help them to do this. Whatever service is offered, a person-centred approach will ensure the individual's preferences are always taken into account.

ACTIVITY

The following three people have specific needs.

- Charlie is 27 years old and has Down's syndrome. Charlie has moderate learning difficulties.
- Robin is 75 years old and has dual sensory loss. Robin is sight and hearing impaired.
- Jasmine is 14 years old and has cerebral palsy. Jasmine has difficulty with coordination and movement.

1 On your own, research more about each disorder and make some brief notes.

2 Then, in your group, discuss each individual's needs. Discuss the suitability of each of the services in Table 2.4 for each individual. You could share your ideas with another group.

LINK IT UP

To find out more about a person-centred approach when considering the health and wellbeing of an individual, go to Section C in Component 3.

CHECK MY LEARNING

Try to find one local provider that could meet the needs of each of the individuals mentioned in the activity. You could use local council websites, which may have a directory.

Services for older adults

GETTING STARTED

Imagine you only have the use of one arm. List the things you would find difficult. Think about all the activities you would do from waking up in the morning to going to bed at night.

Do you think a grandparent could run as fast as their grandchildren? Your answer is probably 'No'. As we grow older our bodies start slowing down, taking longer doing things.

The problems of ageing

As we age, our body systems function less effectively. Despite that, many people are able to remain fully independent through older age with little or no help. For others, the ageing process means they may start to develop some of the conditions shown in Table 2.5. So they may need to access services for help and support in some aspects of their lives.

Table 2.5: Examples of age-related problems

Problem (or condition)	How it can affect people as they age
Arthritis	• Joints can suffer wear and tear and arthritis can develop. • The joints swell and movement can become difficult and painful.
Cardiovascular disease	• Blood vessels become less elastic and fatty deposits can build. • The heart becomes less effective and there is a higher risk of heart attack and stroke.
Osteoporosis	• Older people are more likely to have deficiency of vitamin D and calcium, which weakens the bones. • Bones can break more easily due to hormone changes as we age.
Cancer	• Older people have usually had more exposure to cancer-causing substances. • Their cells have had more chance to develop genetic mutations and become cancerous. • Their immune systems are also weaker.
Breathing problems	• Reduced respiratory (breathing) function can lead to conditions such as chest infections, chronic bronchitis and asthma.
Dementia	• Memory loss can be a problem. • The risk of developing dementia increases with age.
Depression	• Older people may suffer from depression caused by retirement. • They may suffer depression caused by loss of loved ones, friends, independence, home and social network.

Choices for older people: accommodation

Where we choose to live as we get older often depends on:

- our preferences
- our health and social care needs
- availability of accommodation.

Older people needing support may choose to stay in their home with the help of a carer or personal assistant. (A personal assistant may be able to help with using online services such as shopping and banking and other light duties around the house.) Others may decide to move into a residential care home for older people.

Jack and Winston, the two men featured in the case studies on the next page, have similar needs but have made different choices. Why do you think this is?

Case study 1: Jack

Jack is 82 years old and has arthritis. He has limited mobility but can get about using a walking frame. Jack has no family nearby. He loves the company of others and led the local dominoes and darts teams for several years.

Jack is mostly independent but needs a little help with personal care. He has decided to move from his own home into a local residential home, where he will not have the worry of paying bills and shopping. He wants to be able to enjoy life fully without the responsibility of running his own home.

Jack has many people around him for company. But he also has the privacy of his own room, where he can have quiet time as well.

Case study 2: Winston

Winston is 87 years old. Recently he had a fall. He is recovering well and can walk with a frame.

Winston's wife died 5 years ago and his daughter lives about 50 miles away. He is a keen gardener and loves to watch the birds from his living room.

Winston likes to visit a local club where he sees friends. He has lived in his home since he was in his 20s. He planted the trees in his garden when he first got married. He also has a vegetable plot and likes to give his produce to friends and neighbours.

Winston has chosen to stay in his home with the help of a carer who visits twice each day to help him with personal care.

ACTIVITY

Read the scenario and answer the questions.

Daisy is 76 years old and has had a stroke. Her mobility is good, but sometimes she gets confused. She lives alone, but has many friends in the neighbourhood. She is trying to decide whether to stay at home supported by carers or move into residential care. Daisy has requested information about both options.

1 In your group, research Daisy's two options. Find out the care and support each offers.
2 Write an email to Daisy explaining what domiciliary care and residential care homes offer. Ensure equal amounts of information are given. Do not say which option you think is best.

CHECK MY LEARNING

Write another reply to Daisy, giving your own opinion about which care option would suit her better. Clearly list what you think are the advantages. You should also list the things she might find difficult at first.

Informal social care

GETTING STARTED

Sammy's grandmother cannot see very well. He goes to visit her regularly after school. How do you think Sammy can help his grandmother when he visits?

Not all carers get paid for what they do. Some people volunteer to help others. They are known as informal carers and social care services would struggle without them.

Who are the informal carers?

There are many types of informal carers such as partners, family, friends and neighbours. Each can play a valuable role in giving up their free time to support others.

- **Spouse or partner:** When you live with a person and have a close relationship with them, it will feel natural to want to care for them if they need help and support.
- **Son or daughter:** Children can feel a sense of responsibility as their parents age or become disabled. They often reflect on how their parents looked after them when they were young. In some cultures, caring for ageing parents is expected of sons and daughters.
- **Friends:** Often, the bond between friends (especially if they have known each other a long time) can be very strong. Good friends usually want to give a helping hand.
- **Neighbours:** Good neighbours are invaluable. Having someone nearby who can quickly respond to needs and problems gives peace of mind to a person in need. Here is an example of how a neighbour can support an elderly person:

Mr Chinery is 80 years old. He is a wheelchair user but is independent and lives alone. Mr Chinery has a good neighbour who calls each day after work to make sure that he is fine. Mr Chinery is pleased to have company and likes to talk about the old days. He also likes to know what is going on locally, because he does not get out very often, especially in the winter months.

One evening, Mr Chinery was making a piece of toast. His toaster tripped the fuse box and his bungalow was in darkness. Luckily, he had a torch near the back door. Mr Chinery phoned his neighbour who responded immediately and reset the electrical trip, so he had lights and power again.

Who would you call in this situation?

ACTIVITY

The care people receive is often given by unpaid carers (informal social care). The care that friends, neighbours and relatives give often goes unrecognised and unnoticed, yet informal care is crucial in the lives of some individuals.

1. In your group, create a poster titled: 'Informal carer of the month'. Include made-up characters who are informal carers who will be nominated for the award.
2. Write a short account for each character explaining why they have been nominated.
3. Look at posters by other groups. As a class, vote for who should be nominated as 'Informal carer of the month'.

What informal carers do

Informal carers can provide a range of support, including personal care such as washing and dressing. They can do practical jobs around the house and garden, and help with collecting prescriptions or taking individuals to the doctor or hospital appointments. They can also assist with paperwork and managing correspondence, as well as tasks such as shopping, cooking and doing the laundry.

Being there to provide company for older people is also a need that informal carers can fulfil. It is often the small acts of kindness given by informal carers that make a big difference to the health and wellbeing of an individual.

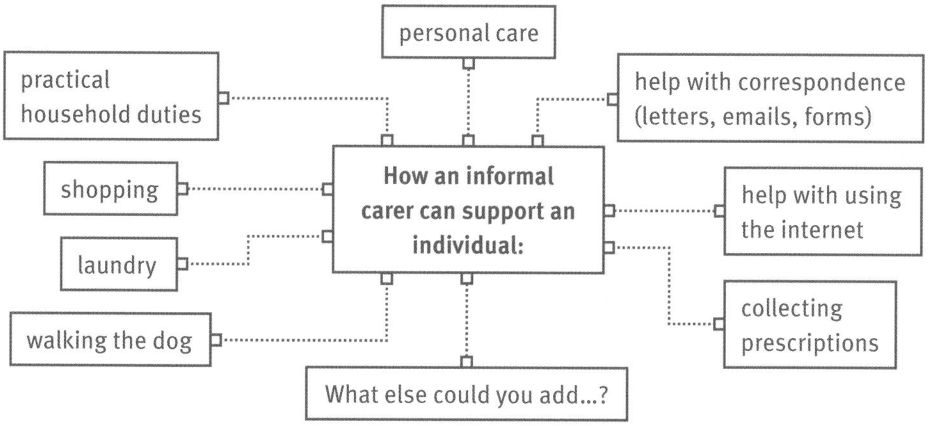

Figure 2.3: Examples of informal support

The future of informal care

For many reasons, the number of informal carers is declining.

- People retire from work later, so they have less time to give to their ageing or disabled parents, friends and neighbours who need support.
- People tend to have fewer children. This means that sometimes a grown-up child could have all these people at once to care for – a parent, a grandparent and their own children.
- People sometimes move away from their birthplace, which creates a geographical distance between them and their family.
- Communities are changing and many people do not know their neighbours.

CHECK MY LEARNING

Using the lesson titles so far in this component, create a mind map of what you have learned. Highlight any areas you are unsure about for your teacher to see.

DID YOU KNOW?

Unpaid carers save the UK enough money each year to fund a second NHS. It costs in excess of £100 billion per year to run the NHS.

Physical barriers

GETTING STARTED

Imagine you need to use a wheelchair to get about. What difficulties do you think you would face? Think about getting to and from school and going out to the shops or to the cinema.

LINK IT UP

To find out more about barriers to accessing services, go to Section C2 in Component 3.

Have you ever thought how frightening and frustrating it would be to have difficulties getting in and around places if you are unwell or have a disability?

Why people struggle with access

People can struggle when accessing care services, even when the building they need to go to has been adapted. The individual has to be able to get there in the first place, which can mean overcoming many physical obstacles. Look at the following case study examples. These people are all independent, but have some problems getting about. Access to many places is not always easy for them.

Blanche needs a little assistance with walking. She uses a rollator both indoors and out. A rollator is like a walking frame with wheels.

Cynthia can walk but not for long distances. She has limited use of her hands and has an electric wheelchair to help her to get around outdoors.

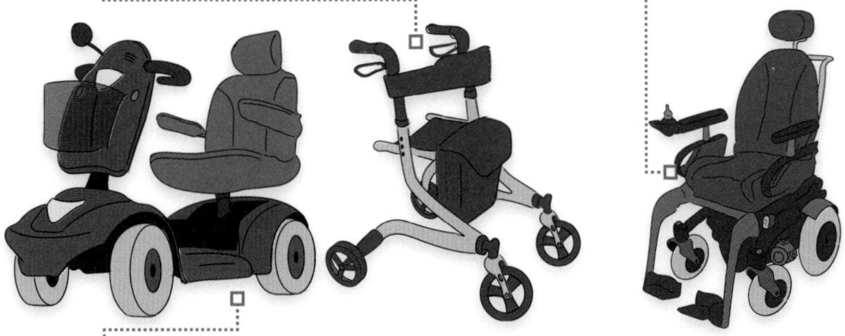

Patrick has limited use of his legs but has good upper body strength. He uses a mobility scooter.

Rahi has an arthritic hip. He can walk independently with no aid but needs to take his time and be careful not to trip or fall.

Figure 2.4: Examples of people who may have access difficulty

Overcoming access difficulties

As you saw above in the case studies, the individuals all have the equipment they need to support their movement. However, they are still likely to encounter a number of barriers such as:

- uneven and rough pavements and surfaces
- buildings with narrow doors and corridors
- small bathroom facilities with low toilets and high mirrors
- busy shopping areas with lots of people
- getting on and off public transport
- bins on pavements on collection day, which can make the route difficult to navigate
- (sometimes) the attitudes of society
- lifts that are not working
- being nervous that their wheelchair or scooter will tip over
- having to recharge batteries on their mobility equipment
- getting up steep slopes
- bad weather, including rain, snow and ice
- litter, debris and slippery leaves.

Overcoming other difficulties

Physical barriers are not always about mobility. Some people who need to access health and social care services may encounter other types of problems. For example, a person who has arthritis in their neck, back pain or breathing problems may find lying in a dentist's chair or on a treatment table painful and difficult.

Consideration, careful planning and small adjustments can make all the difference to someone with physical difficulties, as the diagram below shows. Additionally, providing feedback to local councils and health and social care services may also help to drive improvement.

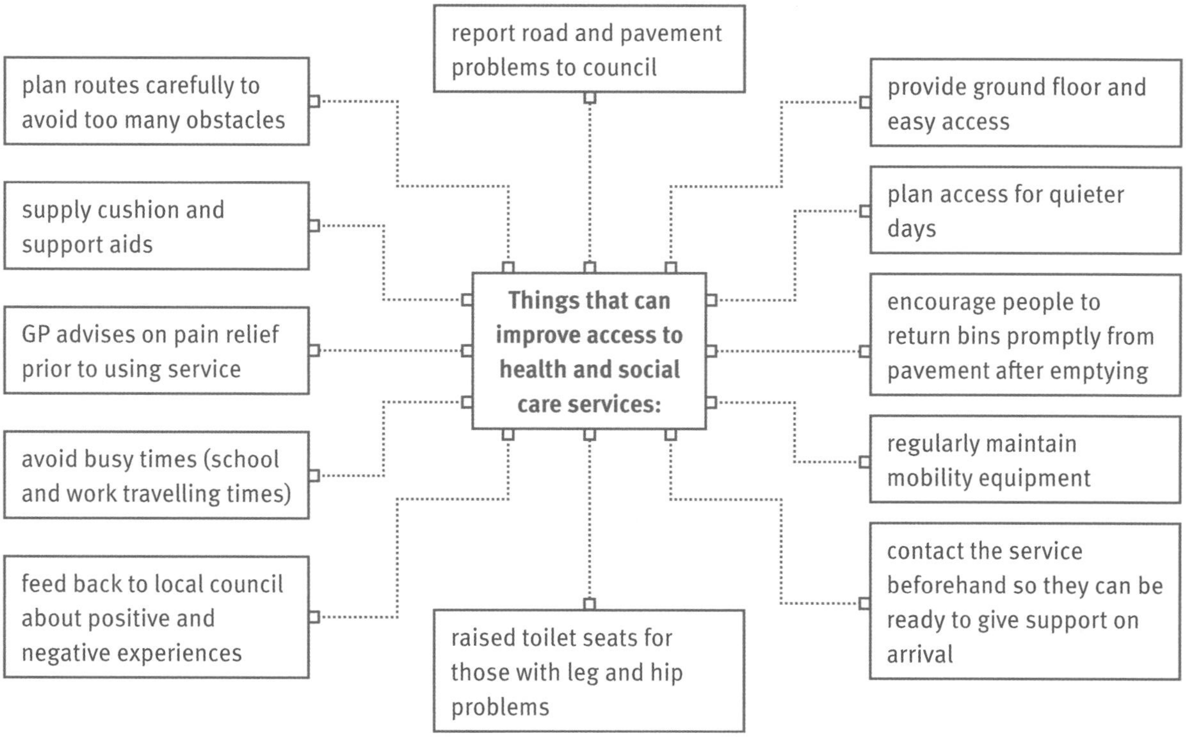
Things that can improve access to health and social care services:
report road and pavement problems to council
plan routes carefully to avoid too many obstacles
supply cushion and support aids
GP advises on pain relief prior to using service
avoid busy times (school and work travelling times)
feed back to local council about positive and negative experiences
raised toilet seats for those with leg and hip problems
provide ground floor and easy access
plan access for quieter days
encourage people to return bins promptly from pavement after emptying
regularly maintain mobility equipment
contact the service beforehand so they can be ready to give support on arrival

Figure 2.5: Examples of accessibility

ACTIVITY

Some areas are difficult for people to access because they cannot walk or balance properly. They may need to use a wheelchair, mobility scooter or walking aid. Often there are differences in floor levels with steps and changes of surfaces. Small areas such as bathrooms can be particularly difficult to access.

1 In your group, carry out an access audit of your school for an individual who uses a wheelchair or mobility scooter. Your access audit should identify where physical barriers to access may occur.
2 Present your findings to the class and be prepared to answer questions from others.

DID YOU KNOW?

Sometimes, official audits take place to make sure buildings and other environments meet the correct guidelines for disabled people. They may also be referred to as Disability Discrimination Act Audits or Disabled Access Audits.

CHECK MY LEARNING

Imagine that someone who has mobility difficulties is coming to visit you in your home. Carry out an access audit before they arrive.

Sensory barriers

GETTING STARTED

Close your eyes for 2 minutes and carry on listening to what is going on around you. Then discuss with your partner how you felt not being able to see things.

Imagine if you cannot see or your vision is blurred and if you cannot hear what people are saying? How would you feel? Many people live with these sensory difficulties.

The importance of senses

Our senses are important because they allow us to see, hear, taste, smell and touch. However, sometimes we can have difficulties with one or more of our senses either because of age or because of a physiological problem (a problem that relates to the body).

Sensory impairments (difficulties with our senses) can often be a barrier to accessing services. When we access health and social care services it is usually because we have a health need or problem. We often need to give and receive complex information clearly and accurately. Having a sensory impairment can make this process more difficult and frightening.

LINK IT UP

To find out more about physiological issues, go to Section B1 in Component 3.

Types of sensory impairment

Any of our senses can alter. We may notice, as we get older for instance, that we need stronger glasses or cannot clearly hear people talking. Here are some of the ways sensory impairment can affect individuals.

Vision

A person who wears glasses relies on them to be able to function properly and safely. Someone who has lost their glasses will not be able to drive to an appointment safely. Similarly, a person may not be able to read important information and instructions. They may even find signing a prescription difficult.

Some people have profound sight problems and can see very little. They may use Braille to communicate. Not all services provide sufficient information in Braille format.

LINK IT UP

To find out more about Braille and its importance, go to Section B1 in this component and Section C2 in Component 3.

Hearing

Hearing loss is common. Like sight loss, it can affect both young and older people. Individuals may experience varying levels from mild hearing loss to complete deafness. Having a hearing impairment can be isolating. Not being able to hear what is going on around you can be frightening.

Many of us find understanding complex medical instructions difficult, but imagine how it feels for a person who cannot hear very well. Procedures such as undergoing an eye test could prove a real challenge for a hearing-impaired person.

ACTIVITY

1. In groups of three, choose one to blindfold. The remaining two carefully guide the blindfolded person to a place in the classroom, for example, leading by the hand, clear verbal instructions or both.
2. Remove the blindfold when you have reached the place. Discuss the difficulties/feelings of *either being the sight-impaired person or supporting them.*
3. Next, in your groups, choose one person to wear headphones/earplugs. The remaining two go through instructions (for example, buying online) with the person wearing headphones.
4. Once completed, discuss the feelings/difficulties experienced as the 'hearing impaired' person and those giving the instructions.

Helping people who have sensory difficulties

Health and social care providers should make their service accessible to those who have sensory difficulties. This can be as simple as:

- providing information in large print for the sight impaired
- using good communication skills to help the hearing impaired
- if possible, trying to learn some sign language (a way of using your hands and fingers to communicate visually).

Imagine you are a care provider. Look at Table 2.6, which gives information about how to help and communicate with people who are sight or hearing impaired.

Table 2.6: Tips for care providers when communicating with sight- or hearing-impaired people

Sight-impaired people	Hearing-impaired people
Introduce yourself. Greet the person and use non-verbal communication, e.g. a supportive hand placed on their arm or handshake. If there are other people present, introduce them too.	Introduce yourself and anyone else present.
Continue using supportive non-verbal communication as this often helps to display an empathetic tone of voice. Smile; although the person may not see this, it will come through in your voice.	Sit facing the individual so they can see your face and lip read if necessary.
Communicate in quiet areas away from external noise and maximise the use of natural light. Speak naturally and clearly. You do not need to raise your voice unless the person is hearing impaired.	Choose a place where it is quiet and with good natural light. Speak clearly but not too slowly as this makes it difficult to lip read.
Be clear about instructions, e.g. 'the toilet is ahead of you and immediately on your right-hand side'.	Avoid jargon. Help the person to understand by paraphrasing if necessary. Check the person's understanding regularly and repeat if necessary. If another person is present (e.g. an interpreter) talk to, face and address the service user, not the interpreter.
If the person wears glasses, ensure they have them, as well as any other aids that they use. Make sure that the glass lenses are clean.	Do not cover your mouth while talking. The individual may be lip reading. Keep your facial expressions and gestures natural. If the person uses a hearing aid, ensure they have it and that it is clean and working properly.
Tell the person when you are leaving.	Clearly indicate to the person when you are leaving.
Make sure the person has the call bell or other method of alerting care staff before you go.	If the individual uses any other aids, ensure that they have access to them before you leave.

CHECK MY LEARNING

1 Annie is sight impaired. How could a care provider help her when going for a hospital appointment?

2 Josef cannot hear very well and goes to the pharmacist for some advice. How can they make sure communication is effective?

DID YOU KNOW?

In 2003, the UK Government officially recognised British Sign Language as a minority language.

Would you be prepared to learn this language to help the hearing impaired?

DID YOU KNOW?

There are lots of technologies and apps to help people who are visually impaired or blind; for example Text to Speech, magnification, navigation and object identification. More are being developed all the time. Check your phone to see what apps you can find that could help.

Social, cultural and psychological barriers

GETTING STARTED

On a piece of paper, write the words 'social', 'cultural' and 'psychological'. What do you think these words mean? Write definitions. Use a dictionary or the internet if you need help.

Imagine visiting a dentist after a previous terrible dental experience. You could be very nervous going back. People accessing services might also feel nervous because of social, cultural or psychological barriers.

Anxiety about accessing services

Having a phobia about accessing a service can create a great deal of anxiety. It could lead to panic attacks or avoidance of going altogether. There can be many social, cultural and psychological reasons why people do not want to, or cannot, access health or social care services, as Table 2.7 shows.

Table 2.7: Why some people find access to health and social care services challenging

Reason	Example
Self-diagnosis	There may be avoidance of going to the doctor because of fear of the outcome.
Stigma	This occurs especially around conditions relating to sexual health or fear of a physical examination.
Drug and alcohol problems	Fear of not only what the practitioner might think but also other service users.
Fear of giving in to the illness	For example, a person who has profound memory loss, fears the diagnosis of dementia.
Opening hours	Many individuals work during standard daytime opening hours of some services, which creates a problem.
Cultural barriers	Some people have specific cultural barriers, for example, in some cultures a woman may wish to see a female doctor/pharmacist.
Negative experience	A person having had previous negative experiences of using the service.
Mental health difficulties	The individual may feel embarrassment and shame; they may avoid accessing services for fear of being judged and labelled.

KEY TERMS

Stigma is when you feel that others disapprove of your circumstances and you have strong feelings of shame or embarrassment about something.

Cultural considerations

People from different cultural backgrounds might find accessing services difficult. They could be worried that their cultural needs lead others to judge them. They might also feel they are not being taken seriously.

Health and social care workers must be sensitive to people's preferences and choices. Specific cultural preferences should be respected. Meet the people on the next page who all have different cultural preferences and are using health and social care services. It is worth remembering that cultural preferences can include regular praying and specific diets. If someone was staying in a hospital or care home, or even had carers in their own home, these preferences need to be properly understood and respected.

'My name is Eliora. I am Jewish. I would prefer another female to support me with hygiene but would accept a male if necessary. If I were an Orthodox Jew like my mother, I would most definitely wish to have another female.'

'My name is Raakin. I am a Muslim. We all consider cleanliness desirable but Islam insists on it. I cleanse my teeth and nostrils regularly. I trim my nails and remove armpit and pubic hair where dirt might collect. I do not leave excess hair untrimmed for more than 40 nights.'

'My name is Parmita. I am a Hindu. Please may I have a female to help me with my hygiene. If my husband were the patient, he would be very offended if a female helped him. I am pleased there is a bidet available because I like to use running water to cleanse myself after using the toilet. While I am having a period I am considered unpure. So I take a ritual bath when the bleeding stops. This is a very private matter and I prefer not to talk about it.'

'My name is Devinder. I am a Sikh. I do not cut my hair, so I like to use conditioner to keep my hair and beard smooth and glossy. I wear my turban at all times.'

Figure 2.6: Examples of cultural requirements

ACTIVITY

There can be many reasons why some people may not wish to, or cannot, access facilities because of social, cultural and psychological reasons. Look again at the section on 'Cultural considerations' and the speech bubbles above. Let these stimulate ideas around barriers and information about cultural preferences.

1 In your group, create a poster that shows a range of potential social, cultural and psychological barriers to accessing services.
2 Suggest how each barrier could be overcome.
3 Present your poster and ideas to others in your class.

Breaking down barriers

A few simple things, including building a trusting and understanding relationship, are often enough to break down most barriers.

- Individuals should be given opportunities to share their concerns and have them taken seriously.
- Ensuring that different gender practitioners, and facilities to worship, are available shows respect and understanding.
- More service providers are open for longer periods of time for people who work during traditional hours. This means they can access services before and after work.

CHECK MY LEARNING

Have a look at each group's poster about social, cultural and psychological barriers. For each poster, use a sticky note to write:

1 two positive points
2 one suggestion that would have made the poster even better.

Language barriers

GETTING STARTED

Make a list of modern words like 'hashtag' and then share with the class.

Do you struggle to understand some terms older people use? They may not understand some words that you use either. Language changes over time and this can make communication difficult.

The problem with language

Several thousand languages are spoken throughout the world. Considering how people travel for both work and pleasure, it is not surprising that this can create potential barriers when individuals access health and social care services.

Figure 2.7: How many of these words do you know?

When a person is unwell, it can put a strain on communication. For example:

- a person with dementia may revert to the first language they spoke as a child making things difficult for the individual, family and carer
- some people know exactly what they want to say but find it hard to get the words out because they have a stutter or another speech difficulty
- someone who falls ill in another country may not understand what they are being told and may not be able to ask questions
- carers can become as frustrated as individuals trying to find a common understanding.

It is not just the language that can create a barrier; words and phrases change over time. This can be challenging even for speakers of their home language. The use of words and phrases that are not readily understood creates barriers for both the service user and the provider.

DID YOU KNOW?

The *Oxford English Dictionary* is updated four times a year. A recent update included 500 new words and phrases. That is about 2,000 new words each year.

ACTIVITY

Read the scenario and then answer the questions.

Angelika is 29 years old. She has lived in England for just over a year. She has a 6-year-old son, Cezar, who attends primary school. Angelika's partner works away from home. They have no other family nearby. Angelika speaks very little English. Her son is more fluent in English than she is.

Angelika has found out she is pregnant and is now under the care of the midwifery services. She has received a letter to attend hospital for a scan. Angelika will need to go alone because her partner is away. The hospital is 25 miles away. She does not drive and rarely uses public transport. Angelika is worried.

1. Why do you think Angelika is worried about attending the appointment on her own?
2. What difficulties do you think she may face getting to hospital?
3. How could the hospital reception staff help Angelika get to the midwifery department?
4. How could the person carrying out the scan help Angelika understand what is happening?

Overcoming language barriers

Careful thought and forward planning can help to prevent and overcome most language barriers. Making an effort can go a long way to demonstrating respect for and inclusion of the individual.

- Individuals can be given fact sheets that have been translated into their native language. These can be created using translation software.
- Professional translators and interpreters can be very useful to help convey important information.
- Family members can help to translate or interpret. However, this is an area that needs sensitivity. Family members are not professionally trained. They may also hear information that is sensitive and embarrassing, which *could* restrict how the information is passed on to the care provider/professional. There is also a potential for breach of **confidentiality**. However, family members can be very useful for discussing dietary requirements and for asking and answering general questions.

Children should *never* be used to translate or interpret.

Electronic assistance

There is an ever-growing range of electronic translation application tools. One example is Google Translate. These applications are quick and easy to use. They can also be a very useful day-to-day communication aid. However, electronic translations are not always 100 per cent accurate, so must not be used to convey important or specific information.

CHECK MY LEARNING

Find out about hospital translator services in your local hospital. Then find out about electronic applications that are available. How might they support service users who may experience language barriers?

KEY TERMS

Confidentiality is not passing on information or discussing a private conversation to anyone else.

DID YOU KNOW?

The NHS can sometimes provide fact sheets and information in other languages. For example, it can provide information about diabetes in Bengali, Polish and Welsh.

DID YOU KNOW?

Translators deal with the written word. They help with consent forms and other written documents. Interpreters deal with the spoken word. They help by listening to someone talking, for example, in French, then explain in English what they have said.

DID YOU KNOW?

Mandarin Chinese is the most common spoken language.

Geographical barriers

GETTING STARTED

How did you arrive at school today? What time did you leave home? What transport did you use and how long did it take? Compare your answers with others in your class.

Imagine you needed to get somewhere but had no transport. For some people, getting to local health and social care services can be difficult, especially if they do not drive.

Reasons for barriers

People who need to access health and social care services may have problems that stop them from travelling very far. In fact, for some people, getting to a nearby service can be just as difficult. The diagram below explores some of the reasons why.

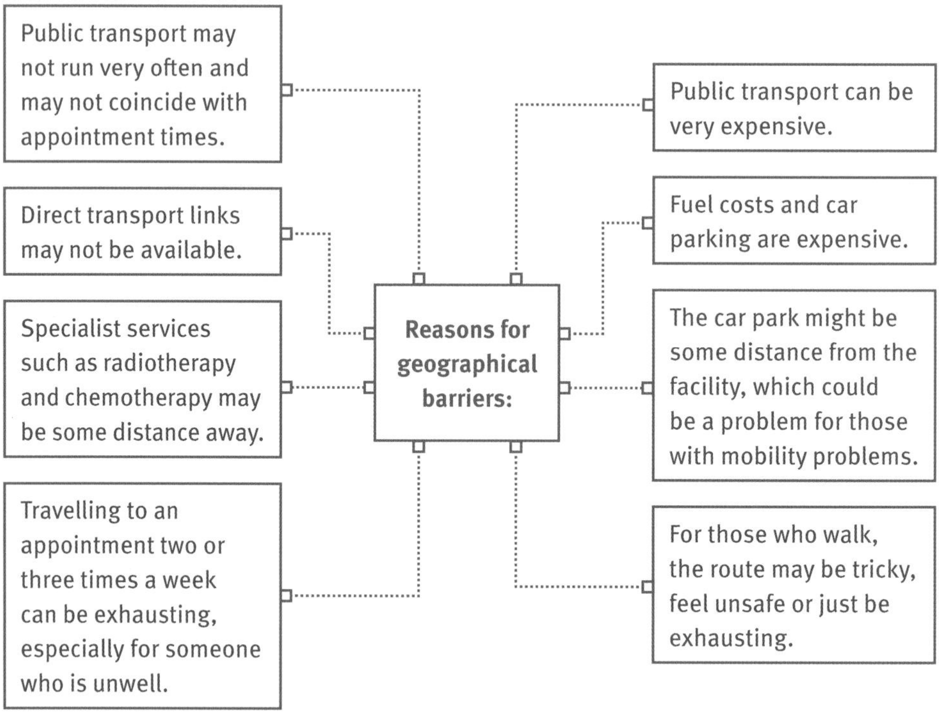

Reasons for geographical barriers:
Public transport may not run very often and may not coincide with appointment times.
Direct transport links may not be available.
Specialist services such as radiotherapy and chemotherapy may be some distance away.
Travelling to an appointment two or three times a week can be exhausting, especially for someone who is unwell.
Public transport can be very expensive.
Fuel costs and car parking are expensive.
The car park might be some distance from the facility, which could be a problem for those with mobility problems.
For those who walk, the route may be tricky, feel unsafe or just be exhausting.

Figure 2.8: Examples of difficulties with travel

ACTIVITY

In your group, read the scenario and then answer the questions.

Mr Patel has an appointment at the dermatology clinic in a local hospital. He needs to be there at 10.00 a.m. His appointment lasts for about 2 hours. Mr Patel lives very close to your school.

1. Research Mr Patel's journey to your local hospital. He is unsure whether to drive or use public transport.
2. Find public transport information about his journey from the road where your school is to the hospital. Will he need to take a bus or a train? Consider his appointment time. How much time should he allow from when he leaves his house? Remember, he will need to first walk to the bus stop/train station. List all timings for Mr Patel to arrive by 10.00 a.m.
3. Mr Patel will leave hospital at 12 noon to go home. How long will his visit take – from when he leaves home to when he returns?
4. Plan a route that Mr Patel can take if he decides to drive. You may need an online street map to help. Think how busy roads are in the morning and where he will park. Do you think his journey will be quicker by car? Do you think his journey will be cheaper? (Include car park costs.)

Overcoming barriers

As you have seen and as the case study of Robert (below) shows, getting to and from appointments can often be difficult. However, there are ways of overcoming these barriers.

- Voluntary services provide direct transport to and from hospitals and GP appointments for a reasonable cost.
- Mobile health surveillance and treatment units travel to local areas. These units, for example, can check for diabetes and some forms of cancer. They can also give chemotherapy treatments.
- Hospitals will often refund car parking charges for patients who are undergoing some specialist treatments such as cancer.

Case study: Robert

Robert has been diagnosed with prostate cancer. He needs to have radiotherapy treatment in a specialist hospital 35 miles from his home. There are no direct transport links. Each treatment takes 10–15 minutes. He needs to attend 5 days a week for 6 weeks – that is 30 sessions in total.

To begin with, Robert was fine driving. But the treatment started to make him tired and feel unwell. So family and friends took turns to drive him there. Hospital transport was available, but the journey took much longer. Robert could have stayed in discounted accommodation close to the hospital to avoid all the travel. But he preferred to be at home with family after his treatments.

Thankfully, radiographers offered appointment times that avoided rush hours.

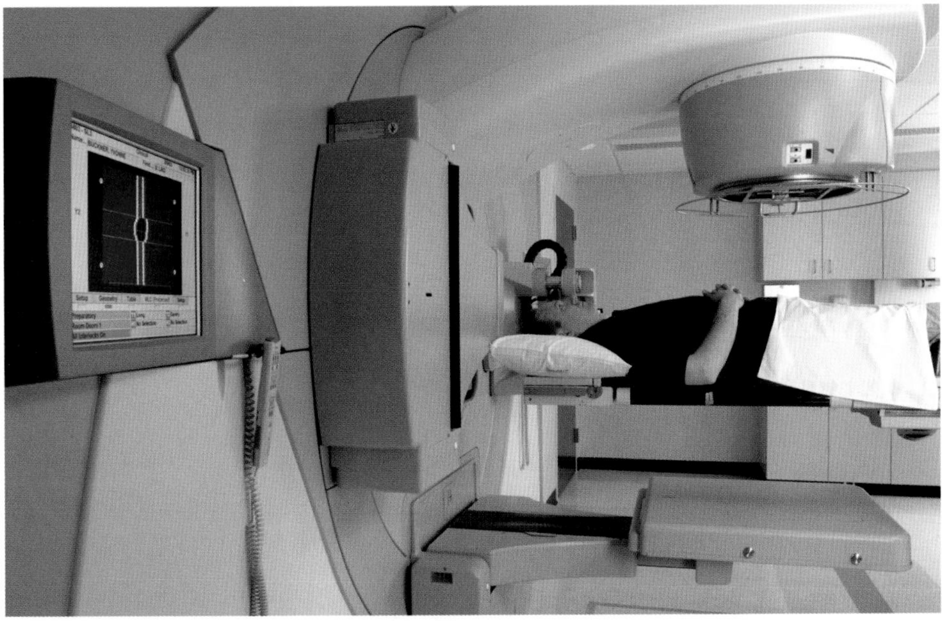

Would you have made the same choices as Robert?

CHECK MY LEARNING

Research the journey from your own home to your GP surgery, the optician, the dentist and your nearest hospital. The journeys can be made by public transport, car or both.

DID YOU KNOW?

There is more expense to running a car than the fuel that is used. The car must be taxed, insured and maintained.

Intellectual barriers

GETTING STARTED

Why might an individual find it hard to read and understand complicated information? Create a mind map with your ideas and then compare your thoughts with a partner.

Some people may find learning and problem solving very difficult. This intellectual disability could lead to physical and mental health difficulties and create barriers to health and social care services.

Understanding intellectual disabilities

A person with an intellectual disability may have problems with:

- intellectual functioning – they may struggle to learn, reason, make decisions and solve problems
- adaptive behaviour – they may find parts of day-to-day life difficult, for example, communicating with people and looking after themselves.

A person may have an intellectual disability because of interference with brain development before, during or after birth. The diagram below gives some more reasons, but sometimes the cause of an intellectual disability is unknown.

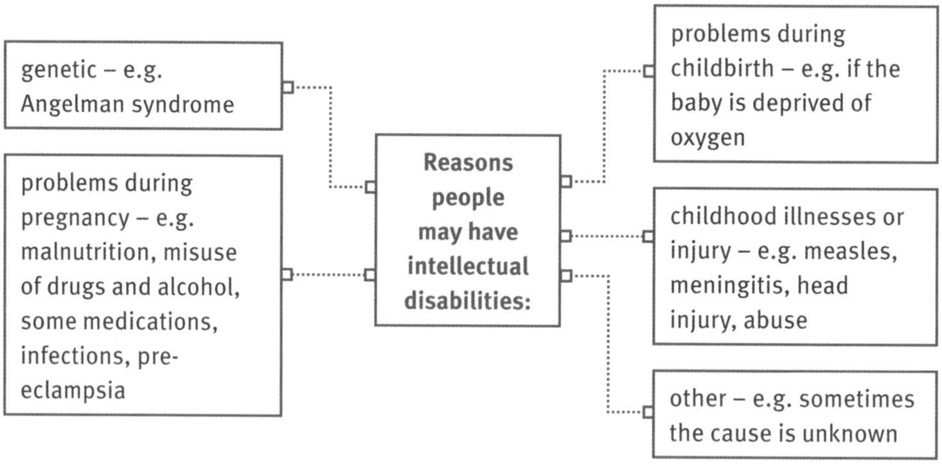
genetic – e.g. Angelman syndrome
problems during pregnancy – e.g. malnutrition, misuse of drugs and alcohol, some medications, infections, pre-eclampsia
Reasons people may have intellectual disabilities:
problems during childbirth – e.g. if the baby is deprived of oxygen
childhood illnesses or injury – e.g. measles, meningitis, head injury, abuse
other – e.g. sometimes the cause is unknown

Figure 2.9: Causes of intellectual disability

LINK IT UP

To find out more about genetic inheritance, go to Section A2 in Component 1 and Section A1 in Component 3.

Detection

People with intellectual disabilities usually have delayed development as a child. So intellectual disabilities are generally detected in children. Genetic reasons can be confirmed through a simple blood test.

Effect on someone's health

An individual may not be aware of the significance of their symptoms. This can result in delayed diagnosis and treatment of conditions. The individual may have a carer. However, carers themselves can create barriers to the individual's good health. For example:

- a carer may not understand why the individual should have regular eye tests if they do not appear to read
- a long-term carer may not notice the gradual decline of the individual's hearing
- parents of children with intellectual disabilities may feel embarrassed by the behaviour of their child in a dentist's waiting room and stop taking them.

Support

A range of people can support an individual with intellectual disability. Table 2.8 shows some examples.

Table 2.8: Who can support individuals with intellectual disabilities?

Carer/Practitioner	Support they can offer
GP/doctor	Ensures the person and their family receive the most appropriate support and refers to other professionals if necessary
Learning disability nurse	Works with the individual and their family to provide specialist health care
Speech and language therapist	Offers support to develop speech and language skills
Occupational therapist	Offers support to develop independence for daily living activities
Dietician	Offers support on nutritional health
Physiotherapist	Supports physical movement

Good communication is crucial when supporting individuals to access services. The individual needs to feel that the relationship is based on trust and respect. Communicating with a person who has intellectual disabilities can be a challenge, but there are ways to help. For example:

- avoid noisy areas
- speak slowly and allow more time to exchange information
- speak clearly, but do not shout
- involve family or a carer, but always focus your conversation directly towards the individual
- avoid jargon and keep sentences short and simple
- use a language level appropriate for the individual (this will differ depending on the disability, but a care plan should show more detail)
- use visual aids and gestures
- be aware that the individual may quickly become distracted if they have another need – for example, to use the bathroom
- be prepared for delayed responses and for answers to 'just appear'
- be aware that some individuals may have a strong understanding but are less able to express their responses
- be aware that the individual may appear to understand even though they do not; rephrase what you are saying to check understanding.

Support with reading and writing

Forms and documents can be complicated and difficult to fill in at the best of times. A person who struggles with literacy skills may feel that completing a form about their health care is impossible. An individual who struggles to read and understand might avoid accessing the services they need because they would feel embarrassed if they had to read or write something. Support can be given by writing and presenting information as clearly as possible. Family, friends or a carer who have good literacy skills can also support an individual.

ACTIVITY

Some important documents for health and social care use complex language and can be difficult to understand.

1 In your group think of a list of documents that might be difficult to read and understand. Examples include: a passport application; applying for money to care for a family member.

2 Find a range of documents and measure the readability of each one. You could look online and print them out. Alternatively, you might receive forms through the post (for example, for taking out a magazine subscription) or from school.

3 Share your findings with the class.

CHECK MY LEARNING

Write a set of instructions for a simple task – for example, how to make a cup of tea. Your instructions need to be clear and easy for an individual who finds reading difficult to understand. (You could include images.)

Resource barriers for service providers

GETTING STARTED

What services do you think a hospital provides and how much do you think those services cost?

Think about how many people access health and social care services at one time. Thousands? Millions? So it is not surprising that sometimes not everyone can access what they need.

What resources are needed

As the population ages and more disorders are being successfully treated, there is a huge strain on health and social care service resources. For example, think about all the services provided by a hospital, care home and in a person's own home at any one time. Think about the buildings that may need to be constructed or adapted and the range of staff, equipment and consumables (such as food and medication).

This is just a selection of the resources needed by health and social care services. However, resources are very stretched and much is still needed. Look at the list of resources below. What other things can you think of that have not been included? Any resource that cannot be provided will create a barrier to someone accessing the health and social care services they need.

Paying for resources

The NHS is mostly funded through:

- taxation (individuals pay tax on their income plus some other items such as tobacco and alcohol)
- National Insurance contributions (most people who earn an income pay this).

LINK IT UP

To remind yourself about primary care, look back to Section A1 in this component.

The UK Treasury allocates money to the UK Department of Health, which then gives money to NHS England. Some money is retained to pay for primary care such as GPs. The rest is passed on to Clinical Commissioning Groups (part of the NHS). These groups are responsible for funding care in their local area.

The list below gives you an idea of the wide range of different resources that need to be paid for out of money allocated to the NHS:

- maintenance of buildings
- vehicles, e.g. ambulances
- specialist clinical equipment, e.g. X-ray machines, monitoring equipment
- staff wages and uniforms
- equipment for hospital wards, e.g. beds, hoists, commodes
- food
- surgical equipment, e.g. disposable gloves, surgical dressings
- medicines
- mobility equipment, e.g. walking aids
- laundry service
- office equipment, including computers and stationery.

Barriers created by lack of staff

Staff are the most expensive resource in the health and social care sector. Without staff, other resources would be of no use. Staff resources can be in short supply in some areas, especially in the caring sector. A shortage of staff creates barriers because:

- not enough people who need help will get it
- it can prevent other resources being used – for example, if a radiographer is not available, someone needing radiotherapy will not be able to receive it.

Shortage of staff often means that the remaining staff have to work harder and longer hours; this can lead them to become exhausted and they may experience '**burnout**'. When staff are under great pressure the quality of care that individuals receive often decreases, and the workers' own mental health can be negatively affected as well. Therefore managers need to be aware of staff workload and stress.

LINK IT UP

To find out more about the availability of resources, go to Section C2 in Component 3.

KEY TERMS

Burnout is when a person becomes exhausted and stressed, usually due to excess pressure and frustration at work.

ACTIVITY

In your group, read the scenario and answer the questions.

Miss Cooper is staying in a nursing home while her bungalow is fitted with handrails and ramps. She recently broke her hip and is recovering at the nursing home.

She used the phone in her room to make an optician's appointment at 10.00 a.m. tomorrow. She asked for a carer to go with her because she needs physical assistance.

The nurse in-charge informed her that no one can take her then - all care staff will be helping other residents to wash, dress and have breakfast. The home is also short-staffed.

1. Why are the care team particularly busy in the morning in nursing homes?
2. How might Miss Cooper feel about not being able to attend her optician's appointment?
3. How can the care team help her attend an appointment that will be acceptable to her and put less strain on staffing resources?

Making the most of what is available

A number of things can be done to make the most of resources available to health and social care services – for example:

- organising the skills and time of staff to make the most of them
- developing and using digital technology, which can make working more efficient
- ensuring that patients can arrive on time for appointments and are properly prepared beforehand with correct information
- educating and training staff to work more efficiently and know how to do their jobs properly (this may also avoid official complaints from users who are not happy)
- promoting good health and early treatment to avoid long, complicated and expensive treatment
- reducing waste
- being open to ideas about how the service could improve and run more efficiently.

CHECK MY LEARNING

With your partner, suggest resources that might be in short supply, which could be a barrier to the efficient running of health and social care services.

Financial barriers

GETTING STARTED

Make a list of what you think is free on the NHS and then make a list of what you think has to be paid for.

Generally, there is no such thing as a service that is free. Although some parts of health and social care services cost nothing, the service user usually pays for others.

Who pays and who goes free

In the UK today, residents do not pay for many of their treatments on the NHS. For example, seeing a doctor and using the emergency services are all free. Some visitors and non-residents may have to pay for some of the services.

But some health and social care services are not free – for example:

- optical care
- dental care
- complementary therapies (such as massages and reflexology)
- chiropody (treatment of the feet, sometimes for painful conditions that make walking difficult)
- care and support services.

Some people who cannot afford the cost of this care or therapies may decide to go without, which could make their condition worse.

Many people also pay for their prescriptions (the medicines prescribed to them by doctors), although others may be exempt (not have to pay because of their age or circumstances). Table 2.9 gives more details about who can get help with health care charges.

DID YOU KNOW?

Some people may choose to pay so that they can access services quicker and have a wider choice. However, not all areas have these extra facilities, therefore limiting access to services of their choice.

Table 2.9: Who gets help with health care charges?

Free prescriptions	Free dental care	Eye care
People over 60		People over 60
People under 16	People under 18	People under 16
People under 19 in full-time education	People under 19 in full-time education	People aged 16, 17 and 18 in full-time education
Pregnant women	Pregnant women	People registered as partially sighted or blind
Women who have had a baby in the last 12 months	Women who have had a baby in the last 12 months	People diagnosed with glaucoma or diabetes and/or who are over 40 with a family history of glaucoma
Some people on low income and benefits	Some people on low income and benefits	Some people on low income and benefits
People with cancer	If you are in an NHS hospital when you need treatment	A prisoner on leave

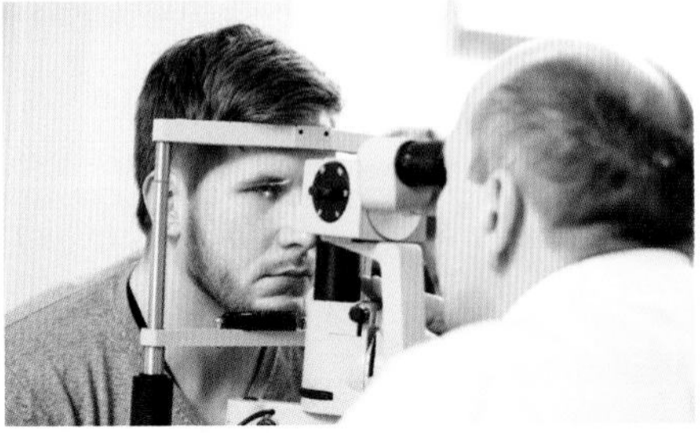

This person is having a free sight test because they are aged 18 and in full-time education

Barriers to accessing a needed service

- Some people may not be able to afford the services they need – for example, a new pair of glasses because their eyesight has changed. Often, regular dental and eye checks can prevent further more serious and expensive issues. Although these checks can be free for some groups of people using the NHS, others might have to pay. Having to pay for treatment is a serious financial barrier for many in society and may prevent them getting the health and social care treatment they need.

LINK IT UP

To find out more about how finances can affect health and wellbeing, go to Section A1 in Component 3.

ACTIVITY

1 Using the NHS website (www.nhs.uk) find who is exempt from dental and optical care costs.

2 In your group, read the scenario and answer questions:

Josephine is 30 years old. She needs to pay for NHS dental and sight tests. She made an appointment for both. Her first appointment is at the dentist. She needs to have one filling.

a How much will she pay?

The next day Josephine has her sight test. She needs to wear glasses.

b Research local opticians and their charges (choose the frames and lenses).

c What will be the cost for the sight test and glasses?

3 Compare answers with others in the class.

Travel costs

Most individuals accessing services will need to pay their own travel costs. These costs can be expensive and may include:

- bus and train fares
- taxis and other private transport
- petrol and parking fees.

Some people may be able to claim back costs if they meet the correct criteria – for example, through the NHS Low Income Scheme. However, others will need to pay themselves. The more frequently they need treatments, the more it will cost them.

ACTIVITY

Some people need to pay for their own care and this can be expensive. Find out how much it costs to stay in a residential care home for a month; research local providers.

LINK IT UP

To find more about income and its positive and negative effects on health and wellbeing, go to Section A1 in Component 3.

Loss of income during treatment

Some people needing treatment such as chemotherapy or physical care (because of an accident) may need to take time away from work. In some instances, this can mean that their income will stop. In other cases, a family member who is acting as a carer may also need to take time away from paid work.

Fear of losing income can be a serious barrier to health care for some families.

DID YOU KNOW?

If you need to pay for many prescriptions, you can save money buying an NHS prescription prepayment certificate. The certificate covers dental prescriptions. You can pay by direct debit (regular monthly payments) to make it less of a financial strain.

CHECK MY LEARNING

What other financial costs might people incur when accessing services?

Learning aim A: assessment practice

How you will be assessed

In this component, you will need to show your understanding of the topics by completing two internally assessed assignments; one to cover Learning aim A and one for Learning aim B.

You have now studied all the topics in Learning aim A. You will need to demonstrate that you know about the different types of health and social care services and the barriers to accessing them by completing the activities.

CHECKPOINT

Strengthen

- Give one example for each type of care: primary, secondary, tertiary.
- Identify four allied health professionals and explain their roles.
- Describe two physical and two psychological barriers to accessing health care services.
- Give a definition and one example each of who might use: foster care, residential care.

Challenge

- Think about someone you know and assess how one of the health services meets their needs.
- Explain two ways an 85-year-old man with hearing difficulties can overcome barriers to accessing health services.
- What barriers to exist for children in foster care? Suggest how they could be overcome.

TAKE IT FURTHER

- Have you considered the positives and negatives of each of the services and thought about how suitable they would be for 6-year-old Millie?
- Have you made realistic suggestions about how the barriers could be overcome?
- Have you provided clear justifications for your answers?

TIPS

Think about the types of primary care Millie could access. Do you think Millie might be referred to secondary care services? How would they help to meet her specific needs?

ASSESSMENT ACTIVITY LEARNING AIM A

Part 1:

Millie is 6 years old. She has had many infections recently and has been very tired. She has had a lot of time off school. Millie's mum is worried today: Millie has a very high temperature and is weak.

Millie lives in a small village on the outskirts of town. Her mum does not drive. The bus service is limited. Millie has a brother who is 3 years old.

Her mum feels that Millie needs to see a health care practitioner soon, because her condition seems to be getting worse. Millie is very afraid of new situations.

1 Research information and write a report about the different services suitable for Millie to access.

2 Assess the suitability of each service for Millie and her family.

3 For one health service you have described, where there are barriers to access, make justified suggestions how the service provider or Millie/her mum can overcome them.

ASSESSMENT ACTIVITY | LEARNING AIM A

Part 2:

Mrs Johnson is 72 years old and lives in a rented home. Until recently, she has been fully independent and had a cleaning job at her local pub. But then she had a mild stroke which resulted in some loss of mobility. Things are getting difficult; she needs some assistance with personal care. Mrs Johnson is considering the social care services available to help support her needs. She is considering domiciliary, residential and informal care that could be supported by her daughter who lives nearby.

Mrs Johnson loves gardening and she has many friends. She likes to visit the hairdresser regularly, but because of her stroke she has not been out to the salon lately to have her hair and nails done. Mrs Johnson does not have many savings.

1 Research information about services that are available to meet Mrs Johnson's social care needs.

2 Include details of the service they provide and consider the suitability of each option based on the information that you know about Mrs Johnson.

3 For one of your suggestions of a care service, are there any potential barriers? Make justified suggestions as to how these barriers could be overcome.

TAKE IT FURTHER

- When researching the different providers, did you discover any services that were provided within the service, for example, leisure activities?
- Did you consider what local services could support a person having domiciliary care?

TIPS

- Consider Mrs Johnson's lifestyle/preferences. How suitable is each option?
- For one of the services, what barriers exist? Make justified suggestions as to how they are overcome by the service provider or Mrs Johnson.

Empowering and promoting independence

GETTING STARTED

Try to write definitions for the words 'empower' and 'independence'. Then check your definitions against a dictionary. Were you right?

Rules for how health and social care practitioners' work with individuals are very important. These 'care values' can help individuals feel empowered to make independent decisions.

Care values

When our health is being looked after, we should all be able to keep our **self-respect**, dignity and safety. But this can be difficult for weak or vulnerable individuals. They may feel a loss of independence because they have to rely on others to help them. This is where care values can help. Carers/practitioners use these 'rules' (or guidelines) to help individuals retain what is important to them.

KEY TERMS

Self-respect is valuing yourself.
Person-centred approach is respecting and empowering individuals.

Take a look at the seven care values in the diagram below. These values can be put in place when practitioners/carers use a **person-centred approach**. It is important to recognise what each of the care values means so that individuals can be supported in the best possible way.

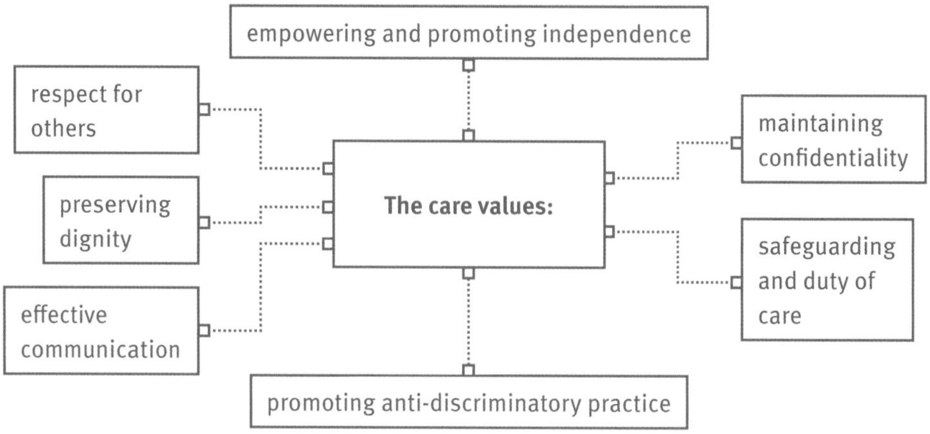

Figure 2.10: Delivering best pratice support

LINK IT UP

To find out more about a person-centred approach, go to Section C in Component 3.

Empowerment

Empowerment is when you feel in control of your life. Imagine if other people made all your decisions for you. How would you feel? No matter how limited our abilities may be, we should all be able to 'have a say' about our own lives. Some people may need help with empowerment, because of their age, circumstances or levels of confidence – for example:

- children and young people
- children and adults with specific needs
- individuals who have learning disabilities
- individuals with physical disabilities
- older people.

Empowerment is important for individuals using health and social care services. It allows them to make choices about treatment and services. They will have been given the information they need to:

- think through the advantages and disadvantages for them
- make safe choices.

Some individuals may need the help of an advocate to empower them. An advocate is someone who can help them put forward their views when they are unable to do so themselves.

This man is being empowered to make decisions about his life; an advocate is helping him to make decisions

Independence

Independence is about having control of our life, being able to do things for ourselves, and not relying on others.

Many of us will experience independence in our lives. But events can happen to some people that will take their independence away – either totally or in part – as the diagram shows.

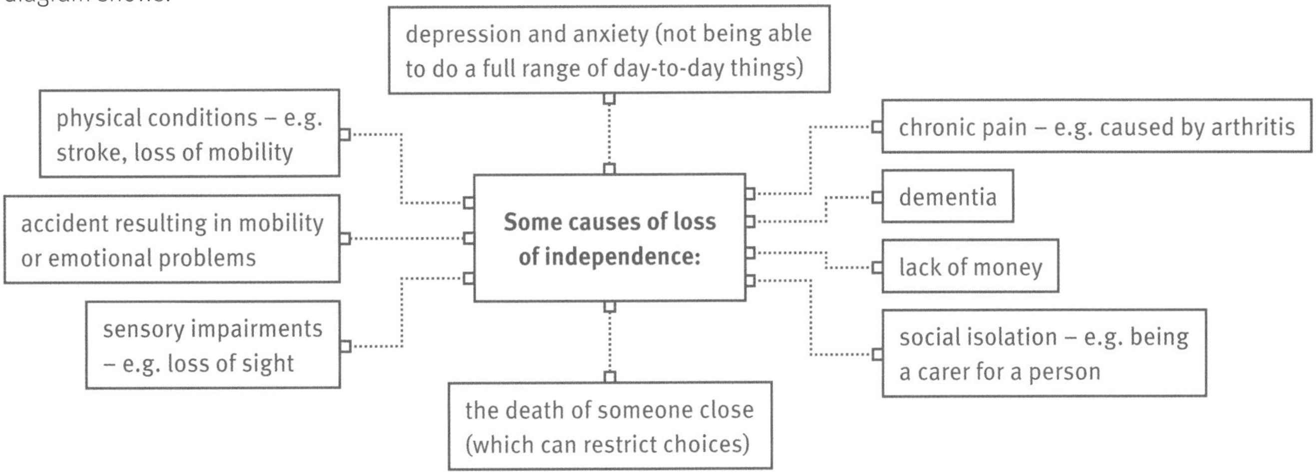
Some causes of loss of independence:
depression and anxiety (not being able to do a full range of day-to-day things)
physical conditions – e.g. stroke, loss of mobility
accident resulting in mobility or emotional problems
sensory impairments – e.g. loss of sight
the death of someone close (which can restrict choices)
chronic pain – e.g. caused by arthritis
dementia
lack of money
social isolation – e.g. being a carer for a person

Figure 2.11: Examples of how independence can be compromised

Caring for individuals who lose independence

When people lose part or all of their independence it is important to be patient with them. There may be a temptation to do everything you can for them – for example, feed them, dress them, wash them and talk on their behalf. Instead, the individual needs to be given tools to:

- do what they can for themselves
- express their wishes.

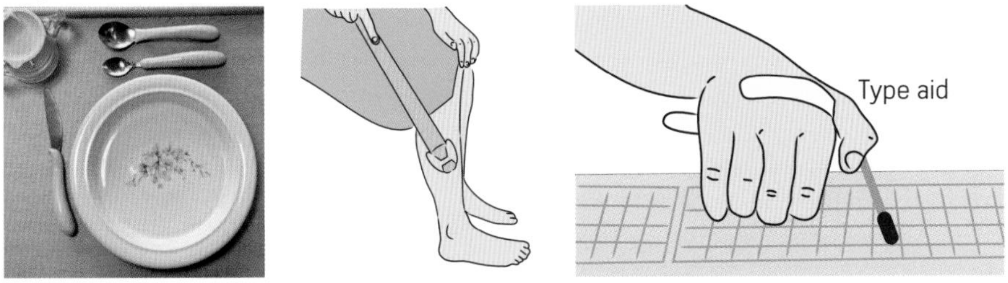
Type aid

How can the tools shown empower people who have lost independence?

ACTIVITY

1. For each of the three images above, give one example of how the item could empower and promote independence.
2. In your group, read the scenario and answer the question.

   Mr Ahmed has arthritis. His joints are sore and swollen. He used to be a solicitor and write a lot, but his fingers have become very stiff and sore.
3. With a partner, role play how you would empower a person to express their choices at mealtimes and to be as independent as possible while eating.
4. Research useful equipment that will give him empowerment and independence with eating, moving, hygiene and communication. Present your findings on a poster and share with the class.

CHECK MY LEARNING

Imagine you only have the use of a couple of fingers on just one hand. What computer and other equipment could help you to continue with learning? Research your options.

Respect for others

GETTING STARTED

What does 'respect' mean to you? Think about times when you have shown respect for someone else. Maybe you let a parent with a small child on the bus ahead of you. Make a list and compare with your partner.

Do you consider other people's feelings? Do you treat them in a courteous way? This is being respectful. Being respectful when working in health and social care shows we care.

Tolerance and acceptance

It seems that most people are very quick to judge others and form opinions. We might even fall out with family and friends because we do not agree about our thoughts, actions and beliefs. Respect is about trying to reach an understanding of someone else's views and opinions. It is about:

- being tolerant of others
- accepting their views (as we hope they would accept ours)
- accepting and keeping an open mind about different behaviours and faiths.

ACTIVITY

Read the scenario and answer the questions.

Nathan will soon celebrate his 14th birthday. He has made a list of who he wants to invite to the party and is preparing invitations, including his friend Jon, a Jehovah's Witness – they do not celebrate birthdays. Nathan invites Jon anyway; he does not want Jon to feel left out. He includes a note with the invitation saying he understands if Jon chooses not to come. He values his friendship and also asks if Jon would like to spend a day with him at the weekend.

1 Do you think Nathan was being a good friend and showing respect? Give your reasons.
2 How do you show respect and tolerance towards other people who have different views from yours? This might include your friend. Give three examples.

Respecting privacy

Respect can also be about privacy. For example, how would you feel if someone read your text messages without your permission or came into your bedroom without knocking? The diagram shows some other ways of respecting privacy.

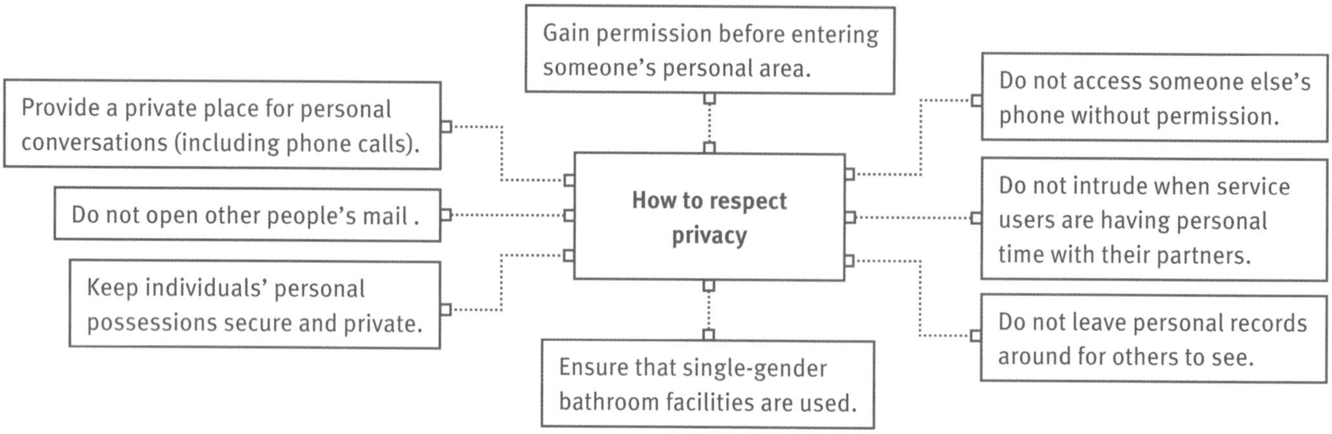

Figure 2.12: Examples of respecting the privacy of others

Respecting mental health needs

People sometimes find it hard to understand mental health problems. Because of this, those needing help with mental health issues may experience a poor quality of care. The views, care and opinions of people with mental health problems must be respected. This will help the individual return to positive mental health.

The attitude of care staff towards individuals with mental health problems can influence whether a person continues or stops their treatment plan. So care staff must ensure they:

- respect the person's views and ideas
- understand that these views and ideas may change
- promote independence
- do not treat the person as less of an individual
- involve the person in decision making
- support the person's choice of treatment without imposing their own views
- are approachable and sincere; a person who has anxiety issues can often find it difficult to talk to people.

Respecting older people

Older people have wisdom and experience that we can all learn from. Many will have lived through harsh and difficult times (perhaps war, food rationing and economic difficulties). Many will also have the experience of bringing up a family, then becoming grandparents and perhaps even great-grandparents. They will have seen many changes throughout their lives. It is helpful, when caring for older people, to try to understand this background.

Some older people's values may differ from younger ones. They may prefer to be more formal, for example, about being called Mr or Mrs. Or they may not like people visiting without an invitation. When we care for individuals, it is respectful to find out about these things and abide by them.

Respecting adolescents

Some people find relating to adolescents difficult. Adolescents may feel they are treated as a child one day and as an adult the next – depending on the circumstances or context of the situation. It is not surprising that a young person might find it difficult if they need to use a care service. For example, an individual may have experienced changes in living arrangements, perhaps being with people they do not even know. Care workers must be mindful of the difficulties that some adolescents face and demonstrate respect and tolerance.

ACTIVITY

Read the scenario and then do the tasks.

Tom lives in a residential school. He has challenging behaviours. Tom has previously been disrespectful towards care workers by swearing, damaging equipment and stealing.

Olwen is about to become Tom's key worker (the main person within social care that he will have contact with). She has a son Tom's age. Her son is respectful towards others and property. Olwen knows she must respect Tom and respect that he is different from her own son.

Olwen's mentor has given her some tips to help her to demonstrate respect towards Tom, including:

- *give time for communication*
- *take an interest in Tom's life*
- *do not make assumptions (especially about previous behaviour and responses to situations)*
- *give Tom a chance to trust and to be trusted.*

1 In your group, list more ideas to help Olwen demonstrate respect towards Tom.
2 Then, in pairs, role play the scenario.
3 Share your ideas with the class.

CHECK MY LEARNING

Speak to an older person about their life when they were your age. Ask them about preferences they had, for example, what they watched on TV. How can you demonstrate respect for what they told you? Give three examples.

Maintaining confidentiality

GETTING STARTED

We all have information that we would rather not share with others. What kind of things do you think people would mainly like to keep private?

Imagine telling a friend something private which they then told someone else. Would you trust them again? Carers know about individuals they care for. Individuals trust them to keep it private.

Confidentiality and rights

It is a person's right by law to have information about them kept confidential (private). It is important that those who work in the health and social care sector know why they must keep information confidential. For example:

- service users can be vulnerable (because of age and circumstance)
- their information is often sensitive
- they may become embarrassed, upset or risk danger if their private information is exposed.

They must also know *how* to keep information confidential – for example, where to store the information and who can retrieve it.

DID YOU KNOW?

The Data Protection Act 1998 strict rules about how to treat private data and how it should be stored.

Those who work in health and social care learn a lot about the individuals they care for:

- by talking to them
- from their records.

The diagram shows the kind of private information a practitioner/care worker may have access to or need to know about.

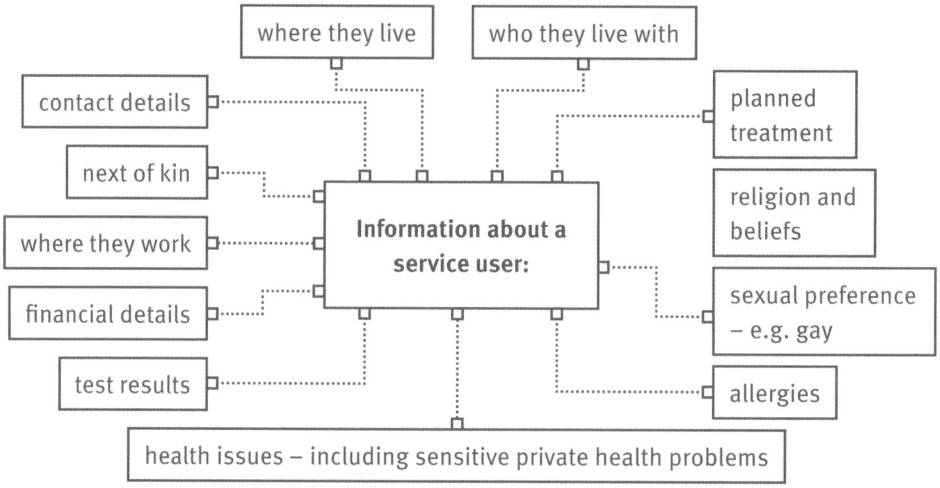

Figure 2.13: What carers may know about the people they support

ACTIVITY

1. Read the information on the diagram outlining what carers may know about service users.
2. In your group, suggest how a service user could be vulnerable or in danger if their information were to get into the wrong hands. (For example, a gay service user from a strict religious background/community could be harassed if their address is known.)
3. Share your ideas with the class and feed back on other suggestions.

Breaches of confidentiality

Care workers are not allowed to talk about one service user to another. If they do, they would be breaching confidentiality (passing on private information). However, some breaches can be accidental. Some examples are listed on the next page.

- A private conversation in a public space between a worker and a hearing-impaired individual might be overheard.
- A friend or neighbour who appears genuinely concerned about the results of a patient's operation may be given those details.
- A sexual health worker may find they are treating a friend's sister/brother.

A breach in confidentiality is serious for the worker. The consequences for the service user could be devastating. An individual's information is protected in law. Therefore, a worker who does not uphold confidentiality could face:

- disciplinary and/or legal proceedings
- lack of trust (for both the worker and organisation)
- depression, anxiety and other mental health problems
- causing a negative reputation for the service.

Social media and breaches of confidentiality

Social media is a great way to share useful information. Many health and social care organisations share valuable information relating to good health and raising awareness of disease.

Many individuals use social media to communicate personal information. But it is easy to forget how many people this information reaches out to. Consider this example: a care worker posts a photograph of children in a nativity show she has been working on. But the children are all from the residential home where she is employed. She has breached confidentiality – even if she did it without thinking. The children are now at risk and she faces disciplinary proceedings.

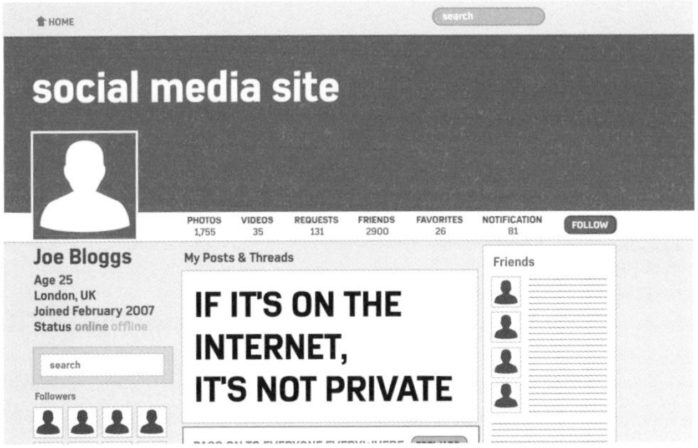

Figure 2.14: Information on social media and other places on the internet is not private

Keeping information private

Health and social care workers can keep information private by:

- not sharing information with people who do not need to know
- being aware of who is around them when talking about private matters
- not sharing information with other service users
- keeping written information in a safe place away from prying eyes
- being careful not to share passwords for anything
- changing passwords regularly
- shutting down applications and logging off when online work is complete
- being careful when using social media.

If a worker thinks they have breached confidentiality, they should tell a supervisor (the person who checks their work).

ACTIVITY

1. Produce a leaflet that could be used by new staff in a health or care setting that explains how to maintain confidentiality. Use everything you have learned in this lesson to help you.
2. What can you find out about the Data Protection Act 1998? What does a health or care setting and the people who work there need to do when handling information?
3. A young adult accesses a sexual health clinic and is worried about their information being shared. Role play how you would reassure the individual that their information is kept secure.

DID YOU KNOW?

Sometimes we need to share private information, for example if a person is at risk of harm. It is important, though, that we only share that information with the right person, such as a nominated safeguarding officer. Can you think of the sort of information that may need to be shared?

CHECK MY LEARNING

How can you keep your personal information secure when using social media applications? Share your findings with the class.

Preserving dignity

GETTING STARTED

With your partner, write down any reasons you can think of why people might become embarrassed.

KEY TERMS

Dignity is being respected and treated with care.

Imagine at school the stitching comes loose on your uniform. You might be embarrassed by what is exposed. This is how service users might feel when exposed to others.

Preserving an individual's dignity

Allowing someone to keep (preserve) their **dignity** is about considering their feelings. Think about this example: a classmate is desperate to go to the toilet – so desperate, they do not make it in time. Other classmates poke fun at them. How do you think the person feels about themselves? They are likely to feel embarrassed and ashamed. Service users who cannot get to a bathroom in time feel embarrassed too. Those who care for them need to be both sensitive and understanding when this happens.

Dignity is respecting a person's self-worth and treating them with care and respect. Some people are unable to preserve their own dignity. For example, a person with physical disabilities may not be able to:

- take themselves to the toilet
- wipe spilt food from their mouth and clothes while eating
- wash or dress themselves.

Those who care for them need to think ahead and protect their dignity.

Why an individual might lose their dignity

Sometimes, a person might not care about having dignity. For example, an individual with a mental health problem such as depression may not care what they look like – even though their appearance and personal cleanliness used to be important to them.

In these cases, it is important that a carer helps them to restore (get back) their dignity by encouraging and supporting them to maintain their personal hygiene while they are unwell. However, a carer should not force their own standards of hygiene on others.

How carers can demonstrate dignity

Carers can show they care about a person's dignity in a number of ways, as Table 2.10 shows.

Table 2.10: Demonstrating dignity versus not demonstrating dignity

Demonstrating dignity	Not demonstrating dignity
Using appropriate equipment for the individual – for example, adult feeding utensils	Using, for example, children's feeder cups and bibs instead of age-appropriate equipment that has been adapted
Involving the person in their own care	Not discussing with a person what their care will be
Helping the person go to a toilet/bathroom	Telling the person they should use a bed pan or incontinence pad
Checking with the person what they like to be called (e.g. by their first name, by their last name or any other name they suggest)	Calling a person 'love', 'darling' or 'dear'; or assuming it is fine to use their first name without their permission
Giving the person the time they need	Rushing a person
Making the person feel valued	Making the person feel they are being a nuisance

There are other ways that a carer can demonstrate dignity and respect, for example:

- closing doors and curtains when an individual is washing, bathing and going to the toilet
- keeping their private areas (for example, their genitals) covered
- using professional language and speaking quietly when discussing personal, sensitive things so that others cannot overhear
- making sure an individual's clothes are clean
- dealing with embarrassing situations sensitively and professionally.

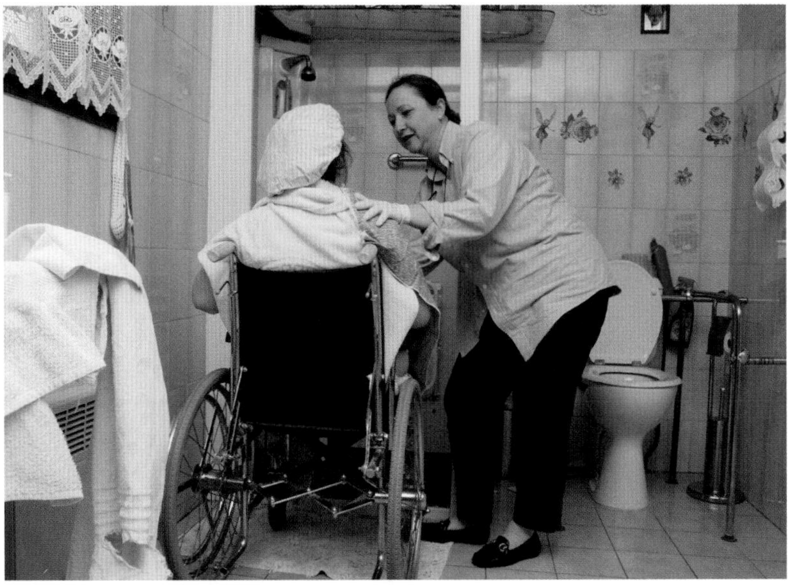

How would you feel if you were not treated with dignity?

ACTIVITY

Read the scenario and then do the tasks.

Ana is in a hospice. She is having palliative care. Previously, she had a course of chemotherapy treatment, which caused her to lose her hair. Ana has a wig, which she always wore after her hair loss. In fact, no one saw her without it. She had always been very particular about her appearance. She would hate to be seen without make-up, nail polish and nice clothes.

Ana is nearing the last days of her life. She is very sleepy and unable to communicate. Justine, who works at the hospice, helps Ana with personal care. She keeps Ana's door closed and talks to her, even though Ana is unable to answer. She washes her with care and respect, keeping her body covered as much as possible. She cleans Ana's teeth, puts her in a clean nightdress, fits her wig on her scalp, gives her a hand massage and paints her nails. Before Justine leaves the room, she puts on a piece of Ana's favourite music.

1 Discuss with your partner how Justine respected Ana's dignity. Make a list.
2 Role play the scenario with your partner or write out what you think Justine might have been saying to Ana.
3 Show your role play or script to others in the class and ask for their feedback. You will have a chance to feed back on their work, too.

CHECK MY LEARNING

Give an example of how a carer could respect the dignity of the following people:

- a child
- an adolescent
- an older person
- a person with mental health problems.

Effective communication

GETTING STARTED

How many different ways do you communicate with people? (Think about written communication as well as spoken communication.) Write a list of examples.

Do you communicate the same way with older people as with friends? Do you adapt how you communicate with people? If so, you are practising effective communication.

Why we communicate

Communication is a basic need. It is the key to all relationships – for example, with family and friends, in work, at school, socially and formally.

Poor or ineffective communication between individuals can often lead to problems. You might have heard the phrase 'a breakdown in communication' to describe a relationship that has failed. Building trusting relationships in health and social care is crucial. Trust can easily be lost if the care worker appears not to care or be interested.

Electronic communications

These days, it is common for carers to communicate electronically both with service users and with colleagues. It is important to consider tone and impact, especially in short messages. For example:

- using capital letters gives a feeling of shouting or impatience
- short statements may appear cold and too direct
- the message might be misunderstood by the reader (communicating electronically does not have the supportive body language that verbal communication does).

How might this be helping to communicate with a person who is living with dementia?

DID YOU KNOW?

We may look like we are listening but our minds can often be somewhere else. Active listening is about concentrating on what the person is saying. Active listening shows an individual that they are being listened to properly.

Who needs help with communication

Sometimes, carers will need to adapt how they communicate with service users. For example, a service user:

- may not communicate well in the English language
- may have visual difficulties or be blind
- may have hearing difficulties or be deaf
- may have problems understanding because they have dementia or other brain damage
- may have a combination of these issues.

Carers will need to adapt to the situation for example to:

- show their enthusiasm too, if the person is happy and excited about an event they are attending
- show they understand the pain of an individual who has experienced the death of someone close.

Recognising different communication needs and trying to overcome them shows that carers (and all of us) respect the individual.

ACTIVITY

1 In your group, you will be allocated an individual who has one communication difficulty: they speak a different language; they are hearing impaired; sight impaired; or have learning disabilities. Research a range of methods that may help that individual to overcome their communication barriers. To help, you could use the websites of organisations such as the Royal National Institute of Blind People and The Makaton Charity.

2 Present the information on a poster and share with the class.

ACTIVITY

3 In further group discussions, identify the positives and negatives around each method of communication.

4 With a partner, create a role play around communication differences to demonstrate how you would communicate effectively to find out information about the person. The conversation could include, for example what they like to do in their leisure time, dietary choices, favourite music/TV.

Good communication

An effective care worker will be able to:

- adapt their communication style to suit the situation
- make service users feel respected.

For example, if a carer is working with someone who cannot speak, is deaf or does not understand English, they can show the person things. A care worker can use body language to help with understanding and use non-verbal communication such as smiling and nodding to show they are fully engaged.

A person who is both sight and hearing impaired can be given something to feel, or can be gently touched (if they give their approval) as ways of communicating. These things all show that the individual is being valued. Some more examples of valuing a person through communication are shown in the diagram.

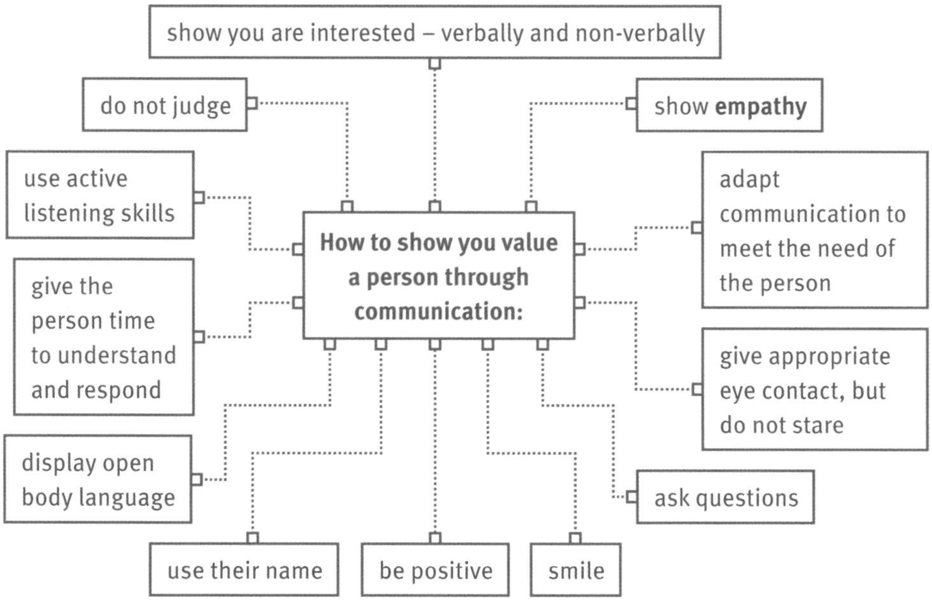

Figure 2.15: Supporting difficulties with communication

KEY TERMS

Empathy is being able to understand and share the feelings and views of another person.

CHECK MY LEARNING

1 Observe a range of individuals communicating. Note down the different methods of communication that they use.

2 How effective is the communication?

3 What could you suggest to make it better?

Safeguarding and duty of care

GETTING STARTED

Make a list of examples of unkind treatment to individuals. Then share your ideas with the class.

DID YOU KNOW?

Anyone who works with vulnerable people must provide references and have a Disclosure and Barring Service check; this helps to ensure that the worker is trustworthy.

What would you do if you witnessed someone being unkind to another person? Would you recognise they were doing something wrong? Would you know what to do?

Why do we need to safeguard?

Safeguarding is about keeping people safe from harm.

- Service users have a right to be safe.
- Care workers have a legal duty to protect service users.
- If a carer understands the signs of danger and harm, they will be able to protect their service users.

Types of abuse

There are many types of abuse, as Table 2.11 shows.

Table 2.11: Types of abuse

Type of abuse	What happens
Physical	Hitting, pulling, pushing, holding down, rough handling
Emotional	Bullying, calling names, threatening, putting the person down
Sexual	Touching an individual in private places, making suggestive comments, showing sexually related materials, e.g. pictures and videos
Financial	Spending their money, stealing
Neglect	Not giving the person enough food, personal care or attention
Institutional	Not giving individualised care, working to a routine that suits the workplace rather than the individual
Domestic violence	Violence or aggression in the home, usually by a partner
Modern slavery	Human trafficking, forced labour, sexual exploitation, prostitution, debt slavery (being forced to work to pay off debts)
Discriminatory abuse	Unequal treatment, denying basic rights, derogatory terms
Cyberbullying	Using electronic and social media to bully people

There are some warning signs that someone is being abused, as the diagram shows.

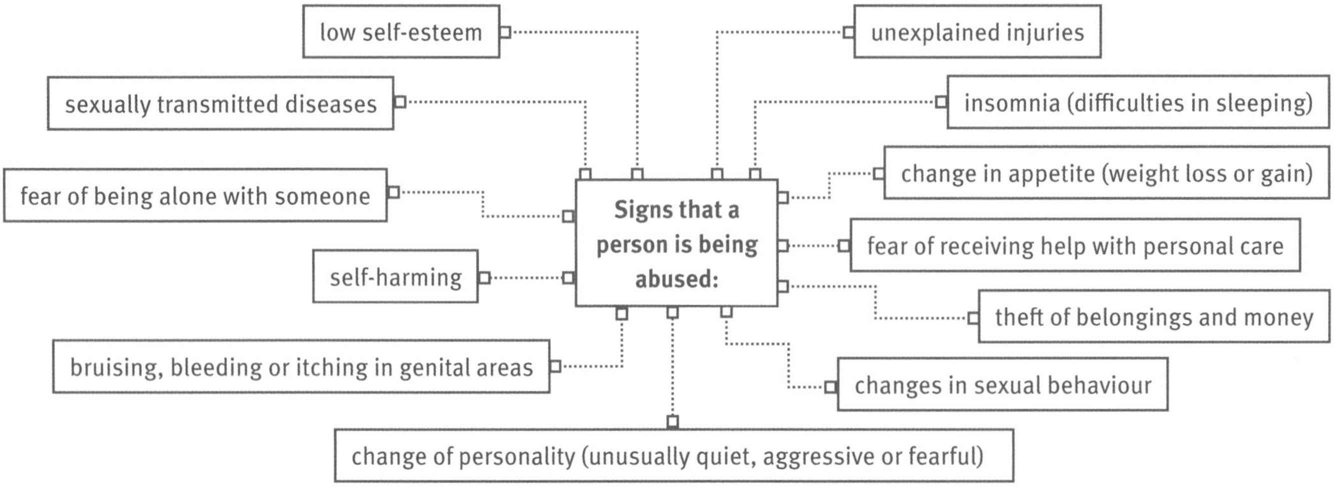

Figure 2.16: Everyone should be aware of these signs of possible abuse

Safeguarding individuals

It is important that care workers recognise the signs and symptoms of abuse so they can protect people. Symptoms on their own do not always indicate abuse. Carers need to look at the whole picture. For example, an individual with bruises could have fallen recently. But several unexplained bruises at different stages of healing would make you suspicious. Several signs together would make you strongly suspect abuse.

What to do

If you were a care worker and you suspected someone was being bullied or abused, here are some things you would do:

- report the abuse – the person could be in danger
- never promise to keep the abuse secret
- make it clear that you need to tell someone more senior than you – for example, your supervisor. (Each workplace will have a procedure telling you what to do)
- if you could not talk to someone in the workplace, you would tell a responsible adult who would help to contact the inspection team – a team that checks a care service is being properly run.

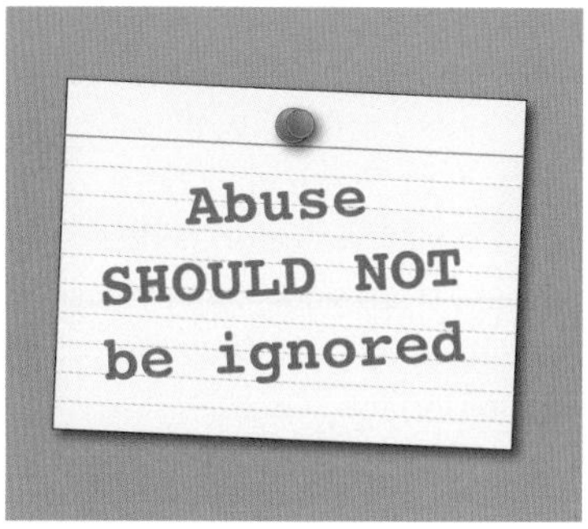

Figure 2.17: Would you know what to do if you suspected abuse?

ACTIVITY

Look at the scenario and then answer the questions.

Lakeside View is a day centre for individuals with learning disabilities. Kim is 23 years old and lives with her parents and two brothers. She attends the centre several times each month and does many activities there.

Recently, Jenny, a carer at the centre, noticed Kim was unusually quiet. Jenny observed that Kim had chosen to sit on her own rather than join in with other people. Jenny encouraged Kim to join a group that were painting some views of the lake, which could be seen from the activity room.

When Kim was painting, she knocked over a jar full of dirty water and it splashed onto her trousers. Jenny took her to the bathroom to help clean her trousers and Kim put on some spare jogging pants that she had with her. It was while Kim was changing that the carer noticed some signs of abuse.

1 What might make Jenny suspect that Kim had been abused?
2 What types of abuse might Kim have experienced?
3 What should Jenny do next?

Duty of care

Care workers must work in ways that never put individuals at any risk of harm. They need to know the responsibilities of their role and only do things they were trained to do. Their duty of care to safeguard people means that they:

- know their role and responsibilities
- follow all procedures properly
- deliver care as the individual care plan states
- always report and record any concerns about an individual, even if it appears minor.

CHECK MY LEARNING

Your friend has an older relative with dementia moving into a residential care home and is worried they may come to some harm. Putting their mind at rest, write a note how their relative will be safeguarded in the home.

Promoting anti-discriminatory practice

GETTING STARTED

With your partner, write a definition of 'discrimination' on a sticky note. Use a dictionary to help with your definition. Place your note on a board/wall alongside others from your class. Have you roughly got the same definition?

Have you come across these words 'discrimination', 'discriminate', 'discriminatory' and 'anti-discriminatory'? They are words that need to be understood and taken seriously in health and social care services and values.

What is discrimination?

Discrimination means treating a person or groups of people unfairly or less well than others. Discrimination may be obvious. However, sometimes it is more subtle or hidden. It is against the law to discriminate.

The following are known as 'protected characteristics'. The Equality Act of 2010 makes it illegal to discriminate based on these points. For example, it would be illegal to discriminate against someone in a job interview based on their:

- age
- disability
- gender reassignment
- marriage and civil partnership
- pregnancy and maternity
- race
- religion or belief
- sex
- sexual orientation.

Why people discriminate

When someone discriminates against another person it may be because they have a stereotyped idea of what the person is like. They do not see the person as an individual; they see them as a member of a group based on, for example, their religion, race or gender. They make assumptions about the individual based on what they think they know. For example, they may assume that all older people are frail and weak. This is having a prejudiced attitude.

In childhood, we learn from the people around us. If those people have prejudiced attitudes, then we may grow up believing those attitudes are right. Often, we are unaware of our prejudices, but they can make us act in ways that discriminate against other people. We need to think about our attitudes and make sure we do not use discriminatory behaviour.

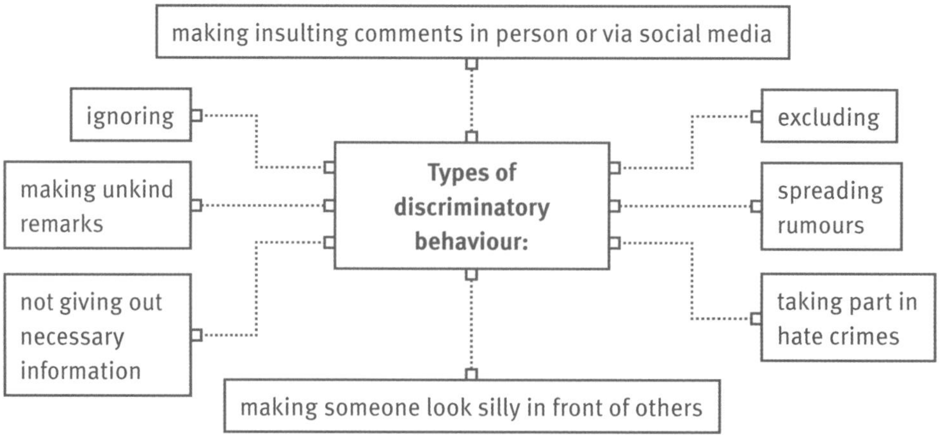

Figure 2.18: Examples of discrimination

Effects of discrimination

The effects of discrimination are devastating for the victim and for others who know them. Can you imagine how it would feel if someone who was special to you was a victim of discrimination? Discrimination can result in:

- feeling isolated and depression
- disempowerment (loss of control over life)
- physical health problems such as digestive, heart and skin problems
- low self-esteem and mental anxiety
- suicide.

Anti-discriminatory practice

Look at this example of anti-discriminatory behaviour.

Paulina, who is Polish, is 14 years old. She has been in the UK for 6 months and is new to the local school. The students are celebrating Christmas and listening to carols. They ask Paulina about Christmas songs in her country and how she celebrates. They talk about different traditions and beliefs. Then they find some examples of traditional Polish carols and listen to them.

There are many ways of promoting anti-discriminatory practice in health and social care, for example:

- having patience with others who do not speak English very well
- communicating in a way that the person will understand
- showing tolerance towards people who have different beliefs from you
- respecting the health and care choices that individuals make
- not getting involved in the discriminatory behaviour that others show
- challenging unkind behaviour.

Working in an anti-discriminatory way will demonstrate that you value a person and their differences.

ACTIVITY

1 Working in your group, produce a poster that could be used in a young person's setting for a campaign to fight discrimination. You must emphasise the idea that discrimination should never be tolerated and that people should be valued for who they are.

2 You need to include on your poster information about:
- behaviour that positively welcomes differences
- how to demonstrate tolerance
- how to support people who are being discriminated against.

3 You have a young person who is new to the setting. In pairs, role play how your organisation actively promotes anti-discriminatory practice. You can use the information on your poster to help you.

Figure 2.19: How can you make sure you promote anti-discrimination?

DID YOU KNOW?

Settings can also discriminate against a person. For example, a person with a physical disability may not have an equal opportunity to access some kinds of buildings.

DID YOU KNOW?

Working in an anti-discriminatory way is about being positive about differences and preventing discrimination.

CHECK MY LEARNING

Hospitals need to promote anti-discriminatory practice. Research information about your local hospital. What can you find out about how they prevent discrimination in their service?

Applying care values in a compassionate way

GETTING STARTED

If you were to ask someone to describe your character (what sort of person you are) what do you think they would say? Write down your ideas and then ask a partner for their opinion.

How you present yourself says more about you than what you say or do. How would a health and social care worker present themselves to demonstrate the care value of compassion?

Care values and how we apply them

In recent lessons, we looked carefully at the care values when working in health and social care services:

- empowering and promoting independence
- respect
- maintaining confidentiality
- preserving dignity
- effective communication
- safeguarding and duty of care
- promoting anti-discriminatory behaviours.

In the caring professions, those care values need to be applied in a way that shows compassion. For example, promoting dignity and respect would be difficult if we did not demonstrate a true desire to care.

Imagine you are a care worker who is helping a person in hospital. This person is incontinent (has no control over passing urine and faeces). You could probably carry out the task efficiently – for example, by covering the patient, enabling them to do as much as possible for themselves and offering choice. However, it is not just your actions that count. It is how you come across as a person while caring for people that is important too. You need to be able to demonstrate compassionate care to show you are sincere.

As a care worker, you might be able to find the right words. For example, you can tell an individual you understand how difficult things must be for them. But if your body language does not support those words, then you will lose the trust and respect of the individual.

DID YOU KNOW?

About 90 per cent of a person's emotions are shown non-verbally. So we need to have good self-awareness of how we come across.

Empathy and caring

Empathy is about putting yourself in other people's situations. When caring for a person, you should think about how you would feel in the same situation. Putting yourself in this mind-set will help you to understand the situation a service user is in. It will help you to develop the skills to be caring and empathetic.

You can show you really care by:

- being patient
- showing sensitivity
- understanding
- actively listening
- having a positive outlook
- being encouraging
- having genuine concern for other people.

Figure 2.20 on the next page shows the six Cs of compassionate care. Table 2.12 takes a closer look at what each 'C' actually means. Workers can check themselves against lists like these to make sure they are applying care values with compassion.

DID YOU KNOW?

A report exposed poor practice in a hospital that needed to change because the caring focus had been lost. A plan was put together for all health and social care staff to work in a compassionate way – known as compassionate care.

Table 2.12: Understanding what the six Cs cover

The 'C'	What it covers
Care	Helps to improve an individual's health and wellbeing. Care should be tailored to each person's needs and circumstances
Compassion	Shows the care worker understands what the individual is experiencing. Being empathetic to their situation shows care and value to the individual
Competence	Shows that care workers can safeguard and protect individuals from harm
Communication	How to adapt to individuals and their circumstances to ensure important information is given and shared – keeping the individual at the heart of everything that is done
Courage	Protecting individuals by speaking up if you think something is wrong; being brave enough to own up if you have made a mistake
Commitment	Carrying out your duties to care for others to the best of your ability

Figure 2.20: Compassionate care and the six Cs

ACTIVITY

In your group, read the scenario and then complete the tasks.

Sharna is 52 years old. Until recently, she had her own business. Then she had a stroke and can no longer work. Her mobility and speech have been affected.

Sharna was in hospital to begin with, but has now been discharged. She is at home and is having domiciliary care support. Sharna has regular visits from practitioners – for example, care workers, a nurse, a physiotherapist and an occupational therapist. Sharna also has close family support.

Because Sharna has difficulties communicating, she and her family have decided to create a small poster for the professionals who visit to say how she wants to be treated in a compassionate way.

1 Using the six Cs of compassionate care, create a poster that could be displayed in Sharna's house to remind those who visit how she would like to be cared for. Remember to include things such as what she likes to be called, what foods she prefers to eat and cultural preferences around personal care.
2 Display your poster alongside those of other groups. Take a look at the work that everyone has produced.

CHECK MY LEARNING

1 Self-assess your poster. Write two positive points and one that would have made it better.
2 Peer-assess a selection of other posters in your class, noting two positive points and one that would make it better.

Working together

GETTING STARTED

Refer to the list of care values in the previous lesson. Choose a health or care worker. Give examples of how each care value is demonstrated by the health or care worker chosen. (For different care roles, look at previous lessons.)

All care workers have a responsibility to uphold care values. If everyone works together, doing their 'bit', service users and colleagues alike will all be able to have positive experiences.

Every care worker counts

A good health or social care provider will ensure that everyone is working to the care values. For example, a housekeeper will show respect for an individual's dignity by knocking or asking if this is a good time to clean their room. The senior consultant can empower an individual by encouraging them to make choices about their treatment and care. And all the carers in between will demonstrate the care values in many different ways.

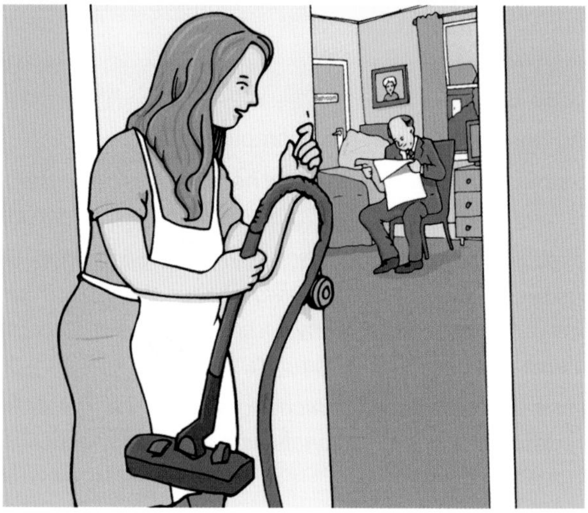

Figure 2.21: How is the housekeeper demonstrating care values?

A good health or social care provider also understands they may face situations that are not easy. For example, an individual may show anger or blame – and sometimes even violence. (There are many reasons why they might react in this way.) The key to being a good care worker is being able to:

- put any feelings and emotions to one side
- continue to work in a way that respects each of the care values.

Staff training

Staff training to keep everyone updated is vital. Even if someone has already had training in care values, further training will remind them of their importance. Having the opportunity to talk to other workers about experiences and difficulties can also be helpful; it is a way of discovering better ways of working and possible solutions to difficulties.

What service users think

Health and care providers are keen to know what service users think about their:

- experiences with staff
- levels of satisfaction
- positive comments as well as negative ones.

This feedback can be given to the care team or shared in staff meetings. Feedback that is not so positive can also be addressed at training sessions.

Seeking feedback can help you to know what you are doing well and how you need to improve. Here are some comments from service users and their families. As you read them, make a mental note of whether they deserve a thumbs up (positive) or a thumbs down (needs work).

'The porter who took me to theatre was brilliant. She introduced herself. She knew I was scared. She just seemed to know what to say to make me feel better.'

'The mental health team were great. They made sure my daughter was safe when we were worried about her.'

'One of the staff forgot to give me my tablets. I was cross at the time. But looking back I really admire his courage because he owned up to his mistake.'

'The nurse was so committed. She stayed after her shift had ended to help me speak to my daughter who lives in Australia.'

'The man who cleans my room always knocks before coming in. He makes sure he knows where things are. I can't see very well and he even brought in some large print books that his sister doesn't need any more.'

'Part of my treatment was in another hospital. The communication between the two places was terrible. Neither seemed to know what the other was doing.'

'My son has problems with communication. The care worker went out of his way to draw pictures to make sure that he understood what was happening.'

'My godmother lives in a care home. She has dementia and can be difficult at times. The care staff were very abrupt and ignored her.'

'When my grandad was unwell, the care worker sat with him and gently held his hand. She talked to him even though my grandad was unable to reply.'

'My brother would not have been able to walk again had it not been for the staff working together to encourage him to do as much as he could for himself.'

Figure 2.22: Examples of positive and negative feedback

ACTIVITY

Focusing on care values reminds us of their importance.

Imagine you are working in a health or social care setting. The manager wants all staff to have a leaflet that will remind them about the care values. The manager has asked you to develop that leaflet.

1. With your partner, choose a health or social care setting – for example, a hospice.
2. Design a leaflet explaining what care values are and how they could be applied in your setting. The leaflet is aimed at staff at all levels, so keep the information clear, concise and relevant to the setting.

CHECK MY LEARNING

Adapt the content of your leaflet to a different type of setting. Even though the same values exist, see how you can apply them in a different way.

Making mistakes

GETTING STARTED

Health and social care workers occasionally make mistakes. With your partner, write a list of potential mistakes that they could make. Think about all parts of their job – not just their contact with service users.

Though you try your hardest, sometimes you might make mistakes. We all do. When following instructions, we might make mistakes. The same can happen in health and social care settings.

The consequences of mistakes

Health and social care staff work hard to do their jobs well. But occasionally they might make mistakes. These mistakes may not be life-threatening, but they could have serious consequences. For example, a nurse caring for a patient in hospital may not record when the patient last passed urine. A doctor looking at the patient's notes might conclude their kidneys are not working properly and give them medication they do not need.

It is important that staff own up to mistakes, no matter how minor they appear. This is part of the duty of care to safeguard individuals; it also demonstrates respect for individuals.

ACTIVITY

Read the scenario and then answer the questions with your partner.

Alex works with the drugs team and is a support worker. Alex is there to help people when they are coming off drugs. It can be very difficult for those trying to withdraw from addictive drugs. It can result in the person being restless, anxious and having difficulty concentrating.

Alex goes to work one day. He has been working long hours, is tired and his young child is not sleeping well.

Sam is a new service user and Alex is introducing him to the service.

Sam becomes very angry and starts shouting at Alex. Alex shouts back, telling Sam how tired he is. Alex says he will not tolerate Sam's outbursts.

Afterwards, Alex reflects on the situation and recognises he did not react in a professional way or demonstrate the care values.

1. What care values did Alex not demonstrate?
2. How should Alex have responded to Sam?
3. Role play the scenario with your partner. You could even role play it to the class.

Dealing with mistakes

Making mistakes can make us feel terrible. We may experience a range of physical and emotional feelings (as the diagram on the next page shows). The difficulty of working in health and social care is that mistakes are likely to be related to an individual. The important thing is being able to deal with a mistake in the correct and professional way.

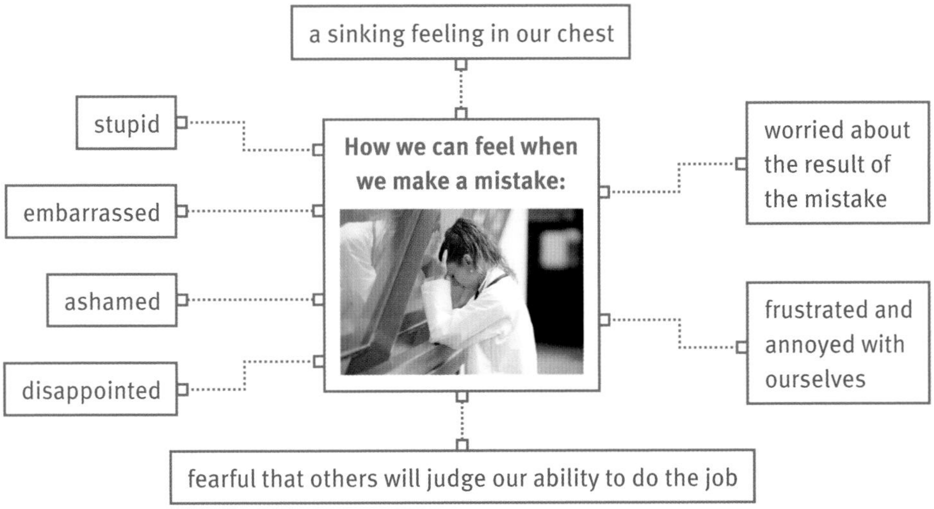
a sinking feeling in our chest
stupid
embarrassed
ashamed
disappointed
How we can feel when we make a mistake:
worried about the result of the mistake
frustrated and annoyed with ourselves
fearful that others will judge our ability to do the job

Figure 2.23: Personal consequences of making mistakes

Most mistakes are easily remedied, as long as you go about things in the right way. For example, it is important that you:

- are honest about your mistake
- do not pretend that it did not happen
- do not blame someone else.

When working with vulnerable people, the consequences of making mistakes (even though they may be small) can be damaging. Service users can lose trust in the service. They may even avoid returning, which could have devastating effects on their care and treatment. The reputation of the service is also at risk.

If you make a mistake at work, here is the best way to tackle it:

- tell your supervisor, admit your mistake and apologise
- be honest and accurate about what happened
- suggest ways to avoid the mistake happening again
- earn back the trust of the person involved
- prove you can do the job
- do not be too hard on yourself; seek help and guidance from others to manage your own feelings.

CHECK MY LEARNING

Think about a mistake you have made. You could use an example from the introductory activity. What would you do differently if the situation were to happen again?

DID YOU KNOW?

Owning up to your mistakes shows courage and maturity. Although the initial response may be difficult to handle, people will respect you if you are honest and brave enough to own up when you get things wrong.

Reviewing own application of care values

GETTING STARTED

We are all skilled in some areas but not so strong in others. Make two lists: one list for what you think you are skilled at; the other list for things you find difficult and are not so skilled at.

Recognising what you do well and what you need to do better is important for working effectively. This way you build on your strengths and work on your weaknesses.

Learning about our own skills

In a health and social care context, care workers need to be able to look at how they are developing their skills in demonstrating care values. Throughout this component, you have learned what each of the care values mean. You have also had some practice of these values using scenarios and role play.

One way you can improve your skills is to look carefully at:
- the areas you are good at
- what you are able to do well
- things you find difficult or are not quite so good at.

Looking at our own strengths and areas for development is called self-assessment.

Strengths

Have you noticed that sometimes it is hard to give yourself praise for what you do well? It might feel uncomfortable, almost as if you are bragging. However, recognising your strengths is an important part of working in health and social care.

Knowing your strengths will allow you to take on tasks with ease. You will feel confident that you are doing a good job. Sharing your strengths with supervisors lets them know too that you feel you can do some jobs well. For example, you might be very good at communicating with a particular child who has autism. This can benefit the child. It will also give you and your supervisor confidence in your abilities.

Areas for development

Are you aware of the things you find difficult? Recognising these areas is a start to working out how to develop them. In a health and social care setting, sharing your thoughts with supervisors about your areas for development will:
- let them know where you lack confidence
- help them to support you before you carry out tasks in those areas.

Identifying your weaker areas is not a bad thing. In fact, it shows you are able to be open and honest with yourself and others. Look at Table 2.13. It is a self-assessment of how you might have demonstrated care values through scenarios or role plays.

Table 2.13: Self-assessment of how care values have been applied

Strengths (What am I good at?)	Areas for development (What parts do I need to work on?)
• **Dignity** 'When we did a role play in class, I knocked on the door of a service user before entering.' • **Respect** 'I always ask service users how they would like to be addressed. Mr S does not like us to use his first name.'	• **Communication** 'Someone I know has had a stroke and finds it difficult to speak. I don't always know how best to communicate with her. I feel a bit awkward.'

Remember that self-assessments are there to help you – and they are confidential

ACTIVITY

In this component, you have learned about the care values and you have had some opportunities to practise these during scenario work and role-play activities. Now you are going to practise self-assessing – how well you think you have demonstrated your understanding of these values. An important part of self-assessment is to prepare and gather as much information as possible beforehand.

1. Find a list of the care values and write them out.
2. Write a few ideas against each care value about how that value should be demonstrated.
3. Create two mind maps:
   (a) the care values I have shown I can do well
   (b) the care values I have not been so skilled at, or not had the opportunity to demonstrate.
4. Complete the following table by using the information on your mind maps (you will need to explain your ideas in sentences, not isolated words).

Strengths: The values I have confidence in demonstrating *(give reasons why)*	**Areas for development:** The values I do not feel confident yet in demonstrating *(give reasons why)*

Confidentiality

You may feel embarrassed about writing down your thoughts and ideas. Self-assessments are private to you and your teacher or supervisor. The purpose of self-assessment is to help you develop. Knowing it is private will give you the confidence to be honest. An honest assessment is a valuable tool that will help you to grow and develop in your work.

DID YOU KNOW?

When you are at work, you will regularly record self-assessments on your ability to do your job. You will also share this information with your supervisor.

The importance of regular reviews

You will notice that your strengths and areas for development change over time. So it is important to review them regularly. For example, you may work in a small care home, know the residents well and demonstrate most of the care values with ease. But if you were to move to a different area, such as a drug rehabilitation team, you may find some of the care values harder to achieve.

It can be difficult to demonstrate all of the care values, especially if you are new to health and social care work. It can take time to gain the confidence and competence in all of the areas, so you will need to be patient with yourself.

CHECK MY LEARNING

With your partner, discuss the benefits of self-assessing skills in demonstrating the care values.

Share your ideas with the class.

Receiving feedback

GETTING STARTED

Think about a time recently when you received feedback for something you did. From the feedback what did you do well? What areas needed more work? How did you feel about the feedback and did you agree with it?

How often do you think you receive feedback? It may happen regularly as part of your coursework and informally, chatting with friends – for example, they say they enjoyed your baking.

Purpose and types of feedback

The purpose of feedback is to let you know:
- what you are doing well
- what areas might need improvement or extra work.

Feedback from teachers, supervisors and service users can be useful to learn more about yourself and can help you to improve. Feedback can be:
- formal – such as school reports or following an observation in a work setting
- informal – when you are chatting to colleagues about work events during a break or socially.

At some point, you may have received negative feedback on, say, a project. This might have made you feel that it was pointless continuing the project. But feedback is not about making you feel bad about yourself. If it is given correctly, it should:
- encourage you to feel pleased with what you have done well
- motivate you to improve in weaker areas – making you even prouder of your achievements in the end.

For care workers, asking for feedback from service users is the most valuable type of feedback they can receive. This is because service users are the direct recipients (receivers) of their care.

Giving feedback to others

Giving (and receiving) feedback should be a positive experience. It is important that feedback is constructive – that is, it takes a balanced view of the situation. It is also important, when you give feedback, that the other person feels valued rather than negative or bad. Imagine you are feeding back to someone who is giving personal care. To help them feel valued and positive, you could:
- start with something positive, (for example, 'I liked the way you asked Mr Costa if you could help him with a wash this morning')
- suggest they could have offered a bath or shower instead of just a wash
- end on something positive (for example, 'Mr Costa was pleased that you remembered to bring him a newspaper this morning').

This is sometimes known as a 'feedback sandwich'. If a person is given negative feedback right at the end of the session, it might be easy for them to forget any positive points. That is why areas needing work should generally be given in the middle of a session.

Figure 2.24: You can use a 'feedback sandwich' to give people constructive feedback

ACTIVITY

Read the scenario and then complete the tasks with your partner.

Natalia works in Foxglove House, a care home for older people. She is new to care work but has finished her initial training. Natalia is helping Mr Williams with personal hygiene. She helps him wash, shave and dress into clean clothes. Natalia then helps Mr Williams get to the day room and gives him a newspaper. A little while later, Mr Williams calls another carer and asks if they can help him to clean his teeth because Natalia had not offered to do them. This is not the first time that Natalia has not helped people to clean their teeth.

1. Natalia's supervisor is about to give Natalia feedback on how she managed the personal hygiene of Mr Williams (including not cleaning his teeth). How should the supervisor give the feedback?
2. How should Natalia respond to the feedback?
3. Role play the scenario. You could show your role play to others in the class, then listen to their feedback.

DID YOU KNOW?

Service users are usually invited to give feedback on their experiences of using health and social care services. This feedback is used to develop and improve practice.

How feedback helps

Feedback is only helpful if you use the information you have been given. Positive feedback should be noted, so that you know what you are doing well and how to continue to do so. Difficult areas of feedback may often feel uncomfortable to hear or read. But you must not take these personally. You must remember that the person giving feedback is trying to help you to be even better at what you do.

Imagine what might happen if carers were not told how they could improve. They might continue making mistakes that could have a serious impact on someone's health. It is important that feedback is used to help them develop and be the best they can.

CHECK MY LEARNING

With your partner, discuss how feedback can help people to work better in health and social care.

DID YOU KNOW?

You should complete a self-assessment before reading feedback from others; otherwise, your own judgement of the situation will be influenced.

Using feedback

GETTING STARTED

Have you received feedback identifying where you could improve in your work? Did you think you already worked hard on that piece and did as well as you could? How did you feel when told you could have done better?

You have received feedback; some is very positive and some identifies where/how you can make improvements. It is important now to use that feedback to get the most benefit from it.

Turning negatives into positives

Knowing how well you are doing will make you feel good. Having your hard work acknowledged increases motivation and will make you feel positive. So how do you feel when your feedback calls for improvements?

Feedback in the workplace is about helping you to develop. One way of doing this is to:

- point out weaker areas
- give advice on how to improve.

Receiving what seems like negative feedback can feel uncomfortable. But it is actually more useful than positive feedback, because it tells you the areas to focus on to improve. It is also important to remember that feedback is about your work, not you as a person.

LINK IT UP

To find out more about SMART objectives, go to Section C1 in Component 3.

Feedback action plans

An action plan is a good structured way to recognise improvements that are needed and find ways of achieving them.

Imagine you have received feedback identifying some areas for improvement – for example, a recent assignment. A feedback action plan will help you to use this feedback to improve.

- First, you will need to note down information from your self-assessment (how well you think you did and what areas you think you could improve).
- Then note down feedback you have gained from others – positive areas for improvement. Remember to ask questions if you do not understand part of the feedback.
- Now use the SMART acronym to help you create an effective action plan for your improvement – see Figure 2.25.

Involving others

It is good to involve other people when developing your action plan – for example, your teacher or work supervisor. This is because they will also have an active interest in you achieving the goals.

Are your plans detailed, precise and accurate?
Specific
How will you monitor your progress?
Measureable
Can you reach your goals?
Achievable
Are your suggestions possible?
Realistic
Have you set a date to review progress to keep you focused?
Time-related

Figure 2.25 Is your thinking SMART?

An action plan case study

Take a look at the case study below about Josef. Then look at his action plan in Table 2.14 for development and improvement.

Josef is completing a period of work experience at Grange House, a local care home for people who have learning disabilities. Josef enjoys talking to the residents and helping with activities – especially crafts. At mealtimes, Josef confidently helps residents to be independent and set the dinner table.

One resident, Tamir, has cultural restrictions on what he can eat and drink and sometimes when he can eat and drink. Josef knows this and does not want to be disrespectful. However, Josef is aware that he lacks cultural knowledge around these restrictions. He is also not sure about what Tamir does eat and drink. The last thing Josef wants to do is upset Tamir.

Josef recognises this developmental need and creates an action plan.

Table 2.14: Josef's action plan

Goal	To be achieved by	Action	Review date	Evaluation
To know the food and drink that 'T' can consume that will be consistent with his culture	4 weeks from now	• Use the internet to research food and drink preferences for T's culture • Speak to T's key worker further on these preferences (the key worker may have more details) • Refer to T's care plan (which may also have more information about preferences)	6 weeks from now	

Some things to remember...

Notice that Josef has not set too many goals at one time. Having just a few goals will help you to achieve your targets. Too many could make you feel overwhelmed and perhaps demotivated.

When you review your progress, do not be afraid to say that you have not achieved a goal. There are often genuine reasons – for example, you may have been unwell. You can always change the target date or review how you will meet the goal. You could even start again with a different action plan, if that helps you to achieve your goals.

ACTIVITY

Think about a recent assignment or project you have completed on care values. You are about to create an action plan that will help you with areas that you think need improvement.

1 Self-assess how well you think you completed the work. Make a note of the positive parts. Then make a note of areas you think you could improve. Use this information to create an action plan that has SMART goals.
2 When you have completed the action plan, check again that the goals are SMART.
3 Show the action plan to your teacher and ask for feedback.

CHECK MY LEARNING

If you were to follow the action plan, how would it help you to develop in a health or social care career?

DID YOU KNOW?

When working in health and social care, all staff have regular assessments on how they are doing, identifying their strengths and areas for development. They are then given an action plan – similar to the one you completed in the activity.

Learning aim B: assessment practice

How you will be assessed

For Learning aim B, you will be assessed on how well you demonstrate each of the care values, within a health or social care setting. If this is not possible, you may be asked to role play or take part in other scenarios. Your teacher/supervisor will observe this. You will also assess your own performance, then use your teacher's feedback and your self-assessment to review your practice and make suggestions for improvement.

Your teacher will set the assignment, explain the evidence you need to provide and the submission date. The teacher will mark the assignment telling you the grade achieved.

CHECKPOINT

Strengthen

- Identify four health/social care settings.
- List the seven care values. For each, give two examples of how you could demonstrate the care value (from a health/social care setting).
- What is the purpose of assessing your own ability/performance?
- What is the purpose of feedback?
- Why do you complete a self-assessment before receiving feedback?

Challenge

- Give two examples of when it might be difficult to uphold care values.
- What would you do if you experienced difficulties supporting care values?
- How could an action plan help to develop your practice?
- How can you ensure that an action plan is SMART?

ASSESSMENT ACTIVITY LEARNING AIM B

Part 1:
Read the following scenario and undertake the role of the health care worker in a role play.

Millie is 6 years old and will be staying in hospital for a few days because she will be having tests. Millie arrived today but her mum needs to collect her younger brother from nursery. Millie's mum is unable to stay with Millie because she has no one to care for her younger child.

You have been asked to show Millie around the ward and spend some time with her to help her settle in. Millie says that she is thirsty. While you are showing Millie around, she tells you that a little boy came over to her earlier and hit her when no one was looking. Millie loves playing board games and enjoys reading.

TAKE IT FURTHER

- Have you taken into consideration Millie's young age and her family circumstances?
- In your role play, will you use communication that is appropriate for her age and understanding as well as recognise her potential fears?

TIPS

Read the scenario very carefully highlighting important, key points. Use a list of care values to make notes around how you could demonstrate each one in this situation.

ASSESSMENT ACTIVITY | LEARNING AIM B

Part 2:

Read the following scenario and undertake the role of the social care worker in a role play.

Mrs Johnson is a new resident at Barley Fields residential home. She is very quiet and is sitting in her room looking out of the window. Mrs Johnson usually wears glasses but you notice she is not wearing them. You have been asked to spend some time with Mrs Johnson to help her settle in. While you are talking to Mrs Johnson, she says that some foods make her feel unwell but she did not tell anyone because she didn't want to appear to be a nuisance. Mrs Johnson likes to read the newspaper, look at family photographs and to knit.

TAKE IT FURTHER

- Have you taken into consideration how Mrs Johnson might be feeling and why she is quiet?
- Why do you think she is not wearing her glasses? What can you do about it?
- Is it a concern that staff did not know about food that makes Mrs Johnson ill?
- In your role play, will you use communication that is appropriate for an older person?
- How will you show Mrs Johnson that you recognise and understand how she might be feeling?
- How will you adapt communication with Mrs Johnson so that she can quickly trust you and understand that it is fine for her to tell carers and staff how she is feeling and what her preferences might be?

TIPS

When assessing your own performance, be very honest. Do not be afraid to say what you have done well, and – very importantly – recognise what you could have done better.

Use feedback information to the maximum and remember that what might appear to be a negative comment will probably be the most valuable. It will give you the ability to make realistic justified suggestions of how you could improve.

COMPONENT

03 Health and Wellbeing

Introduction

How often does someone ask you how you are and you say, 'Fine, thanks'? Have you ever really thought about what being healthy means? You will begin this component by understanding what we mean by 'health and wellbeing'. You will also learn how it is affected by a range of factors. You will then begin to recognise indicators of possible poor health and understand how to interpret health and lifestyle data. Finally, you will design a health and wellbeing improvement plan, including short- and long-term targets. This will consider obstacles that individuals may face when implementing such a plan.

Because this component builds on the knowledge, understanding and skills you have developed while studying Components 1 and 2, you will need to revisit key elements of these. At the end of this component, you will be asked to assess an individual's health and wellbeing based on a case study and design a health and wellbeing improvement plan for that individual, under test conditions. You will also be expected to identify any difficulties the individual might face when trying to make the changes you suggest and think of ways to overcome them.

In this component you will learn about:	
A	Factors that affect health and wellbeing
B	Interpreting health indicators
C	Person-centred health and wellbeing improvement plans.

Definition of health and wellbeing

GETTING STARTED

Work in pairs to write down what you think the words 'health and wellbeing' mean.

How do you define health and wellbeing? It can mean different things to different people and can change from day to day.

Positive definition

A positive definition looks at how physically fit and mentally stable a person is. You have a positive attitude towards health and wellbeing if you realise there is something you can do to improve your health and wellbeing and do it.

Negative definition

A negative definition looks at the absence of physical illness, disease and mental distress. You have a negative attitude towards your health and wellbeing if you:

- base your attitude on not having anything wrong with you
- continue as you are – including keeping bad habits such as smoking
- assume that because you currently feel fine you will stay healthy in the future.

A holistic definition of health and wellbeing

A holistic definition of health and wellbeing is a combination of physical health and social and emotional wellbeing. It is not just the absence of disease or illness. It looks at all aspects of a person's health and wellbeing. You have a holistic attitude towards health and wellbeing if you look after your:

- physical health – by meeting the needs we have to keep our bodies working as well as they can, such as food, water, shelter, warmth, clothing, rest, exercise and good personal hygiene
- social aspects of wellbeing – by meeting the needs we have to help us develop and enjoy good relationships with others, including mixing with others in appropriate environments and having access to leisure facilities/activities
- emotional aspects of wellbeing – by meeting the needs we have that make us feel happy and relaxed, such as being loved, respected and secure; we need to be able to feel, express and recognise different emotions so we can cope with whatever situations arise in life.

DID YOU KNOW?

We need to keep learning throughout our lives to keep our brains active and healthy.

In addition, we should consider our mental or intellectual health, by meeting the needs we have to develop and keep our brains working as well as possible; these include mental stimulation to keep us motivated and interested.

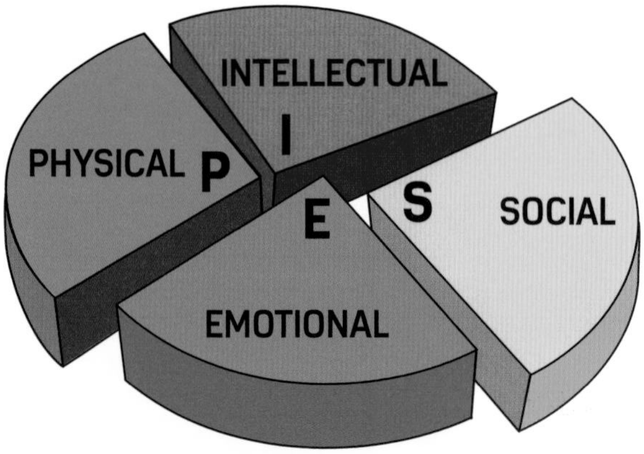

Figure 3.1: Our health and wellbeing needs

ACTIVITY

1. Work in groups to identify physical aspects of health, and social and emotional aspects of wellbeing on a sheet of A3 paper.
2. Share your ideas as a class and add any your group has missed.
3. Work on your own to identify any physical and lifestyle factors that could have a positive or negative effect on your health and wellbeing, now or in the future.
4. If time permits, note down any other types of factor that could affect health and wellbeing.

Life stages and our needs

Our basic needs do not change as we pass through the various life stages. However, different people will need different kinds of support from health and social care services depending on their particular situation or life stage. People also have different views on their needs. For example, an adult might enjoy having time alone to relax, but a child left on its own may feel frightened.

LINK IT UP

To remind yourself of the life stages, go to Section A1 in Component 1.

CHECK MY LEARNING

1. What aspects make up a holistic approach to health and wellbeing?
2. Note down the physical aspects of health and wellbeing.

Genetic inheritance

GETTING STARTED

In a small group, briefly discuss how having an inherited condition from birth such as cystic fibrosis or Down's syndrome would affect an individual's physical, intellectual, emotional and social (PIES) needs.

Physical and lifestyle factors have positive and/or negative effects on health and wellbeing. One example of such a factor is genetic inheritance.

Genetic inheritance

Some conditions or diseases are inherited, which means they are passed down from one generation to another. One example is haemophilia, which only affects males. This would affect the PIES needs in males. A male with this disease would need to make sure he does not cut himself, as his blood would not clot. As a result, he would have to think carefully about:

- what type of work to apply for (physical)
- which type of leisure activities to avoid (social).

This could affect him emotionally and intellectually, because he may be worried and distracted by his condition.

How genetic conditions are inherited

DID YOU KNOW?

DNA, which carries our genetic information, was first discovered in the 19th century.

Most of us have 23 pairs of chromosomes in each of our body cells. One chromosome from each pair is inherited from our birth mother and one from our birth father. These chromosomes contain the genes inherited from our birth parents. There may be different forms of the same gene (alleles) caused by mutations (changes) in the DNA code. A faulty gene can cause a condition to be inherited. There are two kinds of inheritance:

- dominant – if a gene is dominant a child inheriting it from only one birth parent will have the condition – for example, Huntington's disease
- recessive – if the gene is recessive a child would only develop the condition if it was inherited from both birth parents – for example, cystic fibrosis or sickle cell anaemia.

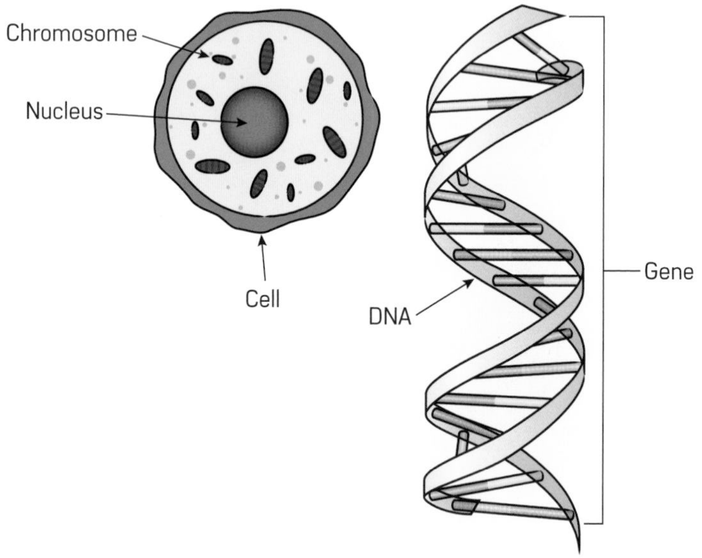

Figure 3.2: Study this image of a gene and cell and try to learn the terms associated with them

Some conditions (such as Down's syndrome) are caused by having more or less than 23 pairs of chromosome. Other conditions (such as coronary heart disease) can be caused by a combination of genes and environmental factors. For example, you can inherit heart disease, but lifestyle factors such as what kinds of food you eat and whether you smoke or drink alcohol may increase your risk.

Any inherited condition affects health and wellbeing, as you can see from Table 3.1.

Table 3.1: Some of the effects of cystic fibrosis on health and wellbeing

Physical	Intellectual	Emotional	Social
• Chest infections • Damaged lungs • Blocked digestive system • Joint, bone and liver problems	• Time missed from school through illness and treatment	• Can cause distress • Can make an individual feel different from their peers	• May prevent person from joining in activities with others • May lead to social isolation

DID YOU KNOW?

Down's syndrome is caused by having an extra (third) copy of chromosome 21.

Predisposition to other conditions

Predisposition means someone is more likely to suffer from a particular condition due to:

- genetic factors
- environmental factors
- a combination of both.

ACTIVITY

1. Work in pairs to research real-life examples of predisposition to certain conditions and the positive and negative effects on their health and wellbeing. Examples could include women who choose to have a mastectomy because they have a predisposition to breast cancer.
2. Produce three PowerPoint® presentation slides on the example you have researched.
3. Be prepared to show your presentation to the rest of the class.
4. Work on your own to research Huntington's disease. Write down how it affects health and wellbeing.

LINK IT UP

To remind yourself of the factors that affect growth and development, go to Section A1 in Component 1.

CHECK MY LEARNING

Imagine you have a predisposition to a condition. Write a piece of creative writing, such as a poem, in a style of your own choosing, to describe how this would affect your health and wellbeing, now and in the future.

Ill health

GETTING STARTED

In pairs, discuss what is meant by the terms 'acute' and 'chronic'. Try to think of some examples of each.

KEY TERMS

Acute illness comes on quickly, is short term and can be cured.
Chronic illness comes on gradually, is long term (more than 3 months) and generally can be treated but not cured.
Short term is less than 6 months.
Long term is 6 months or more.

Ill health is a physical and lifestyle factor that can have positive and/or negative effects on health and wellbeing. Ill health can also be **acute**, **chronic** or sometimes both.

Chronic or acute

Illness may be chronic or acute. An illness may:
- affect physical fitness
- restrict access to varied learning activities (intellectual)
- cause emotional distress
- remove some social opportunities.

All of these things affect health and wellbeing.

Whatever illness a person has, their needs still include all those of a healthy person. However, they have important additional needs (especially access to services) either in the **short term** for an acute illness, or **long term** for a chronic illness. If these needs are met through an enabling environment, the impact of the illness may be decreased.

Table 3.2: Can you think of any other acute or chronic illnesses to add to this table?

Acute	Chronic
Cold	Asthma
Flu	Cystic fibrosis
Pneumonia	Diabetes
Broken bones	Osteoporosis
Rickets	Haemophilia
Measles	Kidney disease
Mumps	Emphysema
Appendicitis	Heart disease
Indigestion	Epilepsy
Heartburn	Hypertension
Heart attack	Bipolar disorder

Some illnesses or conditions are acute but may develop because of a chronic condition. For example, a person may have osteoporosis (a chronic condition that weakens bones) making their bones fragile and more likely to break. Broken bones are an acute condition. Similarly, a person with chronic heart disease (caused by partially blocked coronary arteries) will suffer from angina (chest pains), which can be controlled by medication. If their arteries become completely blocked it will cause a heart attack, an acute condition.

ACTIVITY

1 Work in pairs to research one acute and one chronic condition, affecting the same body system.

2 Produce a table showing the short- and long-term effects of each condition on a person's PIES.

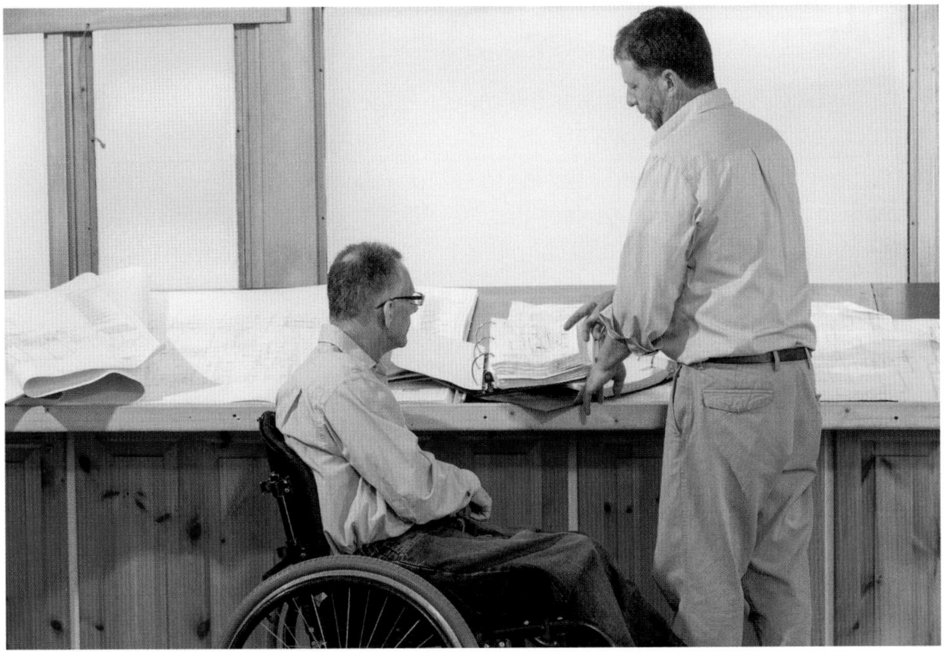

This person has Huntington's disease, which affects the central nervous system. How might his work needs be met?

ACTIVITY

Andrew is 45 years old. He has Huntington's disease, a degenerative disorder of the central nervous system. It causes jerky and uncontrollable movements of the limbs. It will eventually affect his motor skills and speech and lead to loss of physical movement.

1 Which of Andrew's needs is currently met by the job he does in an office?

2 How could his working conditions, such as the layout of his office, be adapted so he can go on working for longer?

CHECK MY LEARNING

1 Discuss which will have more effect overall on a person's health and wellbeing:

- asthma, which is chronic and can be controlled by medication, or
- a heart attack, which is acute.

Diet

GETTING STARTED

Reflect on your own diet. Jot down what you have had to eat and drink since you got up this morning. Do you think your choices were largely healthy or unhealthy?

A balanced diet is one that contains the correct nutrients in the right proportions to keep our bodies and minds healthy.

Diet is often a lifestyle choice. Choosing to eat too much or too little might make us less able to take all the opportunities that life offers. A person who is overweight may:

- be more prone to illnesses and conditions
- have their life expectancy reduced
- be less able to exercise effectively
- miss out on learning experiences
- miss out on some sporting activities, such as skiing
- be less successful in job interviews
- feel embarrassed and self-conscious about their appearance in social situations.

An overweight or underweight person could try to control their weight through a balanced, healthy diet of good-quality food. The essential parts of a healthy, balanced diet are:

- fats (saturated and unsaturated)
- carbohydrates (sugars and starches)
- minerals
- vitamins
- proteins.

We also need to consume the right amount of food and fluids each day.

DID YOU KNOW?

The *Eatwell Guide* outlines what the UK Government suggests we need to eat to keep us healthy. You can find out more by looking at the GOV.UK website and searching for the *Eatwell Guide*.

The *Eatwell Guide* says we should try to:

- eat at least five portions of fruit and vegetables a day
- base meals on starchy foods like potatoes, bread, rice or pasta (preferably wholegrain or wholemeal varieties) to give more fibre; this should make up about one-third of what we eat each day
- have some dairy each day, but lower fat varieties
- eat some beans, oily fish, eggs, meat and other proteins, which also contain vitamins and minerals
- eat small amounts of oils and spreads, most of it unsaturated
- drink plenty of fluids
- reduce our intake of food and drinks high in saturated fat, salt and sugar.

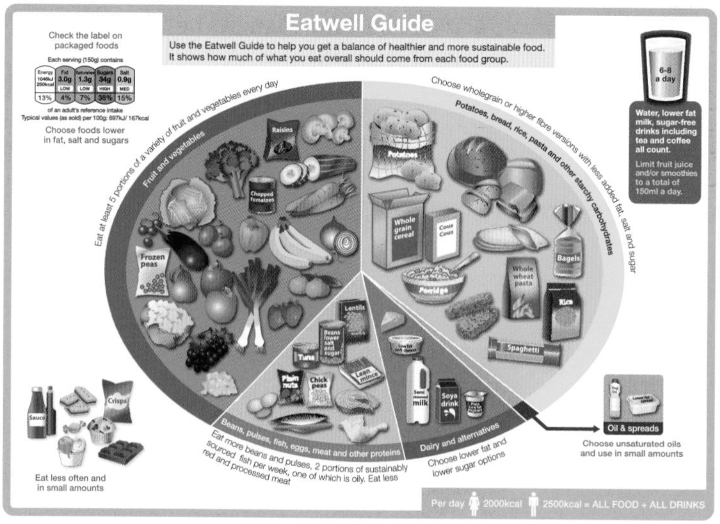

Figure 3.3: The *Eatwell Guide* recommends our diet contains these food items

The food we eat affects the way we feel and look. It is very important for our health and wellbeing.

If we eat more than we need, the body will store it as fat and this, for example, leads to:

- obesity
- heart disease
- high blood pressure
- strokes
- tooth decay
- cancer.

If we eat less than we need, the body does not get enough nutrients to grow and develop properly and this, for example, leads to:

- eating disorders (such as anorexia nervosa)
- anaemia
- stunted bone growth
- heart failure
- depression
- tiredness
- cancer
- rickets.

Some of the above could even lead to death.

DID YOU KNOW?

Our dietary needs vary throughout life. For example, as we get older we may need to eat less food because our bodies are slower to process it.

ACTIVITY

1 Work with a partner or on your own to draw up a concept map using ICT, showing how the balance, quality and amount of food and drink in the diet affects a person's health and wellbeing. Make sure you include positive and negative effects.

2 Print out an extra copy of your concept map to add to a class wall display. Take a look at what others have added to their maps.

3 Reflect on how well you think you completed this task.

CHECK MY LEARNING

Think about what you ate for your main meal yesterday. What will be the long-term effects on your health and wellbeing if you continue to eat like this every day?

Exercise

GETTING STARTED

Discuss, in small groups, an older person you know. How mobile are they? What exercise do they take? How does their mobility affect them?

We need to exercise to ensure we maintain our health and wellbeing. Exercise is a lifestyle factor that can bring many benefits.

Benefits of exercise

Exercise improves our strength, stamina and suppleness, as well as our muscle and body tone. It helps us to:

- concentrate
- relieve stress
- relax and feel good
- gain personal satisfaction
- socialise with others (for example, in a gym or a running club).

DID YOU KNOW?

You should be able to talk, but not sing, during and straight after moderate exercise.

Getting enough exercise is essential and can help prevent heart disease and stroke – two of the UK's top five killers. Doing at least 2.5 hours of moderate physical activity a week, in 30-minute sessions, improves health. Any type of exercise – for example, using the stairs instead of a lift – helps your heart to be healthier. Moderate exercise causes your heart to beat faster, increases your breathing rate and makes you sweat. It can also lower your blood pressure and cholesterol level.

KEY TERMS

Monitor is to check progress over a period of time.

Some 'smart' devices can help you to **monitor** your exercise. They do this by keeping track of, for example, your steps and the speed at which you walk or run. This means you can check your activity level each day or week.

Taking exercise

There are different ways of taking exercise.

- Going for a walk or a jog is free and you do not have to commit to set times.
- Joining a gym or taking a class such as boxercise will cost money. However, some might say that paying for an exercise class makes you more likely to commit to exercise.
- Swimming and cycling are excellent holistic aerobic activities.
- Joining a team (for example, football or netball) may provide a social side in addition to the exercise.

DID YOU KNOW?

Hormones are like messengers, instructing our bodies how to behave. Sometimes they can make us feel better. Sometimes they can make us feel worse, by tricking our bodies into thinking something terrible is going to happen.

Some people are happier to take their exercise alone. For others, it is an opportunity to meet new people or pair up with a friend. Remember, whatever exercise you take part in, your brain will release hormones called endorphins, which provide a feeling of wellbeing.

You do not have to be young or mobile to exercise

Even those with limited mobility can take exercise. For example, residents in care homes are frequently offered gentle standing or armchair exercise. Armchair activities can help people with conditions such as osteoporosis, arthritis and high blood pressure to exercise without putting any strain on their knees or hips.

Not taking exercise

Lack of exercise can lead to conditions such as:

- stiffening of the joints
- poor stamina, strength and suppleness
- obesity
- stroke
- coronary heart disease
- poorly developed heart and skeletal muscles
- sluggish blood flow
- osteoporosis.

Any one of these conditions means that health and wellbeing will suffer.

ACTIVITY

1. Work individually to research exercise. Then draw a mind map of the benefits of different types of exercise.
2. Split into five groups. Share out the life stages covered in Component 1 (combining infants and early childhood) so that each group in your class has a different life stage. Discuss the negative/positive effects on health and wellbeing of exercise for that life stage. Then produce a podcast or script designed to promote the positive aspects of getting enough exercise. Remember to warn of any risks.
3. Be prepared to play your podcast to the class. Alternatively, you could share your script.

CHECK MY LEARNING

1. Self- and peer-evaluate your podcasts or scripts for clarity of key learning points about how exercise affects health and wellbeing.
2. How might exercise help a person with Down's syndrome who is overweight and has poor muscle development?

Substance use

GETTING STARTED

In small groups, discuss what causes people your age to misuse substances such as alcohol, nicotine, illegal drugs and prescription drugs. Also, discuss the possible consequences of making such a lifestyle choice.

KEY TERMS

Nicotine is a powerful, addictive drug found in tobacco.

Addiction is not having control of doing, taking or using something to the point where it could be harmful to you.

Substance use, such as alcohol, **nicotine**, illegal drugs and misuse of prescribed drugs, has a negative effect on health and wellbeing. Regular use can lead to long-term health problems.

Alcohol

Alcohol is socially accepted in many cultures. However, if it is not controlled, it can become an **addiction** for some people.

Excessive drinking of alcohol can cause many illnesses and problems, but if taken in moderation, alcohol is viewed as pleasurable. The first full guidelines on alcohol consumption since 1995, published by the UK Government in January 2016, say that:

- any amount of alcohol can increase the risk of cancer
- men and woman who drink regularly should consume no more than 14 units a week – the equivalent of six pints of beer or seven glasses of wine
- people should not save up their units and drink them in one go (binge drinking).

Nicotine

Smoking tobacco, usually in cigarettes, is legal but banned in public places. All smoking material now carries a government health warning.

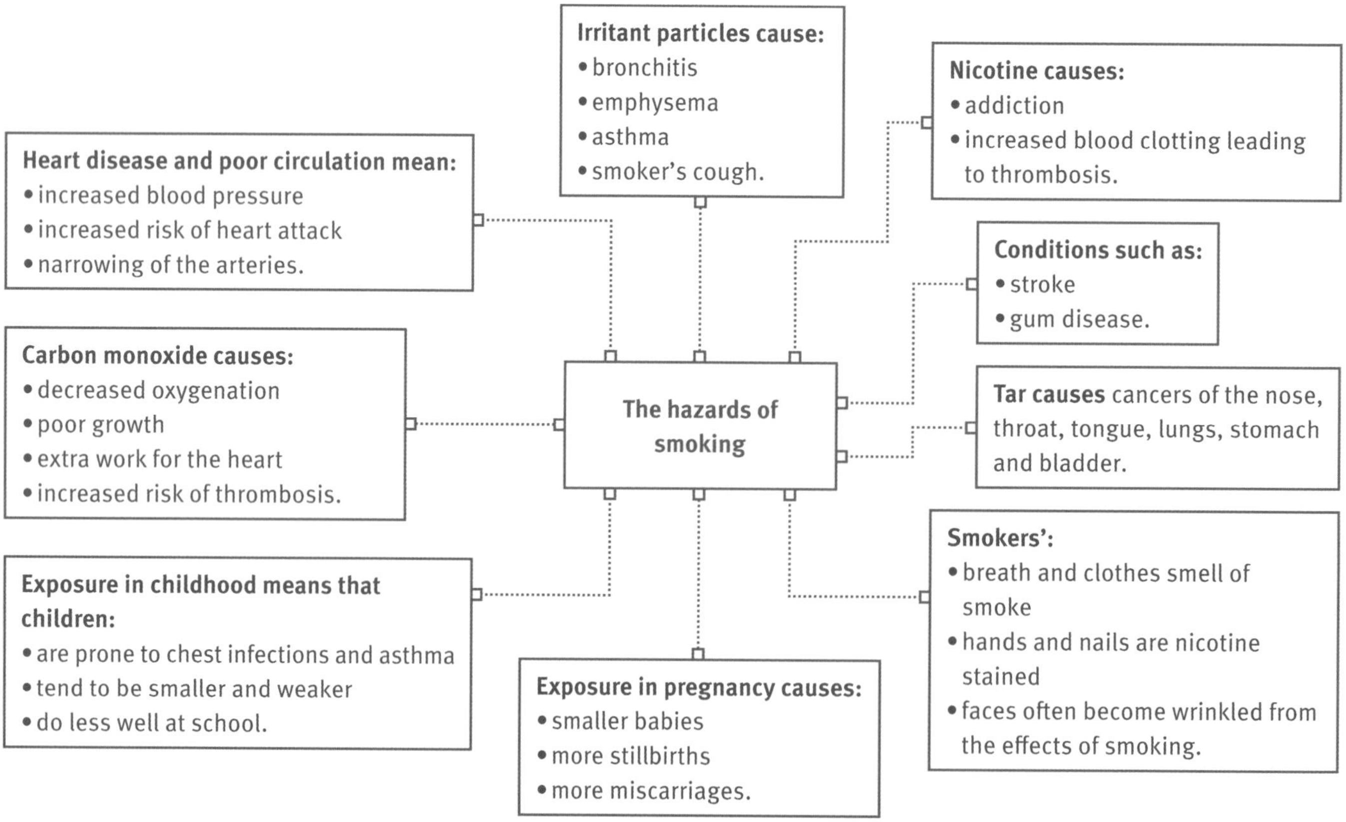

The hazards of smoking
Irritant particles cause:
• bronchitis
• emphysema
• asthma
• smoker's cough.
Nicotine causes:
• addiction
• increased blood clotting leading to thrombosis.
Heart disease and poor circulation mean:
• increased blood pressure
• increased risk of heart attack
• narrowing of the arteries.
Conditions such as:
• stroke
• gum disease.
Carbon monoxide causes:
• decreased oxygenation
• poor growth
• extra work for the heart
• increased risk of thrombosis.
Tar causes cancers of the nose, throat, tongue, lungs, stomach and bladder.
Exposure in childhood means that children:
• are prone to chest infections and asthma
• tend to be smaller and weaker
• do less well at school.
Smokers':
• breath and clothes smell of smoke
• hands and nails are nicotine stained
• faces often become wrinkled from the effects of smoking.
Exposure in pregnancy causes:
• smaller babies
• more stillbirths
• more miscarriages.

Figure 3.4: Smoking causes ill health

Illegal drugs and misuse of prescribed drugs

Substance abuse includes:

- the unsafe use of solvents
- taking illegal drugs such as cannabis or ecstasy
- misusing prescription drugs.

Substance abuse can have profoundly damaging effects on your body. These include a loss of control of your actions and damage to organs such as the brain, liver and kidneys. Many people become addicted to illegal drugs or even prescription drugs if they are misused. Substance misuse and damage to the body could also result in death.

ACTIVITY

1 Divide into four groups. Each group should pick one topic from 'alcohol', 'nicotine', 'illegal drugs' and 'misuse of prescribed drugs'. Do some research and produce a single-page fact sheet giving the positive/negative short- and long-term effects on health and wellbeing of using the allocated substance. (Highlight the effects in different colours.) Your fact sheet should discourage young people from starting, or continuing, to use this substance. In your fact sheet suggest alternative, less harmful activities to achieve the same positive effects.

2 Print copies of your finished fact sheet for each group member to have for their notes.

CHECK MY LEARNING

Use the information from your fact sheet to draw a Venn diagram showing the common effects misuse of these substances may lead to in the long term, in the parts where the circles overlap.

Personal hygiene

GETTING STARTED

Draw an outline of the body and label the areas that are important in personal hygiene. Add notes about how often each area needs attention.

Poor personal hygiene is not only unpleasant but can affect your health and wellbeing.

The importance of personal hygiene

Our bodies offer the correct temperature and moistness for bacteria to grow. Our bodies also provide food in the form of dead skin cells and chemicals in our sweat. We are exposed to bacteria every day. Although many bacteria are harmless, some cause disease. Bacteria can be passed on from one person to another and through food. Bacteria travel when you:

- cough
- scratch
- fiddle with your hair
- rub your face
- sneeze
- do not wash your hands
- pick spots.

Personal hygiene is very important because it helps us to reduce the number of bacteria that live on us. Regular personal hygiene includes cleaning our teeth at least twice a day, having a daily shower or bath, washing our hair regularly and keeping our finger and toe nails clean and trimmed.

Conditions caused by bacteria

We all have various barriers to stop bacteria entering different parts of our bodies. These barriers include skin, tears, mucus and stomach acid. However, if there are too many bacteria, one of our normal barriers will become damaged in some way and we become infected. Some bacteria attack body tissues or release poisons that make us feel ill. They can cause illnesses such as:

- food poisoning
- tetanus
- sore throats
- tuberculosis, or TB
- whooping cough
- meningitis
- syphilis.

ACTIVITY

1 In a small group, make or script a video on the effects of poor personal hygiene on a person's health and wellbeing. Include any changes with age and how these affect the PIES.

2 Be prepared to show your video to the rest of the class. Alternatively, you could share your script.

Caring for others

When caring for others you will need to get physically close to them. If either of you has offensive body odour or bad breath it is unpleasant and may stop better communication taking place. In turn, this could affect:

- your relationship with the person you are caring for
- their health and wellbeing.

As a carer you may also have to touch people, both to comfort them and to treat them. Infection can be spread this way if, for example, you do not wash your hands properly before (and after) you touch them. Young babies or older people are less resistant to diseases and can suffer more damage from bacteria passed on to them.

If a person is immobile for some length of time, pressure on the skin from the hard surface of a bed or wheelchair can cause an ulcer. The ulcer interrupts the blood supply to the affected area of skin, so the skin no longer receives infection-fighting white blood cells. A pressure ulcer, or bed sore, can form and become infected with bacteria, leading to:

- extreme discomfort
- blood poisoning
- tissue death, and
- even death.

This is why it is important that the person's skin is kept clean and dry and they are moved regularly into different positions.

DID YOU KNOW?

If you have normal mobility you automatically make hundreds of regular movements that prevent pressure building up on any one area of your body. You may shift position up to 20 times a night during your sleep.

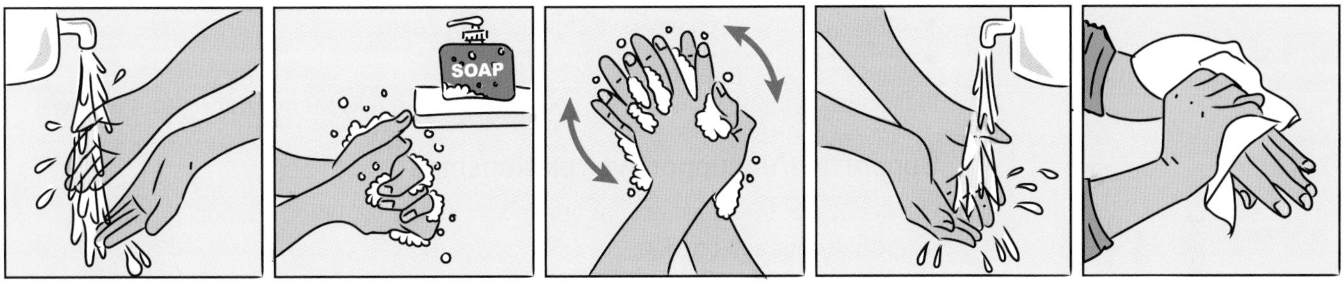

Figure 3.5: Do you always follow these steps to good hand washing?

CHECK MY LEARNING

1 What are the possible problems caused by body changes in adults in later adulthood relating to personal hygiene?

2 How might this affect their health and wellbeing (PIES)?

Social interactions

GETTING STARTED

Working with a partner, discuss the effects that peer pressure or cultural influences can have on an individual's health and lifestyle. Come up with at least two examples and feed back to the class.

LINK IT UP

To remind yourself of social, emotional and cultural factors, go to Section A2 in Component 1.

There are many social, emotional and cultural factors that affect health and wellbeing, one of which is social interaction. What does social interaction mean to you?

Social interaction

Our social needs include the opportunity to:

- mix with others in an appropriate environment
- have access to leisure facilities and activities.

It is important that we have family and friends and belong to groups or a community. These social interactions provide us with a sense of belonging and a feeling that we are accepted. There are many types of social interaction. What other types can you think of?

Relationships

The quality of our relationships influences how we feel about ourselves throughout our lives. There are many different types of relationships:

- some are formal, such as with our boss at work
- others are informal, such as with family and friends.

We form our first relationships with our parents or carers. We usually make our first friends as children. We make more friends through:

- school and higher/further education
- interests and work
- other parents, when we have children of our own
- activities we may take up during retirement.

In fact, we continue to meet new people and make new friends throughout our lives.

Supportive/unsupportive relationships

Our family and friends affect our health and wellbeing. When relationships are supportive they can provide:

- physical support and assistance
- intellectual stimulation
- emotional support and happiness
- a social life.

When relationships are not supportive they can:

- hurt and upset us
- influence us to do things we maybe would not do, such as smoke or turn to crime
- make us unhappy and could distract us from learning experiences
- make us feel lonely and bad about ourselves.

Social integration/isolation

Our relationships affect whether we feel integrated into a community or isolated from it.

Some relationships can lead to social integration – for example, becoming actively involved in a community. One example is working to support a charity, which might result in:

- physical work, such as helping to build benches for a community garden
- intellectual stimulation, such as problem solving
- emotional fulfilment through a new sense of purpose
- social opportunities to make new friends.

Other relationships can lead to social isolation. For example, someone may fall out with a friend who may then bully them. This could lead to the person feeling:

- physically threatened
- intellectually distracted from, for example, their work
- emotionally upset
- socially isolated.

An isolated person could become withdrawn and miserable because they think others find it hard to be friends with them.

Social integration and isolation in retirement

For many people, retirement is an opportunity for social integration because they have more time to meet people. However, others may feel isolated.

Integration includes, for example, meeting people through leisure activities, as long as they remain healthy and active. They might:

- move into a different residential setting
- make new relationships that lead to them being given help with day-to-day tasks (physical)
- take part in stimulating activities (intellectual)
- feel supported and reassured (emotional)
- always have others to mix with (social).

However, some older people become socially isolated as they get older because:

- they may lose friends through illness or death
- they may lose a life partner.

Others who are socially isolated

Others who may become socially isolated include those who are:

- homeless
- physically or mentally ill
- going through a difficult period in their lives
- living with conditions such as autism.

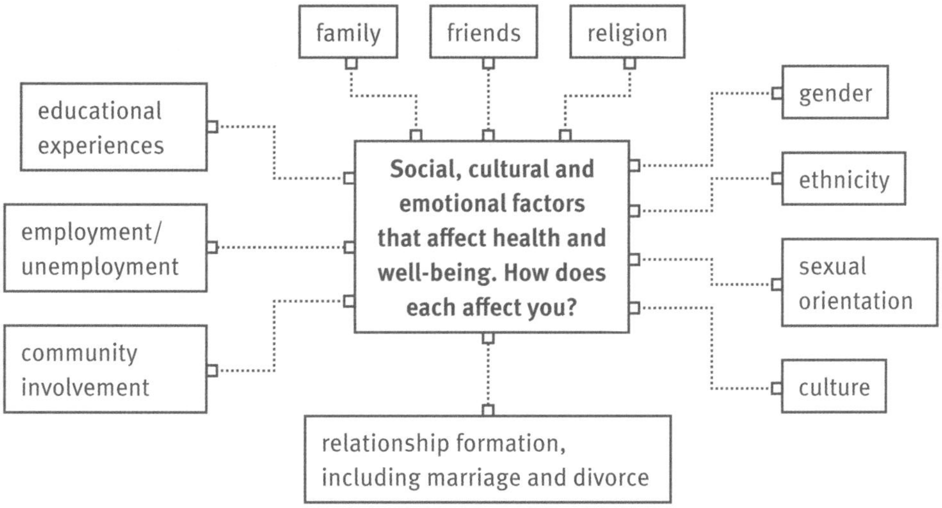

Figure 3.6: Internal and external influences on health and wellbeing

ACTIVITY

1 Work in a small group to identify the different types of relationships.

2 Work individually to identify the positive effects of a supportive relationship and the negative effects of an unsupportive relationship, including social integration/isolation.

3 Write a magazine article about supportive and unsupportive relationships to include family, friends, work colleagues and intimate and sexual relationships. Make the article attractive, well written and informative. Use no more than two sides of A4.

CHECK MY LEARNING

1 Be prepared to share your article with others and to look at theirs. Make a note of any points you have missed from yours.

2 How might your educational experiences affect your health and wellbeing positively and negatively?

Stress

GETTING STARTED

Work in small groups to identify causes of stress in your own lives and (more generally) in the lives of adults.

We will almost certainly have come across the word 'stress' or know what it feels like to be stressed. Learning to control stress can help to improve health and wellbeing.

Stress

Stress occurs when you have to respond to demands made on you. It causes the body to secrete hormones, the main one being adrenaline. These hormones trigger a 'fight or flight' response, which enables you to respond instantly – especially in life-and-death situations. Unfortunately, the response to these hormones can also cause some people to overreact to situations that are not life-threatening. One example includes being stuck in a traffic jam, which could lead to situations such as road rage or physical violence.

Our hormones cannot tell the difference between a life-threatening and a non-life-threatening situation

Everyone gets stressed from time to time and a small amount of stress might even be good for us. For example, you may feel stressed just before an exam, but the stress will make your brain respond more quickly to the demands being made on it. Similarly, if you are about to perform in public, your brain's response to stress may help you to focus more quickly and rise to the occasion.

Stress becomes a problem when it is:

- very intense (caused perhaps, by a bereavement, relationship problem or redundancy)
- experienced over a long period of time (perhaps due to illness).

The stress may affect you:

- physically – you may notice tension in your body
- intellectually – by being distracted and losing concentration
- emotionally – by being upset and unhappy
- socially – by finding it harder to mix with others.

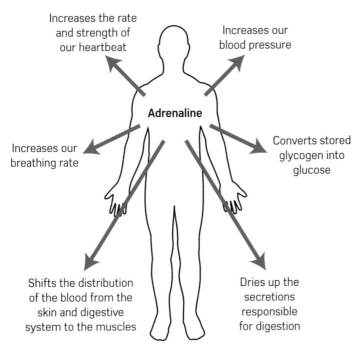

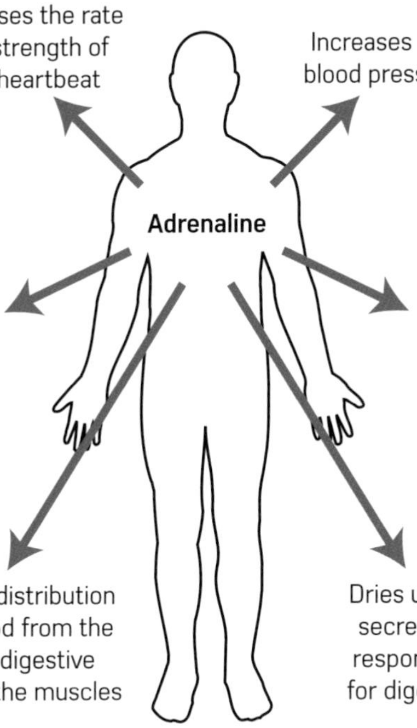
Increases the rate and strength of our heartbeat
Increases our blood pressure
Adrenaline
Increases our breathing rate
Converts stored glycogen into glucose
Shifts the distribution of the blood from the skin and digestive system to the muscles
Dries up the secretions responsible for digestion

Figure 3.7: Are you surprised at the effects adrenaline can have on the body?

Look at Figure 3.7, which shows the effects of adrenaline on your body. Then read Table 3.3, which details the short- and long-term effects of stress. Are you surprised by any of these?

Table 3.3: The effects of stress: which have you experienced?

Short-term effects	Long-term effects
Feeling cold	Sleeplessness
Less sensitive to pain	High blood pressure
More sensitive to touch	Irritability and becoming withdrawn
Tense muscles	Loss of appetite
Faster breathing	Heart disease/ulcers/eczema/asthma
Dry mouth	Poor circulation
Flared nostrils	Nervousness
Wide eyes	Accidents
Pale face	Breakdowns
Body hair standing on end	Aching muscles/body tension
Faster heartbeat	Headaches
Butterflies	Poor sex life
Urge to pass water (urine)	Anxiety
Diarrhoea	Violent tendencies
Sweaty hands	Mood swings

ACTIVITY

1 Working in a small group, identify how various aspects of a person's working life can cause stress. Think about examples such as manual/non-manual work, job satisfaction, career success, mental stimulation, support, work/life balance and level of conflict.

2 Pick a job such as someone working on a conveyor belt in a factory, a doctor, a bricklayer, a manager, a care assistant, a teacher or a farmer. Identify how the stress of that particular job may affect all aspects of a person's health and wellbeing.

CHECK MY LEARNING

Think back to the activity on the effects of work on health and wellbeing. For which work-related factor was it hardest to say why it would affect health and wellbeing? Give your reasons.

Willingness to seek help or access services

GETTING STARTED

Work with a partner to discuss and write down any influences or reasons that may make a person unwilling to seek help or access a service.

The act of seeking help is a social, emotional and cultural occurrence that affects health and wellbeing. This might be influenced by various factors such as culture, gender or education.

ACTIVITY

Research how culture, gender or education may influence a person's willingness to seek help or access a service and the positive and negative effects that willingness may have on the person's health and wellbeing.

Culture

The health and wellbeing of a person, and their willingness to access help or services, are influenced by values, traditions, way of life and beliefs of the society or group into which the person is born. For example, in some cultures:

- it is not the custom for men to be open about their personal health or family circumstances because it could be seen to reflect badly on the family
- diet may be restricted at certain times, which could affect someone recovering from illness
- the use of first names is only acceptable from close family members and friends, so an individual might be offended if they are addressed in this familiar way.

Many older people in the UK, regardless of culture, find it disrespectful if care assistants, for example, call them by their first names. They would prefer if someone asked them what they would like to be called.

ACTIVITY

Manolya is Middle Eastern and in her culture eye contact is considered rude or disrespectful so when she visits her local health centre to make an appointment she looks at the floor when speaking to the receptionist, who thinks she is being rude.

1 How might the receptionist react?

2 How might Manolya's experience affect her willingness to seek help or access services in the future?

Gender

Gender can affect willingness to seek help or access services.

- Men may be reluctant to consult a doctor for something they find embarrassing, such as having a prostate examination.
- Men may feel awkward seeking help with conditions such as depression, anxiety and obesity. They may try to cope on their own rather than talk about their feelings with a professional.
- Women may prefer not to see a male doctor. Some cultures may even prevent women having close contact with men other than their husbands.

All of these gender issues could mean that some individuals delay seeking or accepting necessary help.

How might these people feel about seeking help for a sensitive issue?

Education

Research shows a clear link between education and a willingness to seek help or access services.

A better-educated person is more likely to be aware of and look out for signs and symptoms. They understand the need to seek help early for some conditions – for example, a breast lump. A better-educated person will also be more aware of which services are available. Those with less knowledge might adopt a more negative approach to health and wellbeing. They may think that, because they feel fine now, they do not need to access health monitoring services.

DID YOU KNOW?

Research suggests that better-educated people are more likely to try illegal drugs. However, they are also more likely to give them up because they are aware of the risks of addiction.

Effects on health and wellbeing

If a person is unwilling to seek help or access services, it will negatively affect their health and wellbeing. For example, they may leave it too late to discuss a health issue with a service provider.

- The illness or condition might then become much worse or even life-threatening (physical).
- They may not understand how to cope (intellectual).
- They may become worried (emotional).
- They may be too ill to see friends (social).

LINK IT UP

To remind yourselves about social and cultural factors, go to Section A1 in Component 2.

CHECK MY LEARNING

1 How can personal beliefs and preferences prevent some individuals accessing health and social care services?

2 How can education make a person more willing to seek help or access services?

Financial resources

GETTING STARTED

In small groups, discuss the different sources of a person's financial resources.

KEY TERMS

Wealth is having lots of money and goods.
Social class is a broad group in society having the same social or economic status, most commonly upper, middle and lower class.
Material possessions are objects that can be bought but are not essential to live on, such as jewellery or a large TV.
Income is the money people receive from their work, savings, pension, benefits or investments.

Economic factors such as financial resources (how much money we have) can play a big part in how we live our lives. Not having enough can cause problems.

Income

A person's financial resources are affected by their:
- employment status (for example, whether they are employed by an organisation or company, or whether they are self-employed)
- **wealth**
- occupation
- **social class**
- **material possessions**.

Some people are unable to work because they:
- have a disability or illness
- are caring for someone else.

These people would be able to draw benefits from the state.

The level of **income** a person earns is mainly linked to their level of education, skills, qualifications and talents, how hard they work and their area of work. Income has a major impact on our health and wellbeing.

ACTIVITY

1 Work in a small group to draw up a table showing what having adequate (enough) financial resources allows an adult to do. Include the short- and long-term effects this amount of money may have on the adult's health and wellbeing.
2 Use your table to prepare a role play showing the possible effects on health and wellbeing of not having sufficient financial resources.
3 You could then perform your role play for the rest of your class.

Effects of adequate financial resources on health and wellbeing

If you can afford to buy food that provides you with a balanced diet, you are more likely to be healthy (and therefore, perhaps exercise) and less likely to be ill (physical). You may also be able to afford access to more learning opportunities – for example, further education – and be mentally stimulated (intellectual). Adequate financial resources may allow you to meet up with friends or meet new people (emotional and social).

When adults have an adequate income they can generally afford better-quality housing, with access to services such as good schools to provide a quality education for their children. There will be less stress because they are not worrying about financial problems and so fewer arguments and less chance of relationships failing.

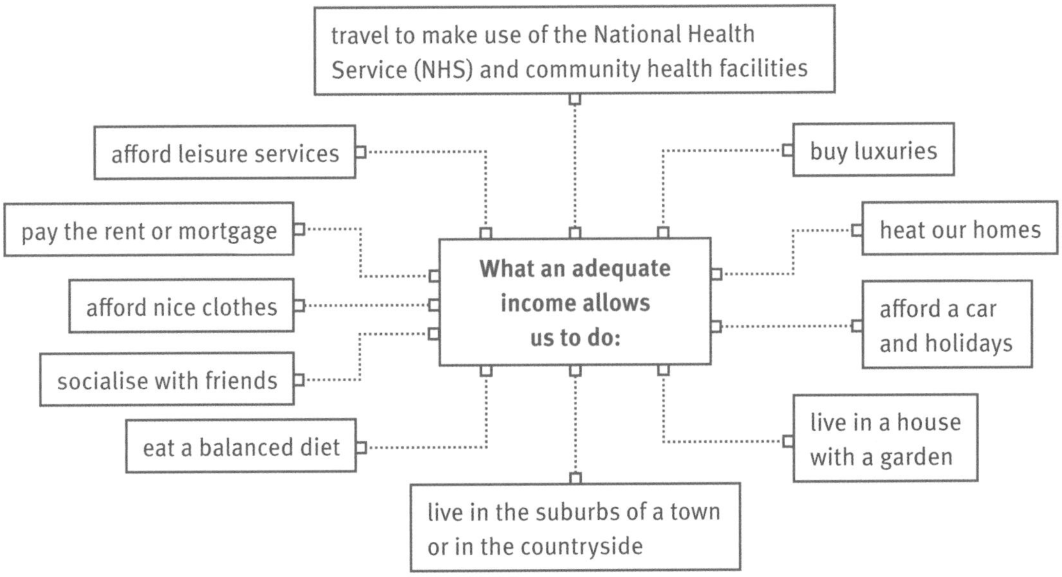

Figure 3.8: The effects of financial wellbeing

Poverty

Some people live in absolute poverty. This means that, despite benefits being available, they do not receive enough money to meet their basic needs, such as food, clothing or housing.

Others live in relative poverty. This means that although they have enough money for the essentials to live, they have less than other people. This will limit their life choices. They also have more chance of suffering ill health and have fewer opportunities for personal development. Their children might:

- miss out on, for example, school trips, new warm clothes and sleepovers
- do less well at school, which could mean they will earn less when they are working adults.

CHECK MY LEARNING

1 How well did your role plays identify the negative and positive effects of having insufficient financial resources? Explain your answer.

2 How can a well-paid job affect health and wellbeing in both a positive and negative way?

DID YOU KNOW?

Poverty affects one in four children in the UK today. There were 3.9 million children (28 per cent of children) living in poverty in the UK in 2014–15.

LINK IT UP

To remind yourself about economic factors, go to Section A2 in Component 1. To remind yourself about financial barriers, go to Section A2 in Component 2.

Environmental conditions

GETTING STARTED

Work in pairs to illustrate in diagram form (no words) as many environmental conditions that can affect health and wellbeing as you can think of.

KEY TERMS

Pollution is the act of introducing harmful substances or irritants that cause damage to living organisms into the environment.

DID YOU KNOW?

On still, sunny days, the sun causes nitrogen dioxide and the ozone to create toxic smog. On cold, foggy days, pollution gets trapped close to the ground, building up to winter smog.

How many environmental factors can you see here?

It is impossible to escape stories about **pollution** of one kind or another. Negative environmental conditions can affect people in a number of ways.

Pollution

We all need clean air, water and proper waste disposal facilities, but our modern way of living means that our air and water can sometimes be affected by chemicals and other products.

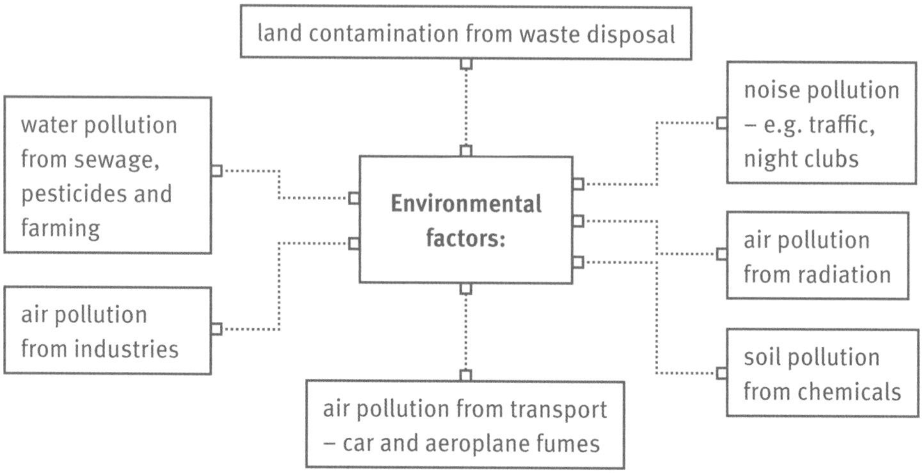

Figure 3.9: The social costs of pollution

Air pollution

Air pollution is a mixture of gases and particles that have been emitted into the atmosphere by human beings. The most common cause is the burning of fossil fuels to give energy. Air pollution in the UK has gone down significantly in recent years because of measures to reduce it. But pollution still exists in and around urban areas (towns and cities).

Air pollution can:

- cause and aggravate respiratory conditions
- irritate the eyes, nose and throat
- severely affect people with asthma and other breathing problems such as emphysema
- include dust that comes from quarries, mines and factories
- be carried from other countries – for example, in dust from the Sahara.

Those who live near busy main roads, airports, seaports and industrial sites are more likely to be affected by air pollution. Events at which large numbers of fireworks are let off can also add to air pollution and smog.

The causes of water pollution include sewage, wastewater, leakages from underground storage, agricultural chemicals and industrial waste getting into lakes and rivers, as well as the dumping of litter at sea. Pollutants from industrial sources include asbestos, which can cause cancer, and lead and mercury, which can poison us.

Fresh air and water can improve health and wellbeing but a polluted atmosphere can make us ill (physical), stopping us accessing learning activities (intellectual), making us feel low (emotional) and stopping us going out with friends (social).

Noise pollution

Noise pollution is excessive noise that may harm the activity of human or animal life and affect health and wellbeing. The noise might come from an aircraft taking off, heavy traffic, or road-mending equipment such as drills. Sustained high noise levels can cause:

- high blood pressure
- sleeplessness
- hearing loss
- increase in stress levels.

ACTIVITY

1. Work in a small group to research how air pollution levels or noise affect health and wellbeing. Produce a TV news report (or script) to show what you have learned.
2. Act out your report to the rest of the class or share your script.
3. Do some research on cities named in Figure 3.10. For example, your research could include population and location.
4. Use your research to explain the shape of the graph.
5. Why is London close to the World Health Organization (WHO) target for healthy air and Montreal at the WHO target?

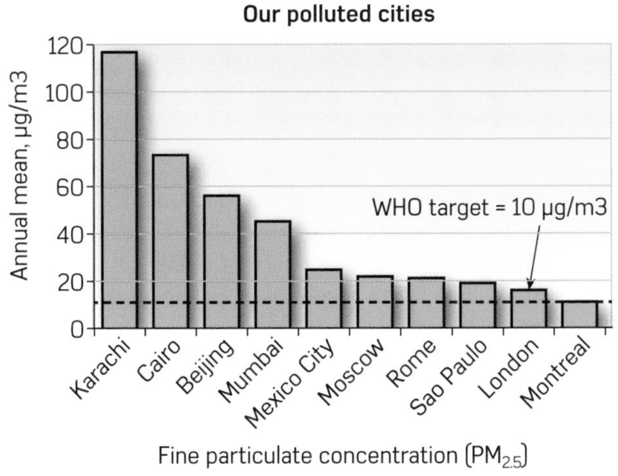

Figure 3.10: Pollution in major cities (Source: WHO air pollution in cities database 2014)

CHECK MY LEARNING

What have you learned about how environmental conditions affect health and well-being?

Housing

GETTING STARTED

Think about a house that is small, cluttered, cramped and dark. How might this affect someone's PIES? Now think about a house that is large, light, airy and uncluttered and answer the same question.

Health and wellbeing is affected by the type of house you live in – its condition and location.

Home environment

Many of us spend a lot of time in our homes. Our home environment can affect our health and wellbeing in a number of ways; see Table 3.4.

Table 3.4: The home environment and how it affects families

Home environment	How it affects health and wellbeing
Type of home	Living in a semi-detached or terraced house means occupants are more likely to be disturbed by noise from neighbours. This can cause children to lose concentration (e.g. when trying to do their homework) and affect the concentration of adults who work from home. It may also lead to arguments with the neighbours.
Condition of home	If a home is cluttered, damp and dirty and has poorly groomed pets, then occupants are more likely to be ill because poor hygiene allows bacteria and other germs to spread and grow. Damp and mould can have a negative effect on respiratory conditions and affect sleep.
Size of home	If a home is small and cramped, illnesses are likely to spread quite quickly. There is also more chance of accidents.
Amount of personal space	If a home is overcrowded (e.g. with siblings sharing a room), there will be less privacy and less space for, e.g. schoolwork, belongings and interests. This might lead to disorganisation and demotivation and may prevent concentration. It might also lead to disturbed sleep.
Location of home	Occupants are more likely to be affected by pollution (including air, light and noise) if they live in urban areas. Living in a high building with no access to a garden or other outdoor space can mean there is nowhere to play or sit outside. Living in a house with a garden in the suburbs or the countryside will be quieter and provide access to the outdoors for leisure activities and exercise.
Influence of others in the home	Others you live with may influence how you eat, dress and behave. Their influence might be positive (they could encourage you to do well at school) or negative (they may lead you into poor habits).
Level of conflict around the home	Living in poor housing areas can cause conflict for many reasons, e.g. living too close to others, embarrassment and resentment at the state of the home and stress.

Rural and urban lifestyles

Living in a detached house with a garden in the suburbs or countryside is more likely to promote better health because of:

- fresh air, opportunities to exercise and low noise levels resulting in uninterrupted sleep (physical)
- improved concentration and alertness (intellectual)
- being more relaxed and happy (emotional)
- a more active social life (social) because families are less likely to be ill or stressed.

For some people, however, living in rural and isolated areas can make access to health and social care services more difficult.

Others may prefer to live in a town or city. If they can afford to live in a high-quality spacious apartment or house, they are likely to notice a positive effect on their health and wellbeing. They are likely to be:

- closer to work, with better transport links or even within walking distance (physical)
- close to amenities such as libraries, theatres and museums (intellectual)
- happy with their life as a result of the other factors listed (emotional)
- close to friends (social).

Urban or rural: where would you prefer to live and why?

ACTIVITY

1. Set out a table showing how living in your ideal home would positively affect your health and wellbeing.
2. Work in pairs to produce an information leaflet based on the positive and negative effects on health and wellbeing of living in the countryside rather than a town or city.

CHECK MY LEARNING

Why do some people prefer to live in the middle of a large town? What positive and negative effects will this have on their health and wellbeing?

The impact of life events relating to relationship changes

GETTING STARTED

Work with a partner to thought shower the different examples of relationship changes. You should include: entering into relationships; marriage; divorce; parenthood; and bereavement.

KEY TERMS

Self-esteem is how good or bad an individual feels about themselves and how much they value their abilities..

We all have relationships of one kind or another. But what happens when those relationships end or change?

Impacts on health and wellbeing

When a relationship changes, it affects our health and wellbeing. These changes can:

- affect our **self-esteem**
- increase our levels of stress and anxiety
- cause us not to function well.

Entering into a relationship

When you first enter into a relationship with someone who may one day become your partner you might:

- be attracted to them (physical)
- be distracted by thinking about them when you are not with them (intellectual)
- feel nervous but happy (emotional)
- enjoy their company as well as meeting their friends (social).

Your new relationship may become serious. You may decide to marry or commit to the partnership in some other way.

Marriage/partnership and parenthood

Marriage/partnership is generally a very positive and happy event. Hopefully, it will lead to a settled and stable relationship with a partner. It can also offer you PIES development, perhaps through:

- shared activities (physical)
- new opportunities (intellectual)
- supporting and looking after each other (emotional)
- developing new joint friendships (social).

You may have children, who will keep you physically and mentally active, giving you love and affection. Children may change your social life to centre more on the home and school. When your children have grown, you may have time again to focus on the two of you. You may take up new interests and friendships. Your self-esteem may be high because you feel more confident and capable as a result of your journey through your partnership.

Beginning a journey through marriage and commitment

Divorce

Divorce is generally a negative event. Even though you might feel relief at ending an unhappy situation, it may still bring negative feelings and other consequences.

- You may enjoy the flexibility of being single and making your own choices (perhaps about what to eat and how to exercise). However, you may have less money, which could affect your general standard of living as well as your opportunities to take part in activities and socialise.
- Although you may be happier single, you may feel lonely and isolated from joint friends.
- Your children may be relieved about a divorce/separation. On the other hand, they may also feel angry and their behaviour may become disruptive.
- Your self-esteem could be affected because you may lose confidence and feel as though you have failed.

Bereavement

The death of a life partner, parent, child or any other family member or friend can:

- cause us to grieve
- make our future uncertain
- raise our levels of stress and anxiety.

Table 3.5 shows how the health and wellbeing of a bereaved person may suffer.

LINK IT UP

To remind yourself more about relationships, go to Sections B1 and B2 in Component C1.

Table 3.5: How a bereaved person who has lost their partner may suffer

Physical suffering	Intellectual suffering	Emotional suffering	Social suffering
• Feels stress • Neglects, for example, a balanced diet • Does not sleep well	• Feels distracted • Lacks concentration • Misses sharing activities/ opportunities with the person they have lost	• Feels unhappy • Feels sad • Perhaps feels angry	• Feels it is harder to socialise as a single person • Feels it is difficult to mix with others • Misses socialising with the person they have lost

ACTIVITY

1. Work in a group and pick one type of relationship change: entering a relationship; marriage/partnership; divorce; parenthood or bereavement.
2. Make notes on the relationship change. Then write the profile of a TV soap character who has the relationship change. Choose any writing style – for example, social media, case study, article.
3. Predict the positive/negative effects of the relationship change on the person's health and wellbeing.
4. Write up and print your profile for yourself and other students, using the notes you made.
5. Read each profile and add any negative/positive effects you feel have been missed.

CHECK MY LEARNING

How might suffering the bereavement of a parent affect a person's health and well-being positively as well as negatively?

The impact of life events relating to changes in life circumstances

GETTING STARTED

Work in pairs to list life events relating to changes in life circumstances.

We all go through changes in our life circumstances. These are expected (starting school) or unexpected (being made redundant) and affect our health and wellbeing in positive and negative ways.

Imprisonment

One example of a change in life circumstances is imprisonment. Being sent to prison may affect the person's health and wellbeing in several ways.

Physical effects

Imprisonment takes away a person's freedom. A prisoner:

- is confined to a cell some of the time and allowed into communal areas with others
- has little privacy
- has little choice of what to eat, drink, wear, when and how to exercise
- has no control over the temperature of their environment
- may also be attacked by other prisoners.

However, for some people, imprisonment may mean three balanced meals a day, warmth, a bed and clothes and the chance to exercise more than they did previously (so they may become healthier and fitter). They will also have access to health and social care services inside the prison.

Intellectual effects

Being imprisoned is likely to cause anxiety and stress. The person may find it hard to concentrate on anything. However, they will be given learning opportunities during their sentence, which could lead to new qualifications and skills.

Emotional effects

They will miss their family and friends. They may feel upset at how life is passing by and what they are missing outside the prison. They may also be worried about issues such as being attacked by other prisoners and finding employment when they leave prison. Although the worry will not disappear, they may decide to give up their old bad habits and try to better themselves. They may become more positive and confident about their new life outside of prison, using their new skills, knowledge and level of fitness.

Social effects

They will have to mix with all kinds of people – including those they do not like. They may find the habits and attitudes of others offensive. However, they may also make friends with a cellmate or other prisoners. They may even enjoy the social life on offer.

Therefore, although being sent to prison will generally be a negative and unhappy event, there may be ways in which health and wellbeing are positively affected. You will usually be able to find some positive effects in most, but not all, changes in life circumstances.

ACTIVITY

1 Work in a small group to discuss any changes that have happened in your life circumstances and how these affected your health and wellbeing. However, you do not have to share your own experiences if you prefer not to. You can keep the discussion very general.

2 Look at the life events shown in the diagram below. Excluding imprisonment and relationship changes, compile a table showing the main effects of each change in life circumstance on an individual's health and wellbeing.

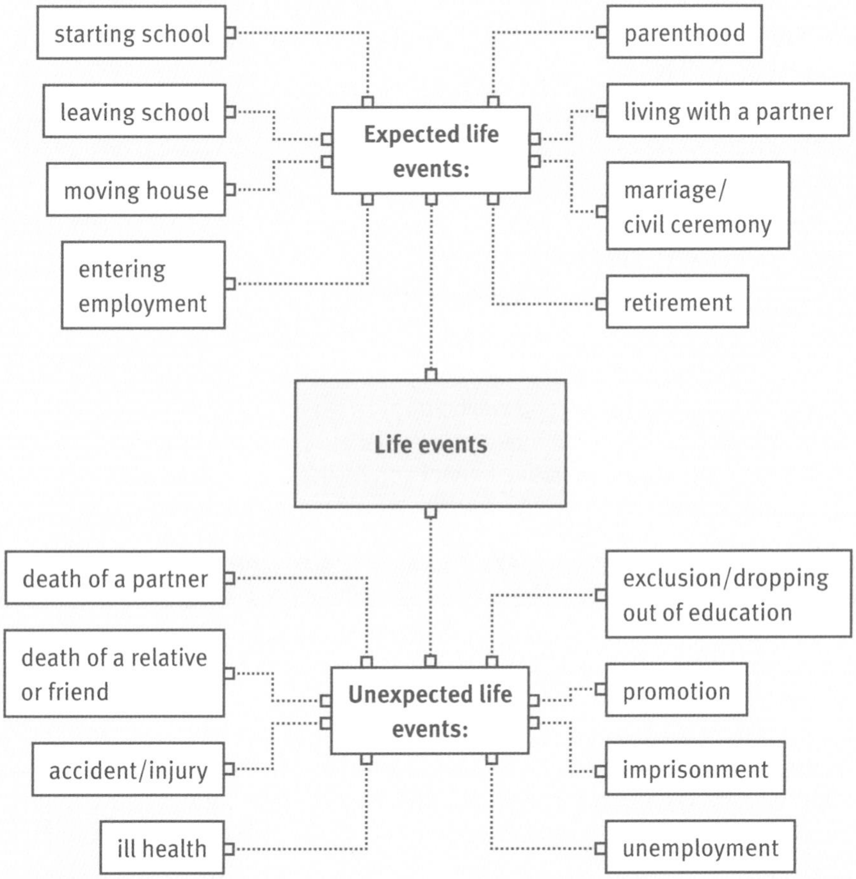

CHECK MY LEARNING

1 How does starting school affect a child's health and wellbeing?

2 How does parenthood affect a person's emotional health and wellbeing, positively and negatively?

A: assessment practice

How you will be assessed

You will be assessed on Component 3 by a written task under supervised conditions. You will have an answer booklet to write into. The task has two sections:
Section A: Assessing health and wellbeing.
Section B: Designing a health and wellbeing improvement plan.

Section A:
Activity 1: asks you to review a case study and to explain factors that can have positive and negative effects on a person's health and wellbeing.
Activity 2: asks you to explain effects a particular event can have on a person's social and emotional wellbeing.

CHECKPOINT

Strengthen

- What do you think you have to do to clearly explain factors that could have a positive/negative effect on the person's health and wellbeing?
- What do you understand by the word 'effect'?

Challenge

- How can you demonstrate a high level of knowledge and understanding of factors that affect health and wellbeing?
- What do you need to do to make your explanation of how different factors can have positive and negative impacts on health and wellbeing, including the impact of a specific life event on wellbeing, as clear as possible?

ASSESSMENT ACTIVITY LEARNING AIM **A**

You are a registered nurse, managing a care home as the nursing home administrator. You are assessing the health and wellbeing of Susan, who is about to move into the care home.

Read the information below. Then complete the activities.

Location: Susan Jones is 82 years old. She lives in a one-bedroom terraced house with a small garden and a short but steep driveway on the edge of a small town.

Medical history: Susan has osteoarthritis and her mobility has recently started to deteriorate and she now uses a stick for support.

Family, friends and social interactions: An old friend comes on the bus once a fortnight to visit and helps with her laptop, so she is able to keep organised and shop for food and other items online. Her niece visits her every fortnight and does jobs like keeping the garden tidy. Her neighbour, who is 73 years old, is often on hand if she needs any day-to-day practical help but has quite a busy life with her own family and friends. Susan has no children and most of her friends have died, are in care homes or can no longer travel. She is often lonely.

Day-to-day life: Susan uses a walking stick to get around the house. She manages the steep stairs by going up sideways with her back to the handrail. She now finds day-to-day tasks such as dressing, washing and cooking increasingly difficult. She does not like to ask her visitors to help, as she does not want to be a burden.

Review the information about Susan.

Activity 1 (a)

Using the information provided, explain **two** factors that could have a positive effect on Susan's health and wellbeing.

(4 marks)

Activity 1 (b)

Using the information provided, explain **four** factors that could have a negative effect on Susan's health and wellbeing.

(8 marks)

(Total for Activity 1 = 12 marks)

Activity 2

Susan's husband Peter died 15 years ago. They used to visit regularly their niece and her family, and her widowed sister-in-law, each about an hour's drive away. They also enjoyed meals out and weekends away in hotels. Susan does not drive and so now only speaks to her sister-in-law on the phone. She now only leaves her home when her niece and family come and take her out for lunch or to attend medical appointments in a taxi.

Explain **three** effects that Peter's death could have on Susan's social and emotional wellbeing.

(Total for Activity 2 = 6 marks)

TIPS

Make sure you spend the right amount of time on each question. Generally, questions with higher marks need you to provide longer answers.

TAKE IT FURTHER

Check your answers. Factors may affect physical health, intellectual, emotional or social wellbeing – you could use one or a combination. Use the information provided as no marks are given for general descriptions. Answers should identify a relevant point from the information provided and then explain how it affected Susan.

Health indicators

GETTING STARTED

Work in pairs to list ways to tell whether someone is well or not and how each way can be assessed.

KEY TERMS

Physiological relates to how a person and their bodily parts function normally.

Health practitioners use **physiological** indicators (certain aspects of a person's health) to assess health and wellbeing. Some can be measured using pieces of equipment, but others are harder to assess.

Health monitoring and illness prevention

Health monitoring means regularly checking that everything is as it should be. Monitoring in this way helps to detect any problems that may arise. These problems can then be dealt with quickly to give the best chance of sorting them out.

- A problem will continue to be monitored during its treatment.
- Support is given to help the person cope with all aspects of the problem.

An example of a problem detected in health monitoring is raised cholesterol. This could then be reduced through eating the correct diet. Lowering cholesterol could, in turn, reduce the risk of heart disease and stroke. Without health monitoring, these illnesses might have been undetected.

Illness prevention services aim to prevent people getting ill. Here are some examples.

- The National Healthy Schools Programme encourages children and young people to make informed health and life choices. It does this by providing knowledge, healthy school dinners, opportunities for exercise and an environment that increases emotional wellbeing.
- Health screening, such as dental and eye check-ups and breast screening, check that certain areas of our bodies are working as they should be or are in the condition they should be.
- Vaccinations help the body to fight infectious disease such as flu, tetanus, diphtheria and polio.

Measurements of health

Measurements of health include measurable indicators, observed indicators and lifestyle.

Measurable indicators

These are shown in the diagram below. Measurable indicators can be measured using purpose-built pieces of equipment – for example, a thermometer to measure body temperature.

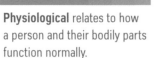

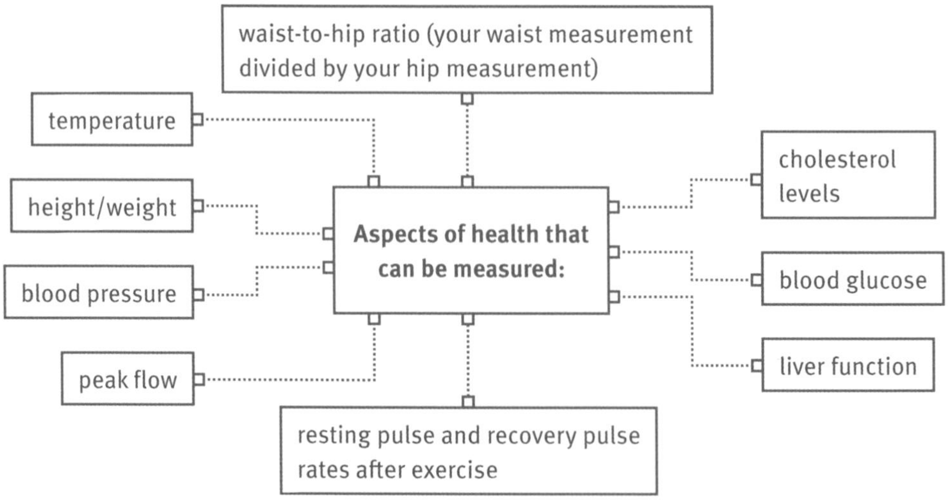

Figure 3.11: Examples of quantifiable health indicators

Positive and negative aspects of lifestyle

Table 3.6 shows the positive and negative aspects of lifestyle. They are less easily measured than the ones shown in the diagram but are useful indicators of health. One way of assessing aspects of lifestyle is to collect the information in a questionnaire or at an appointment with a health practitioner.

Table 3.6: Measuring the positive and negatives aspects of lifestyle

Some positive aspects of lifestyle	Some negative aspects of lifestyle
• Regular exercise	• Genetic inheritance
• Personal hygiene	• Existing chronic conditions
• Supportive relationships	• Substance abuse (e.g. alcohol, nicotine, illegal drugs and misuse of prescription drugs)
• Adequate financial resources	• Social isolation
• Stimulating work	• Stress
• Use of health monitoring and illness prevention services, e.g. screening and vaccination	• Reluctance to seek help or access services
• Use of services such as dentist and optician	• Poor housing
• Risk management to prevent accidents	• Environmental pollution
• Education	• Poverty and/or unemployment
• Leisure activities	• Unprotected sex
• Balanced diet	
• Enough sleep	

Observed indicators

A health practitioner will gain information by observing whether, for example, a person is pale or flushed, sweating, breathless, limping, behaving oddly, twitching, has a swelling, lump or rash and so on.

ACTIVITY

1. Draw a body outline in the middle of a page of A4, leaving enough space to add some labels.
2. Use a height measure, bathroom scales, a blood pressure monitor, a body fat measure, a peak flow meter, a thermometer and a pulse reader or stopwatch to measure your pulse rate, height, weight, peak flow, blood pressure and temperature.
3. Add these measures of health to the body outline, with an arrow pointing to the correct part of your body.
4. You will be adding to this in future lessons so it becomes your health profile.

LINK IT UP

To remind yourself about health care services and their roles (some include measuring health indicators covered here and in the next seven topics), go to Section A1 in Component 2.

CHECK MY LEARNING

How could a GP assess the health of someone who says they feel as though they are getting flu?

Resting pulse rate and recovery after exercise

GETTING STARTED

Reflect on your own pulse rate and what you feel happening to it when you exercise or exert yourself in some way. Discuss with a partner what this may tell you about your level of fitness.

A useful measure of health is to compare your resting pulse rate with the rate after exercise and see how long it takes to return to its normal resting rate.

Pulse rate

Your pulse rate is the measure of how fast your heart is beating. In other words, your pulse rate is the same as your heart rate. This is because:

Every time your heart beats it pumps blood into your **cardiovascular system**.

↓

These beats cause a pulse, or shock wave, that travels along the walls of the **arteries**.

↓

This pulse is strong enough to be measured wherever an artery crosses a bone – most easily in the radial arteries in the wrist and the carotid arteries in the neck.

KEY TERMS

Cardiovascular system is the system that moves blood, nutrients and gases around our bodies. It is made up of the heart, blood and blood vessels; also known as the circulatory system.

Arteries are blood vessels that carry blood away from the heart.

To measure your pulse rate:
- put the tips of two fingers on the radial pulse (just below the base of your thumb) in your wrist
- count how many beats there are in a certain time
- use the number to work out your pulse rate in beats per minute (bpm).

Say, for example, you measure 12 beats in 10 seconds. Multiply 12 × 6 to get the number of beats in 60 seconds. The answer is 72, which means you have a resting pulse rate of 72 bpm. You must use the tops of your fingers, because these are the most sensitive. And remember, the thumb has a pulse of its own, so do not use it to take your pulse anywhere else.

Resting pulse rate

Athletes often use their necks to measure pulse rate but it is easier for you to find the pulse in your wrist

The average resting pulse rate for an adult is about 60–100 bpm. The average for an athlete is lower, about 40–60 bpm. In other words, the fitter you are the lower your resting pulse rate. This is because the heart gets bigger and stronger with exercise, so it becomes more efficient at pumping blood around the body. It can pump more blood round the body with each beat, which means it needs fewer bpm to pump the blood around. Babies and children have faster pulse rates. A new baby's rate can be 70–190 bpm.

The best way to measure your resting pulse rate is to:
- sit quietly for about 5 minutes, so you are calm and rested
- take at least three readings
- work out the average by adding the readings together and dividing by three.

You can also measure your pulse rate using a heart rate monitor on a fitness watch or using an app on your smartphone.

Recovery after exercise

Your pulse rate increases after exercise and then returns to normal. But this can happen at different rates.
- A professional dancer, say, in a TV dance competition can get their breath back and speak almost as soon as a dance has finished because their pulse rate quickly returns to normal.

- Their celebrity partner is often out of breath because they are not so fit and it takes their pulse rate longer to return to normal.

Measuring your pulse rate before and after exercise and seeing how many minutes it takes to return to normal is a good way of measuring how fit you are. The shorter your recovery time, the more fit you are.

The predicted maximum pulse rate is 220 minus your age. A healthy pulse rate during or just after exercise is 60 to 80 per cent of this. Here's an example for a 30-year-old:

$$\text{Predicted pulse rate} = 220 - 30 = 190$$

$$60\% \text{ of } 190 = 60/100 \times 190 = 114$$

$$80\% \text{ of } 190 = 80/100 \times 190 = 152$$

ACTIVITY

1 Check your own resting pulse rate, then exercise (star jumps or running on the spot) for 2 minutes. Measure your new pulse rate immediately afterwards. Take a record of it every minute until it returns to normal and add how many minutes it took to your health profile (started in previous lesson).

2 Draw a graph of pulse rate (*y* axis) against time (*x* axis) to show your own recovery after exercise.

3 On the same graph paper, plot your friend's measurements (if willing to share them). What can you tell by looking at the lines on the graph?

CHECK MY LEARNING

Look at the table. What does this information tell you?

	Before 6 months of regular exercise	After 6 months of regular exercise
Pulse rate (bpm)	84	69
Breathing rates (breaths per minute)	18	16
Heart volume (cm^3)	128	141
Volume of blood pumped out of the heart by each beat (cm^3)	64	76

Blood pressure

GETTING STARTED

Go back to your health profile to find your blood pressure reading. Now look at the diagram below. What range does your blood pressure fall into? Add it to your health profile.

	Systolic (top number)	Diastolic (bottom number)
High blood pressure	140–190	90–100
Pre-high blood pressure	120–140	80–90
Ideal blood pressure	90–120	60–80
Low blood pressure	70–90	40–60

Figure 3.12: This chart helps you to see how healthy your blood pressure is

DID YOU KNOW?

Your blood provides all the organs in your body with the material it needs to stay healthy. Your arteries carry blood *away* from the heart and your veins carry blood *to* the heart.

You might have heard someone say something like: 'You make my blood pressure go up!' But did you know that blood pressure can be a very important health indicator?

Blood pressure

Blood pressure is the pressure exerted by your blood against the walls of your arteries. It is measured in millimetres of mercury (mmHg) as two numbers shown one over the other.

- The top number is your systolic pressure – the maximum pressure in the arteries as the heart pumps blood out around the body.
- The bottom number is your diastolic pressure – the minimum pressure as the heart relaxes between beats.

Normal healthy blood pressure is between 90/60 mmHg and 120/80 mmHg.

High blood pressure

If you have blood pressure between 120/80 mmHg and 140/90 mmHg, you are in danger of developing high blood pressure. High blood pressure is called 'hypertension'. It is 140/90 mmHg or above. Hypertension is a risk to health and needs to be reduced as quickly as possible. This can be done by any of these things:

- removing the source of the stress causing it
- treating the condition causing it
- treating the blood pressure with medication.

Hypertension does not usually have any noticeable symptoms. However, if it is left untreated, it puts extra strain on the blood vessels and organs, which can cause:

- heart disease, attacks and failure
- kidney disease
- strokes
- blindness
- vascular dementia.

The risk of having high blood pressure is increased by all the things shown in the diagram below. Blood pressure can be lowered by making lifestyle changes or through taking medication such as beta-blockers.

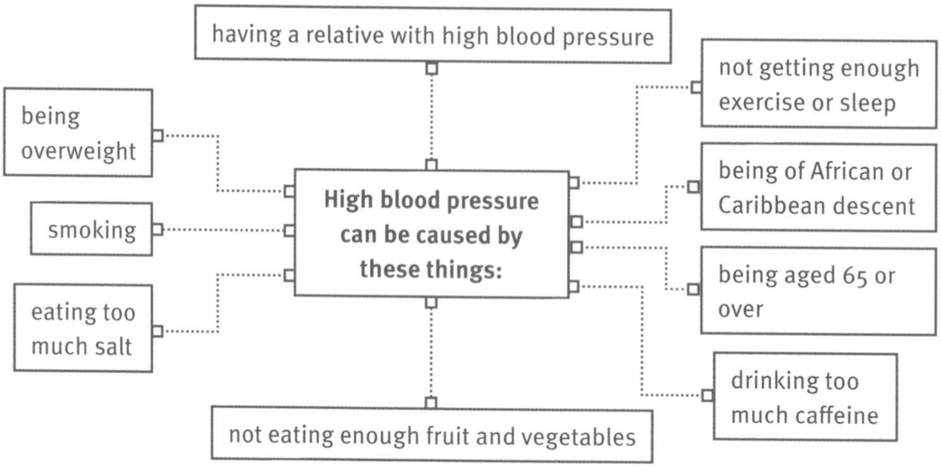

Figure 3.13: Hypertension risk factors

Low blood pressure

Low blood pressure is called hypotension and is 90/60 mmHg or below. Some people have naturally low blood pressure and this can lead to a longer lifespan. Low blood pressure does not normally need treating unless it is causing symptoms. However, reduced blood pressure can restrict the volume of blood flow to your brain, so it can lead to dizziness (perhaps if standing up quickly), fainting or falls. Low blood pressure can also be the side effect of some medication or, more seriously, a sign of a more life-limiting problem such as Parkinson's disease.

DID YOU KNOW?

You can reduce the symptoms of low blood pressure by drinking lots of fluids, eating smaller meals more often, wearing support stockings and standing up slowly.

Measurement of blood pressure

Blood pressure can be measured manually using a sphygmomanometer – made up of a stethoscope, arm cuff, pump and dial. You roll up your sleeve and hold out your arm, which should be supported on something at the same level as your heart. The cuff is wrapped around the arm and pumped up to restrict your blood flow there. This can feel uncomfortable, but just for a few seconds until the pressure is released. The health practitioner uses a stethoscope to detect vibrations in your arteries as the blood flow returns to your arm. This is measured at two points.

These days, blood is also measured digitally using a blood pressure monitor, which automatically puts the blood pressure reading on a digital display. You can have your blood pressure measured at your GP surgery or health centre, at some pharmacies and in some workplaces.

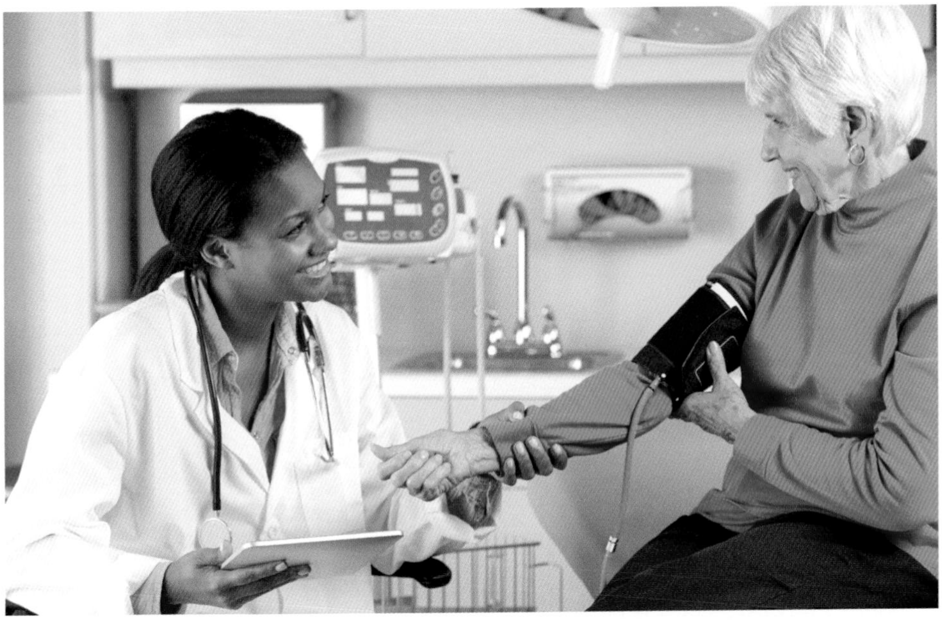

Can you remember the name of the piece of equipment that takes your blood pressure – either manually or digitally?

ACTIVITY

Work on your own to research and produce an information leaflet called 'Blood pressure made simple'. The leaflet needs to be easy to read and attractive. It should include information about: what blood pressure is; high and low blood pressure and their risks; where people can get tested; how the test is carried out; and how to control and monitor it.

CHECK MY LEARNING

1 What is the accepted range for healthy:
(i) systolic pressure and
(ii) diastolic pressure?

2 What are the names for:
(i) high blood pressure and
(ii) low blood pressure?

Peak flow

GETTING STARTED

In pairs, compare your own peak flow reading on your own health profile with the chart shown. What does your reading say about your health? Add the accepted normal peak flow for your age and gender to your health profile.

Peak flow is a measurement of how quickly you can blow air out of your lungs. It is an important health indicator (as people with breathing difficulties may already know).

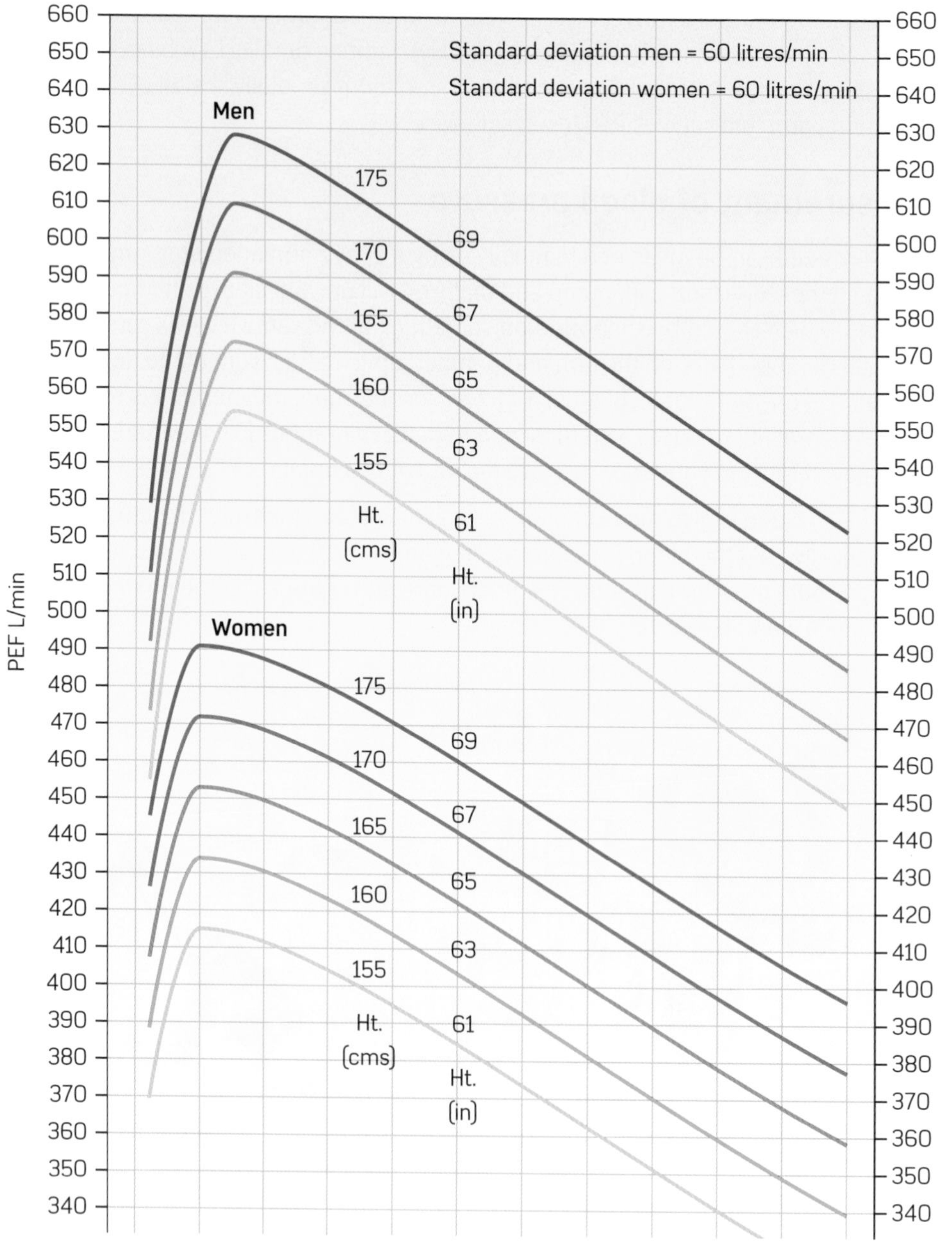

Figure 3.14: Chart showing peak flow against age for people 15–70 years old

Peak flow

This is a measure of the maximum rate, or expiratory rate, in litres per minute (L/min), at which air is expelled from the lungs when you breathe out as hard as possible. Your peak flow reading shows if your airways are narrowed. It is measured using a handheld device called a peak flow meter.

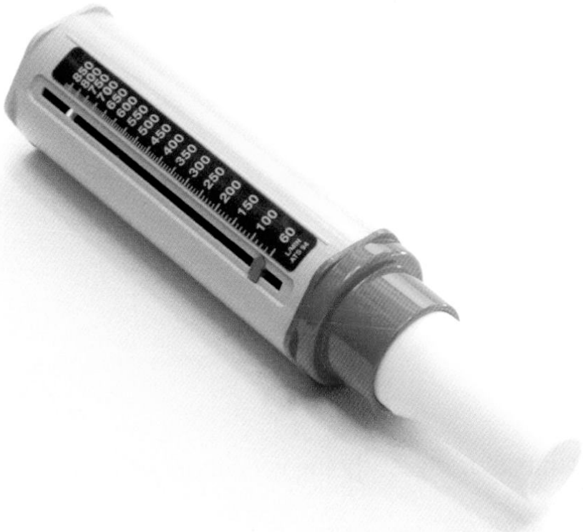

A peak flow meter, which measures air pushed out from the lungs

You draw in a deep breath and seal your lips tightly around the disposable mouthpiece, then blow out as hard and fast as you can. This causes a pointer to move along a scale, so you can read your peak flow at the point it has stopped. You do this three times and take the highest reading.

The most common reason for taking and recording peak flow readings is to monitor a person's asthma, caused by narrowed airways, to make sure:

- it is not getting any worse
- it is being kept under control by the prescribed medication.

If you measure your peak flow before and after exposure to something like animal fur, or before and after a stressful event, a drop in reading can show these things are a trigger for your symptoms. Peak flow can also be used to diagnose and monitor other lung problems, such as:

- bronchitis (a chest infection)
- emphysema (damage to the lungs causing breathlessness)
- cystic fibrosis (a genetic disorder that can affect the lungs)
- lung cancer.

The readings are compared with a chart of expected scores based on age and gender, as shown in Figure 3.14. If you have a lung problem you will have a lower score than expected.

ACTIVITY

In a group, each of you measure your peak flow before and after exercise. Compare your results and discuss what might be causing some of you to have lower peak flows than others.

CHECK MY LEARNING

What conditions could be diagnosed using peak flow readings? Name three.

Body mass index

GETTING STARTED

In small groups, discuss why you think children are having their height and weight measured in Reception class and Year 6 in primary schools as part of the National Child Measurement Programme. Is this a good idea?

BMI is a measure of the amount of fat on your body in relation to your height to tell you if your weight is healthy.

Why measure body fat?

We all carry some body fat. But someone who has too much (they are very overweight) is at risk of:

- cardiovascular disease
- high blood pressure
- diabetes
- arthritis
- stroke.

Having low amounts of body fat (being very underweight) can indicate problems such as:

- an undiagnosed illness
- an eating disorder (such as anorexia nervosa or bulimia nervosa).

Calculating BMI

BMI is worked out using a formula, which divides an adult's weight in kilograms by their height in metres squared.

$$\text{BMI} = \frac{\text{Weight in kg}}{(\text{Height in m})^2}$$

DID YOU KNOW?

For your assessment, you will be expected to know how to use both BMI calculation methods.

It can also be worked out using an online BMI calculator, where you add your weight and height and the calculation is done for you.

The information about your height and weight (and sometimes age and gender) can be used directly to determine which BMI range you fit in. You can do this using a graph (see Figure 3.15) or a table (see Table 3.7). BMI falls into different categories, for example:

- underweight
- normal
- overweight
- obese.

Roughly speaking, a range of 18.5 to 25 is about right for most adults. BMI is calculated differently for children aged 2 to 18. This allows for their BMI to be shown in relation to that of other children of the same sex and age.

BMI only takes into account body shape to give a healthy weight for a certain height. Health care practitioners will take other factors into account. These will be covered later in this component.

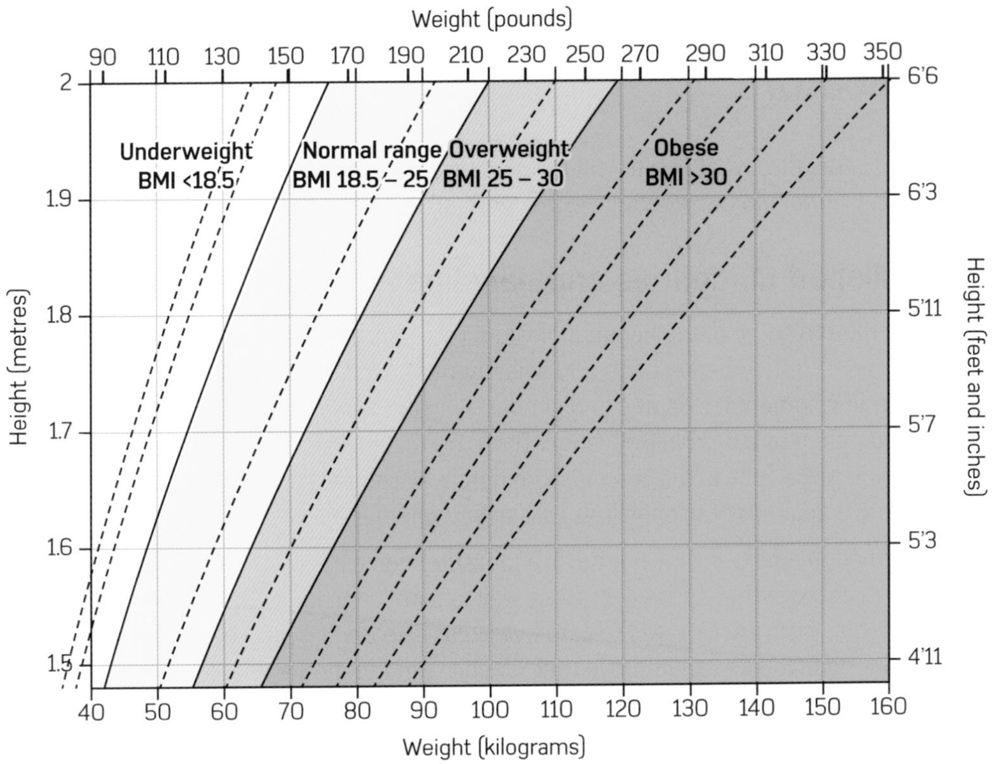

Figure 3.15: Where does your BMI fall?

Table 3.7: Beware: different organisations use slightly different ranges; this one is used by the NHS and is the one that will be used in your assessment

BMI	Meaning
Less than 18.5	Underweight
Between 18.5 and 24.9	Healthy weight
Between 25 and 29.9	Overweight
Between 30 and 34.9	Obese
Between 35 and 39.9	Severely obese
40 or above	Morbidly obese

Test your skills

Ali weighs 76 kg and is 1.89 m tall. Try calculating his BMI, then look at the calculation below.

$$\text{BMI} = \frac{76}{1.89^2}$$

$$\text{BMI} = \frac{76}{1.89 \times 1.89}$$

$$\text{BMI} = \frac{76}{3.57}$$

$$\text{BMI} = 21.3 \text{ kg/m}^2$$

ACTIVITY

1. Work out your own BMI mathematically.
2. Check it online and add it to your own health profile with a note saying what this has shown about your weight.

DID YOU KNOW?

The National Child Measurement Programme (NCMP) measures the height and weight of around 1 million UK schoolchildren every year. The figures for 2014/15 showed one-third of 10–11 year olds and more than one-fifth of 4–5 year olds were overweight or obese.

CHECK MY LEARNING

1. How can you work out BMI?
2. Jo is 94 kg and 1.63 m tall. What is her BMI?

Using published guidelines to interpret health indicators

GETTING STARTED

In small groups, discuss whether you have looked up symptoms on the internet when you have not felt well. How did it make you feel? What are the dangers of doing this?

How do we know what health test results actually mean? What do we compare our results with to find out whether we are 'normal' or not? Published guidelines can help.

Published guidelines and baseline assessments

Think back to some of the health indicators you have already learned about in this component. You will have been told what 'normal' (an average healthy range – depending sometimes on age and gender) is – for example, a normal peak flow measurement or a normal BMI range. These normal measurements, or published guidelines, are called baseline measurements. By comparing a person's health indicators against these baselines we can say whether or not there is a problem.

Even though a person may not be ill, a measurement can give a warning that they may need to improve their lifestyle in some way to carry on being healthy. For example, high blood pressure can lead to cardiovascular disease and stroke, but a person with high blood pressure can improve their lifestyle (and therefore reduce their chances of ill health) through:

- losing weight
- reducing stress, alcohol or salt in their diet
- giving up smoking.

Limitations to published guidelines

Health indicators are vital in diagnosing risks to health but they should never be used in isolation (on their own). For example, BMI is a good way to assess a person's weight in relation to their height. But, BMI cannot tell the difference between excess fat, muscle or bone or whether you are a man or woman. This means that:

- a very muscular person may fall into the overweight or obese category, even though their body fat is low
- older adults may fall into the healthy weight category even though they are carrying excess fat round their middle, because they lose muscle as they age
- women, who generally have more total body fat than men, are measured against the same BMI ranges as men.

Doctors do not use BMI normal ranges when treating people with eating disorders. They also need to consider factors such as age and sexual maturity when taking BMI measurements for children and young people.

Additional calculations may be needed in order to gain a more accurate overall picture than just one measurement in isolation. For example, a person's waist-to-hip ratio and body fat composition can give more information when assessing risks such as cardiovascular disease.

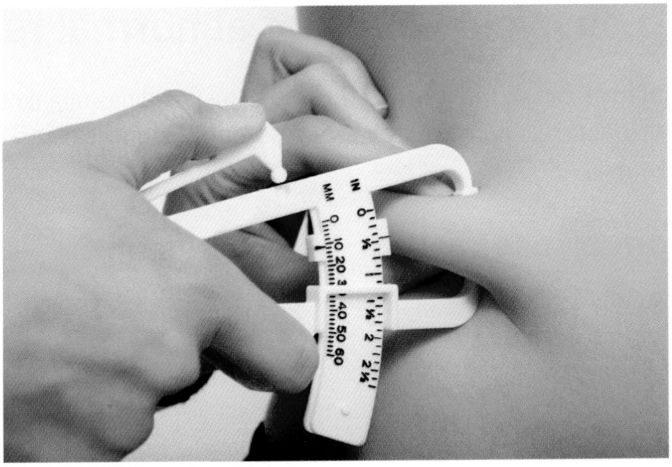

Calculating body fat measurements and adding to other data gives a bigger health picture

Presenting assessments

It is very important that all measurements are:

- accurate and precise
- collected together and presented clearly.

These approaches can help to avoid errors.

It is also important that evidence is validated (checked against something else). For example, if you are having trouble breathing, your peak flow reading should be taken three times and the highest reading noted. Your medical notes should then record:

- that you are having trouble breathing (observation)
- your actual peak flow measurements, which validates (supports) the observation.

Reasoned judgements

Any data collected must be reviewed, taking every piece of information into account. A high total cholesterol level looked at on its own might suggest to your GP that something is wrong. However, if other factors are considered, a GP may feel there is less cardiovascular risk than they first thought. Other factors may include:

- a high percentage of good cholesterol
- a history of high levels of cholesterol in the family with no ill effects.

ACTIVITY

Work on your own to research:

1 the limitations of BMI and the possible alternatives of waist-to-hip ratio and body fat composition

2 blood test results combined with other factors such as family history.

CHECK MY LEARNING

1 Why is it important not to use data in isolation?

2 Why should judgements by GPs and other health practitioners be reasoned and clearly presented?

Risks to physical health of abnormal readings

GETTING STARTED

Work with a partner to reflect on why it is important to take part in health monitoring. Discuss why you should have your health indicators measured and analysed by a health practitioner.

KEY TERMS

Potential significance could develop into something important.

The word 'abnormal' can sound worrying. Abnormal test readings might mean a risk to health. In fact, abnormal readings may indicate **potential significance**. Let us look at blood pressure.

An 'abnormal' case study: blood pressure

Having an abnormally high blood pressure reading means you have very high blood pressure. This could lead to:

- a range of diseases including heart disease, kidney disease, strokes and blindness
- death, because for every increase of 20 mmHg systolic above the normal of 120 mmHg the risk of cardiovascular death doubles
  For example: if your blood pressure is 140/90 mmHg, the systolic measurement of 140 mmHg is 20 mmHg higher than the norm of 120 mmHg, which means your risk of death from a heart condition doubles. If your blood pressure is 160/90 mmHg, the systolic measurement of 160 mmHg doubles again the risk of death.
- even greater risk of health problems such as coronary heart disease if you have other conditions too – for example, diabetes and high cholesterol. Having diabetes may mean the nerves in your heart and blood vessels are damaged, so you may not feel the pain caused by a heart attack as much as someone without diabetes. This makes a heart attack harder to diagnose and therefore, slower to be treated.

DID YOU KNOW?

Around 3.5 million people in the UK are diagnosed with diabetes. But there are many people who do not know they have diabetes because it has not been diagnosed and they may also have high blood pressure.

Abnormal readings: blood pressure

It is very important that blood pressure readings are accurate, so that the right course of action can be taken to reduce it as quickly as possible. Having an abnormally high reading from one test does not always mean you have high blood pressure. Blood pressure can vary during the day depending on what you are doing (for example, exercising) and what is happening around you (for example, situations that may cause stress).

You might also get tense and anxious when you visit your GP or are in hospital, so your blood pressure increases. Your blood pressure may be as much as 30 mmHg higher when it is taken by a health practitioner in a medical setting than when it is taken at home. This is called 'white coat syndrome', because doctors traditionally wear white coats. In this case, you will probably be asked to take part in ambulatory blood pressure monitoring (ABPM). This means you will:

- either take and record readings of your own blood pressure at regular intervals with a home blood pressure monitor
- or wear a 24-hour monitor that automatically checks and records your blood pressure regularly throughout the day and night.

This will establish whether your blood pressure is consistently high.

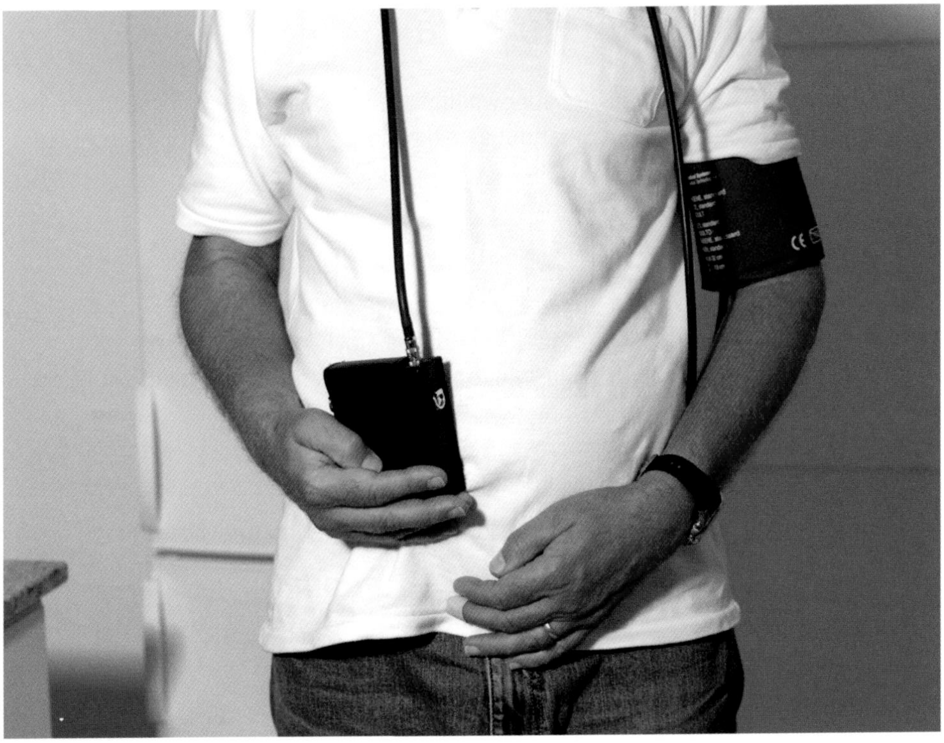

An automatic monitor can measure your blood pressure round the clock

Acting on abnormal readings

Imagine someone has consistently abnormal blood pressure readings. This will need to be acted on as quickly as possible to avoid further health problems. For example, if that person's blood pressure is:

- consistently higher than the threshold figure of 140/90 mmHg, but their risks of other problems are low, they will be advised to make some lifestyle changes
- consistently higher than 140/90 mmHg *and* their risk of other problems is high, they will be offered medication to lower it
- consistently over 160/100 mmHg, they will be offered medication to lower it.

ACTIVITY

1. In a group, pick one of these health indicators: resting pulse and recovery rate after exercise; peak flow; BMI or blood tests.
2. Look back at, and do more research into, the risks to physical health indicated by an abnormal reading in the health indicator you have picked.
3. Produce a 2-minute long script or video of a health promotion advert for TV to highlight the risks. Accompany this with a fact sheet for each member of your class.
4. Show your adverts (or scripts) and give out the fact sheets. Peer- and self-assess each TV advert.

CHECK MY LEARNING

1. Why is it important for a diagnosis not to be made based on one abnormal blood pressure reading?
2. Why is it important for abnormal readings to be dealt with as quickly as possible?

Interpreting lifestyle data

GETTING STARTED

Recap with a partner all the factors covered earlier in this component that can have a negative effect on health and wellbeing. Remember that these negative effects will pose a risk to physical health.

DID YOU KNOW?

- The ONS (www.ons.gov.uk) is the UK Government's largest provider of statistics. The information it compiles provides an evidence-base for policy and decision-making and the allocation of resources.
- NHS Digital (digital.nhs.uk) publishes a range of statistics about health.

Did you know that we can measure our own lifestyle choices against officially prepared data? This can include information about safe limits for smoking, drinking alcohol and taking exercise.

Lifestyle data

If you look for it, you can find a huge range of lifestyle data.

- The Office for National Statistics (ONS) produces official statistics for the UK. It conducts regular surveys on lifestyle topics such as smoking, drinking, obesity and diet.
- NHS Digital collects data from across the health and social care system. This data can be used by, for example, researchers, patients and health care professionals.

It can take a long time for statistics to become available to the public – perhaps up to 2 years. This is because it needs to be:

- collected (through surveys)
- collated (combined)
- analysed
- written into a report.

So information you are reading now, today, might have been collected 2 years ago.

An example of lifestyle data

In 2014, a survey was published giving lifestyle data between 1993 and 2012. It said:

- the number of adults with a normal BMI decreased in that time from 49.5 per cent to 40.6 per cent of women and from 41 per cent to 32.1 per cent of men
- in 2012, 26 per cent of women and 19 per cent of men were classed as inactive, while 67 per cent of men and 55 per cent of women met the new recommendations for aerobic activity
- the number of adults who were obese rose from 16.4 per cent to 25.1 per cent of women and from 13.2 per cent to 24.4 per cent of men
- during 2012–13, there were 10,957 inpatient admissions to NHS hospitals with a primary diagnosis of obesity among people of all ages. That is nine times higher than the same period 10 years earlier.

The survey was repeated the following year but with different areas of focus. Only one statistic was measured in the same way: the number of adults who were obese. It showed a decrease in obese women (23.8 per cent) and an increase in obese men (26 per cent).

This kind of data can be used to develop realistic health and wellbeing improvement plans to tackle obesity. It might be used (for example, by the NHS) in areas of the country that have a high proportion of illness caused by obesity. In order to draw up a plan for a group of obese individuals (regionally or nationally) it will be necessary to:

- assess the present health status of that population by looking at lifestyle data
- set **targets** for health practitioners aimed at improving the situation
- provide support to help meet those targets – for example, trained staff, better buildings, facilities such as larger beds and scanners that will accommodate obese people, and information

KEY TERMS

Targets are goals and aims.

- identify any difficulties that may arise and provide alternative strategies to meet targets to help overcome those difficulties
- monitor and review progress made towards meeting targets and, if necessary, set new targets as time passes.

On average one in ten children is obese and more than a fifth are overweight or obese by the time they start primary school. How will an obese child overcome their weight problem?

LINK IT UP

To remind yourself about lifestyle choices, go to Section A2 in Component 1 and Section A1 in Component 2.

ACTIVITY

1. Your group will be allocated a lifestyle factor from one of the following: diet; illegal drugs; prescription drugs; unsafe sex; and poor personal hygiene.
2. With your group, find the most up-to-date data on your allocated factor on risks to health. Then produce a health promotion poster showing the key data. It is important to use up-to-date statistics from a UK website.
3. Display your poster on the wall and make notes about other posters.
4. Peer- and self-assess each poster.

CHECK MY LEARNING

1. What is meant by lifestyle data?
2. How can lifestyle data be used to help improve the health and wellbeing of a group of individuals?

Interpreting lifestyle data on smoking

GETTING STARTED

In a small group, discuss whether a pregnant woman has the right to smoke.

DID YOU KNOW?

Smoking in pregnancy causes around 5,000 miscarriages, 300 perinatal deaths and 2,200 premature births in the UK each year (Royal College of Physicians, 2010). Perinatal generally means the period of time just before and after birth.

DID YOU KNOW?

Public health refers to the field of medicine concerned with safeguarding and improving the health of the community as a whole.

Smoking is a lifestyle choice. But it comes with many risks to physical health. As you might imagine, there is much lifestyle data associated with smoking.

Who produces lifestyle data on smoking

The ONS (which you read about in the previous lesson) collects data relating to smoking. It publishes both statistics and reports giving key findings.

ASH (Action on Smoking and Health), a public health charity, works towards eliminating the harm caused by smoking tobacco. It uses data about smoking to:

- influence policy (guidelines)
- inform, educate and raise awareness about the risks of smoking
- campaign for tighter controls on the tobacco industry.

ASH receives funding from the British Heart Foundation and Cancer Research UK. It has also received project funding from the UK Government's Department of Health to support tobacco control.

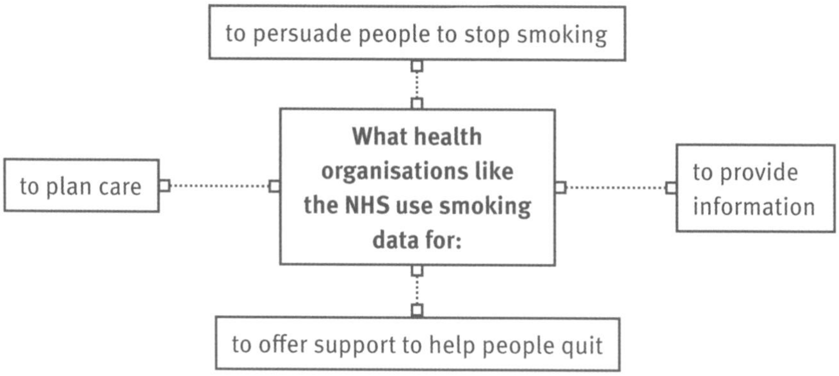

Figure 3.16: The uses of smoking statistics

What the data achieves

The data on smoking provides the UK Government with evidence it can act on by:

- planning national health promotion campaigns to reduce smoking and its associated risks to physical health
- passing laws about smoking (for instance, where you can and cannot smoke).

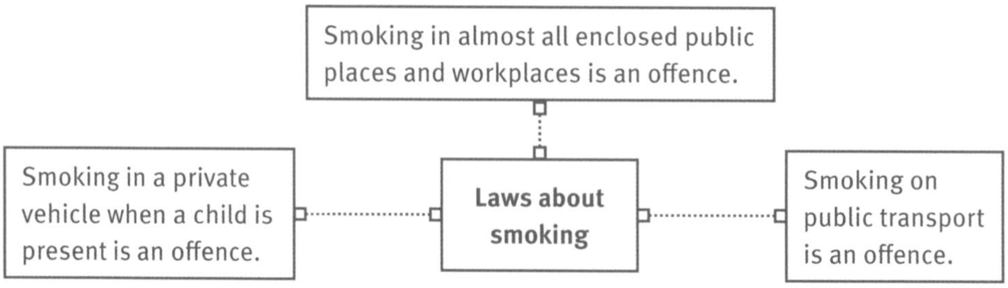

Figure 3.17: Smoking is now banned in many places

Data also delivers hard-hitting anti-smoking campaigns, led by Public Health England. These may be seen on TV, billboards and online. They use graphic images such as:

- cancerous tumours growing from the end of a cigarette (2012)
- blood polluted by smoking products flowing through the body (2013)
- fumes travelling through arteries and veins into the brain (2014)
- smoke rotting the body from within (2015).

What the data shows

ASH identifies that:

- smoking causes around 96,000 deaths in the UK annually
- smokers under the age of 40 are five times more likely to have a heart attack than non-smokers
- smoking causes around 80 per cent of deaths from lung cancer, 80 per cent of deaths from bronchitis and emphysema, and 14 per cent of deaths from heart disease
- more than 25 per cent of all cancer deaths are caused by smoking (for example, lung, mouth, lip, throat, bladder, kidney, pancreas, stomach, liver and cervix)
- on average a smoker will die 10 years earlier than a non-smoker
- women smokers are at greater risk of developing osteoporosis
- smoking is a cause of impotence and can lead to sperm abnormalities
- smokers are more likely to develop facial wrinkles earlier and have dental problems.

ASH also produces fact sheets of smoking statistics and data about, for example, teenage smokers and second-hand smoke.

There is therefore, a wealth of material available on the risks to health of smoking. By providing this information in a suitable format that is attention-grabbing and easy to read, people are more likely to decide to try to give up smoking.

	Men: Cancer risk factor (%)		Women: Cancer risk factor (%)	
1	Tobacco	23	Tobacco	15.6
2	Lack of fruit and vegetables	6.1	Overweight	6.9
3	Occupational hazard	4.9	Infection	3.7
4	Alcohol	4.6	Exposure to sun and sunbeds	3.6
5	Overweight	4.1	Lack of fruit and vegetables	3.4
6	Exposure to sun and sunbeds	3.5	Alcohol	3.3

Figure 3.18: What does this diagram tell you about the impact of smoking on cancer? (Source: Cancer Research UK)

ACTIVITY

1. Download fact sheets giving lifestyle data on smoking from reliable websites such as www.ash.org.uk and www.nhs.uk/smokefree/why-quit.
2. Work in a group to prepare a presentation. The presentation can be in any form your group chooses. Make sure you use the most relevant data to highlight the risks of smoking to physical health. Your presentations must include facts and figures about risks to physical health presented in picture and diagram form – for example, pie charts – so that everyone can easily understand the information you put together.
3. Show your presentation to the rest of the class.

CHECK MY LEARNING

How do organisations such as ASH and the NHS use lifestyle data on the risks to physical health of smoking?

Interpreting lifestyle data on alcohol

GETTING STARTED

In small groups, discuss the example of someone about your age who drinks alcohol. What do you think their positive and negative experiences might be? Reflect on how alcohol may be affecting this person's physical health.

Drinking alcohol is a lifestyle choice. It may seem appealing and social, but it comes with risks to physical health. Lifestyle data about alcohol helps to inform us about those risks.

Who produces and uses lifestyle data on alcohol

The ONS collects information and publishes reports on various aspects of health risks due to alcohol.

The Drinkaware Trust (www.drinkaware.co.uk) is a UK alcohol education charity. It was set up to help reduce alcohol-related risks to health by:

- interpreting available data
- giving people the information they need to make better choices about their drinking – for example, sticking to safe limits and not binge drinking.

The Drinkaware Trust is funded mainly by donations from alcohol producers, retailers and supermarkets.

Alcohol Concern (www.alcoholconcern.org.uk) is a national charity. It works to help reduce the problems caused by alcohol by:

- providing information, advice and support
- aiming to move towards a society where alcohol does no harm.

Alcohol Concern is funded by donations from organisations such as Cancer Research UK. Its website shows a running total of the number of alcohol-related deaths in the UK. It also produces fact sheets giving data on risks to health, such as breast cancer from alcohol.

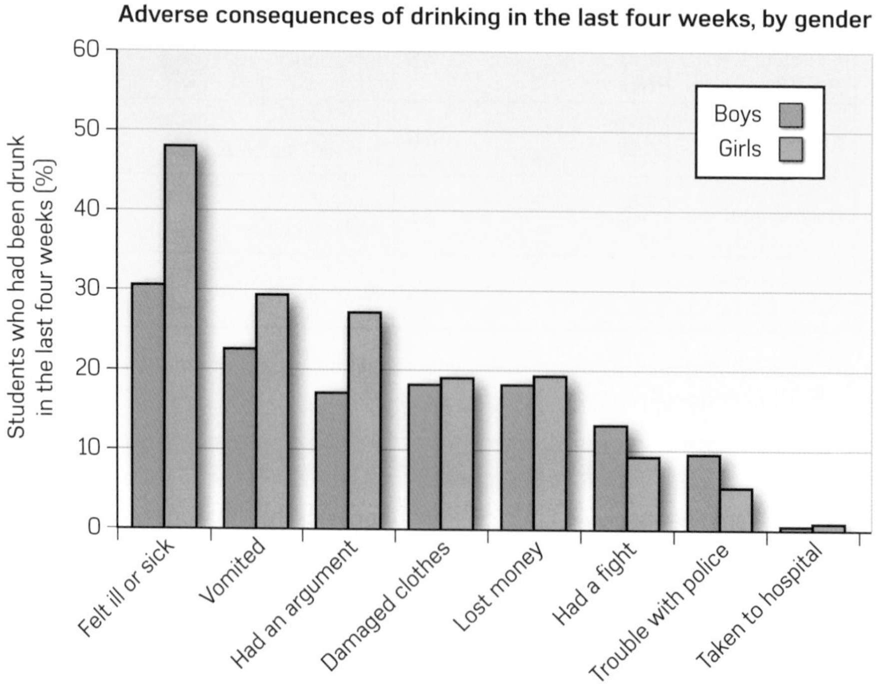

Figure 3.19: Lifestyle data on drinking alcohol can help to produce information like this

What the data shows

Here are some examples of what current lifestyle data on alcohol shows.

- It is strongly linked to at least seven types of cancer. For example, a lifetime of drinking too much alcohol can increase your risk of bowel cancer by 23 per cent.
- Alcohol-related liver disease accounts for 37 per cent of liver disease deaths.
- Two-thirds of cases of chronic pancreatitis are caused by heavy drinking, most commonly in men aged between 45 and 54. (Pancreatitis is an inflamed pancreas that has damaged cells.)
- More than 25,000 people were admitted to hospital with acute pancreatitis in 2013 and 2014.
- Around 1,000 people die from acute pancreatitis every year.
- You are between two and five times more likely to have an accident or injure yourself if you drink five to seven units of alcohol in one sitting.
- Less than one-third of the British public knows about the link between alcohol and breast cancer.
- Each drink per day increases the risk of breast cancer in women by between 7 and 13 per cent.
- In 2011, 3,000 cases of breast cancer were directly caused by alcohol consumption.

This data can be used in health campaigns to show everyone the risks of drinking alcohol, how to lower their consumption and how to reach safe limits.

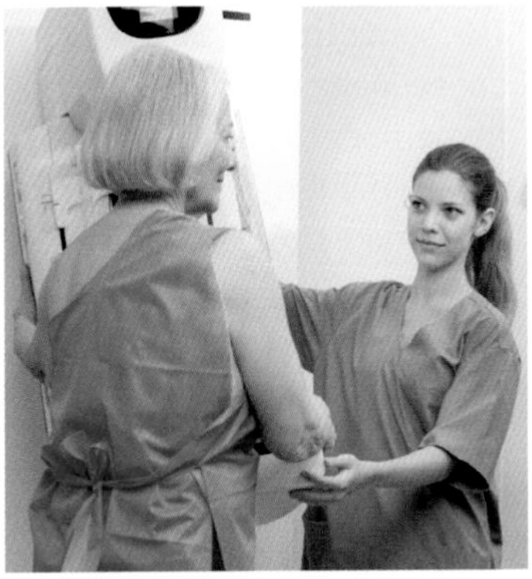

Did you know about the links between breast cancer and alcohol consumption?

New safe limits

In January 2016, the UK Government published new guidelines on drinking alcohol. The guidelines say that:

- any amount of alcohol can increase the risk of cancer
- men and woman who drink regularly should consume no more than 14 units a week (the equivalent of six pints of beer or seven glasses of wine)
- people should not binge-drink all 14 units in one go.

ACTIVITY

1. In a group, share and discuss your ideas for persuading people to reduce their alcohol consumption to at least the latest recommended safe limits, based on the lifestyle data available.
2. Plan a school or house assembly to persuade people your age not to binge-drink or go over the recommended limits. You should do this by highlighting the possible short- and long-term risks to their physical health.
3. Run your planned assembly.

CHECK MY LEARNING

What have you learned that would put you off drinking alcohol?

Interpreting lifestyle data on inactivity

GETTING STARTED

With a partner, discuss how active you and your family members are in a week. Talk about the possible consequences or benefits. Remember to gather your data without making any judgements.

Lifestyle data relating to inactivity lets you know exactly what is meant by inactivity and what you need to do in order to be active enough to make you healthy.

Data on regular physical activity

As you have already learned, activity decreases the risk of many conditions such as stroke, diabetes, cancer, obesity, arthritis and cardiovascular disease. Data says that regular physical activity can make a positive difference, as the diagram shows.

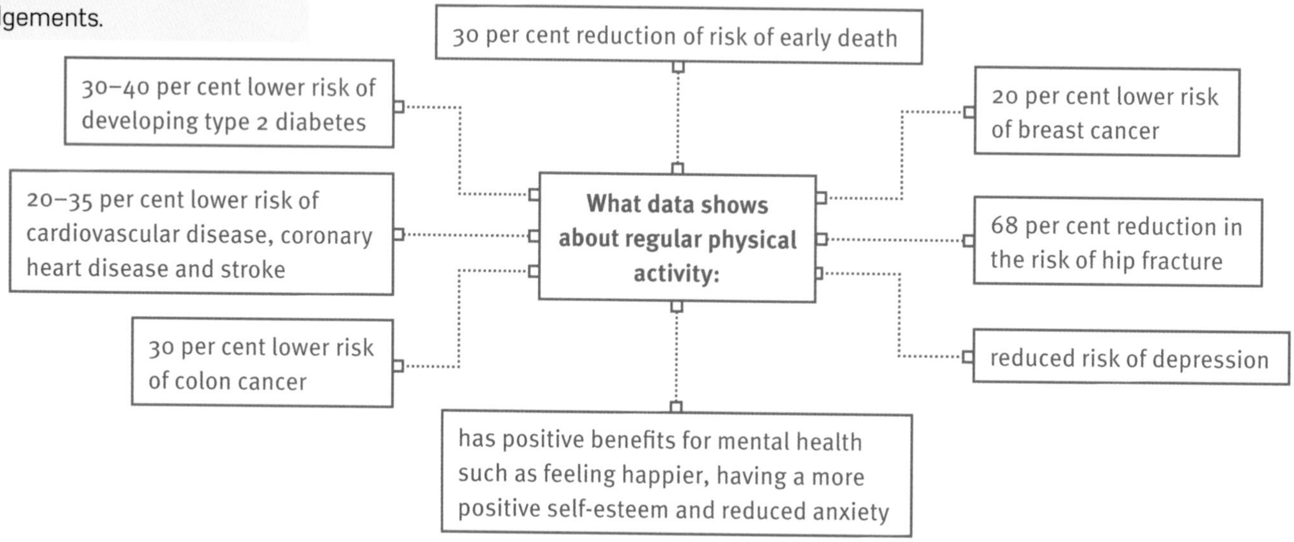
What data shows about regular physical activity:
30 per cent reduction of risk of early death
30–40 per cent lower risk of developing type 2 diabetes
20–35 per cent lower risk of cardiovascular disease, coronary heart disease and stroke
30 per cent lower risk of colon cancer
20 per cent lower risk of breast cancer
68 per cent reduction in the risk of hip fracture
reduced risk of depression
has positive benefits for mental health such as feeling happier, having a more positive self-esteem and reduced anxiety

Figure 3.20: The many benefits of physical activity

Because of data such as this, guidelines were issued by the Chief Medical Officers (CMO) of England, Scotland, Wales and Northern Ireland in 2011 for recommended levels of physical activity for:

- adults aged 19–64 years
- adults aged 65 years and over
- children and young people aged 5–18 years
- children under the age of 5 who can walk.

Adults aged 19–64 should do moderate intensity activity for 2.5 hours a week, according to UK Government guidelines

The physical activity guidelines also suggested that everyone should aim to be active every day. For example, children and young people aged 5 to 18 years should do:

- moderate to vigorous intensity activity for at least 60 minutes and up to several hours every day
- vigorous intensity activities, including those that strengthen muscles and bones, at least three days a week
- less sitting for extended periods.

These (and more) facts can be found on the GOV.UK website by searching for 'UK physical activity guidelines'.

Who produces and uses lifestyle data on inactivity

The ONS produces data in the UK on levels of activity and how these relate to various risks to physical health. Other organisations such as the British Heart Foundation and Public Health England use it to plan health promotion campaigns that encourage people to be more active.

The British Heart Foundation

The British Heart Foundation (www.bhf.org.uk/) is a UK heart charity. It was founded in 1961 and is funded by:

- donations from fundraisers
- money from cardiovascular research projects that help fight heart disease.

The British Heart Foundation aims to prevent people dying prematurely from heart disease. It uses data to highlight the importance of physical activity for cardiovascular health. For example, its report *Physical Activity Statistics 2015* includes data on:

- physical activity levels
- types of physical activity.

This data is broken down by UK country, gender, age and sedentary behaviour. Breaking it down this way means information can be used to target the groups that most need to become more active.

Public Health England

Public Health England (on GOV.UK website) was established to protect and improve the nation's health and wellbeing. It is sponsored by the UK Government's Department of Health. It uses data sources like the annual *Health Survey for England* to provide information on inactivity. This information helps policy makers and practitioners deal with the risks to health such as obesity.

The cost of inactivity

Data on inactivity and its consequences can be used to estimate how much physical risks to health could cost the NHS. This helps the UK Government to plan:

- how to cope financially
- campaigns that reduce inactivity (and therefore reduce the financial strain on the NHS).

For example, data has helped to estimate that by 2050, the health risks created by being overweight could cost the UK almost 50 billion pounds.

ACTIVITY

1. Flora is 9 years old. She is obese, hates exercise and uses any excuse she can to get out of PE. Do some research and draw up a set of recommendations on how much exercise she should be doing. What kinds of exercise would you recommend?
2. Word-process your recommendations in a clear table form. Highlight the benefits of each exercise type you suggest and include at least one relevant statistics at the top of the plan.
3. Swap your plan in class with a partner to peer-assess.

CHECK MY LEARNING

How is data on inactivity used to try to reduce risks to the health of the nation?

B: assessment practice

How you will be assessed

The second part of your externally set assessment consists of one task.

You will be provided with some lifestyle data and physiological data, as well as some guidelines to help you interpret the latter.

You will be asked to explain what the data suggests about the current physical health and risks to future physical health, of the same person featured in the case study for the first part of the assessment in Section A of Learning aim A (see pages 158–59).

CHECKPOINT

Strengthen

- What do you think you have to do to analyse the person's current physical health?
- What do you understand by the words 'risks to future physical health'?

Challenge

- How can you demonstrate a high level of ability to interpret lifestyle and physiological data?
- What do you need to do to use your interpretation of the data provided, to explain clearly and in detail, factors that could potentially affect an individual's current and future physical health?

ASSESSMENT ACTIVITY LEARNING AIM **B**

As in the previous assessment activity, you are a registered nurse, managing a care home as the nursing home administrator. You are assessing the health and wellbeing of Susan, who is about to move into the care home.

Before starting:

- look at the information about Susan from Activities 1 and 2 (see pages 158–59)
- read the information below.

Susan recently had a medical check-up at her local health centre. The practice nurse asked her questions about her lifestyle and took some readings. Susan has given permission for the information to be passed on to you.

Lifestyle data

Susan was a healthy weight before Peter (her husband) died. Since living on her own she has a couple of glasses of wine with her evening meal and afterwards eats her favourite chocolate bar with a third glass of wine. She rarely leaves the house these days.

Physiological data

BMI	28.3 kg/m^2
Blood pressure	140/90 mmHg

Guidance for physiological data

The practice nurse has given guidance below to interpret the physiological data.

BMI (kg/m^2)	Weight category
Less than 18.5	Underweight
Between 18.5 and 24.9	Healthy weight
Between 25 and 29.9	Overweight
Between 30 and 34.9	Obese
Between 35 and 39.9	Severely obese
40 or above	Morbidly obese

Blood pressure

	Systolic (top number)	Diastolic (bottom number)
High blood pressure	140–190	90–100
Pre-high blood pressure	120–140	80–90
Ideal blood pressure	90–120	60–80
Low blood pressure	70–90	40–60

Activity 3

Explain what the data suggests about:

- Susan's current physical health
- risks to her future physical health.

To do this, copy this table.

Lifestyle data	....
BMI	....
Blood pressure	....

(Total for Activity 3 = 12 marks)

TIPS

Roughly speaking there are 3 minutes available for each point. Activity 3 should take about 36 minutes.

TAKE IT FURTHER

You need to have interpreted the data accurately, so it is important to check your answers. You should also have given a clear and detailed explanation of Susan's current state of health and the potential risks to her health.

The importance of a person-centred approach

GETTING STARTED

Discuss with a partner what you think is meant by a person-centred approach. What would a person-centred approach involve?

We are all individuals. So when you help other people to improve their health and wellbeing, it is important to consider their particular needs, wishes and circumstances.

A history of the person-centred approach

Until quite recently, care was done 'to' a person rather than 'with' the person. People receiving care were expected to fit in with the practices that already existed, regardless of their needs. Then, in the early 1960s, the American Psychologist, Carl Rogers developed a person-centred approach. He believed that service users were capable of, and should be trusted with, making decisions about their own care.

This approach continues to develop in the UK. *The NHS Plan* (2000), a document about reform, suggested a need for personalisation and coordination. In 2009, a document called *The NHS Constitution in England* said that:

- 'NHS services must reflect the needs and preferences of patients, their families and carers'
- 'Patients... will be involved in and consulted on all decisions about their care and treatment'.

Today person-centred care is central to the policies of all four UK countries. But there is still work to be done. Services still need to be more flexible; they need to work with people and their families to find the best way to provide their care and support.

Understanding the approach

KEY TERMS

Collaboratively involves working well together.
Empathy is being able to understand and share the feelings and views of another person.

A person-centred approach means that:

- the service user is at the centre of their care and support
- the service user is included in any planning and decision-making about their care and support
- service providers work **collaboratively** with service users
- service providers require **empathy** and a willingness to see things from the service user's perspective.

Benefits of a person-centred approach

It is hoped that adopting a person-centred approach will improve a number of things, as the diagram shows.

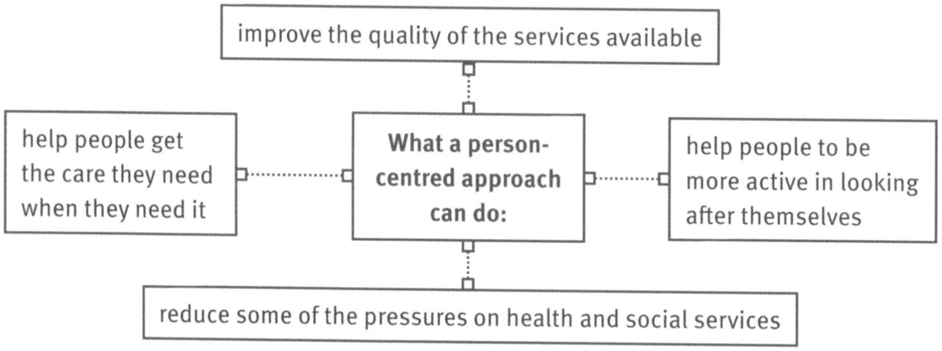

Figure 3.21: Working with people can lead to better services

In the UK, people are living longer and the population is growing. This means there is growing demand on health and social care services, but there are still limited resources. When a person is at the centre of their own care, they are more likely to stick correctly to their treatment plan – including what medication they take, which services they need to access and what surgery they might need. Not only will this improve their health and wellbeing, it may also reduce pressure on the services.

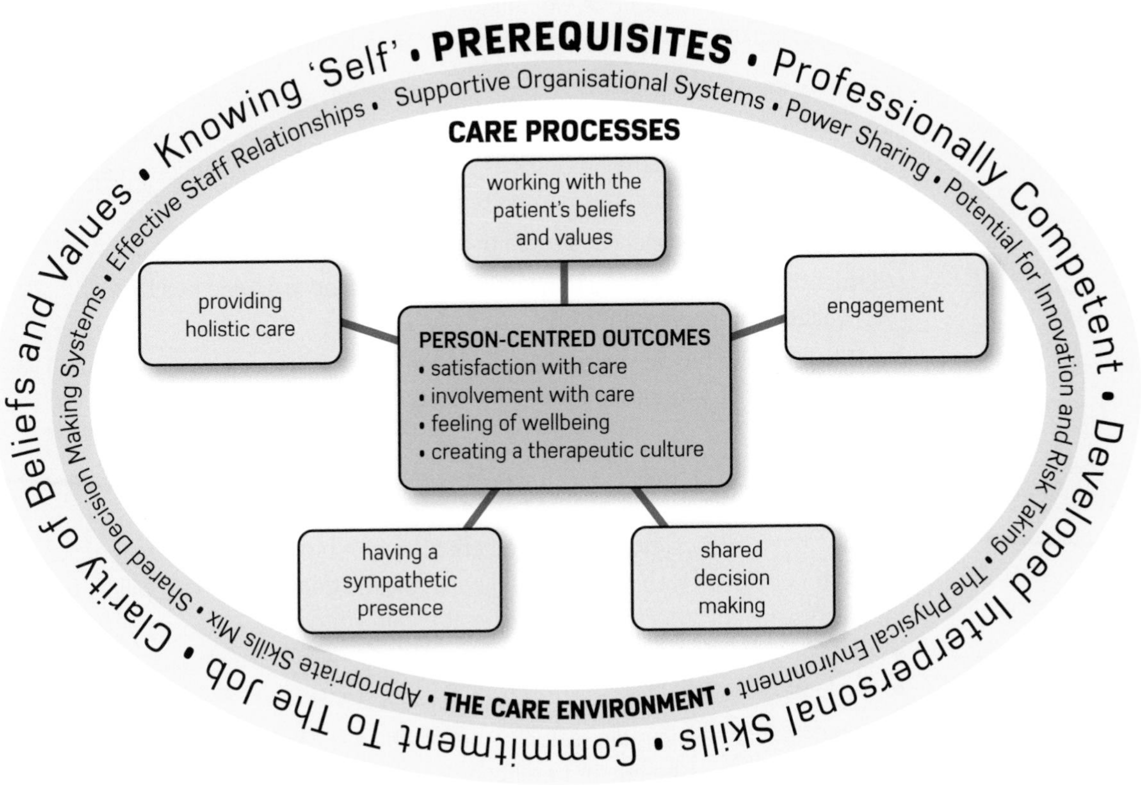

Figure 3.22: A person-centred approach, combined with appropriate resources, training and systems, can lead to improved outcomes for service users

The Health Foundation

The Health Foundation (www.health.org.uk/) is an independent charity. It works to improve the quality of health care in the UK. It does this by, for example, carrying out research and analysis of policy and funding improvement programmes to put ideas into practice in the NHS. It has identified four principles of person-centred care, which are:

- treating people with dignity, compassion and respect
- offering care, support or treatment that is coordinated
- offering care, support or treatment that is personalised
- helping people to recognise and develop their own strengths and abilities, which can help them to live an independent and fulfilling life.

ACTIVITY

1 Work individually to research what is meant by a person-centred approach.

2 Reflect on your own needs. Think back to a time when you have been ill or had a problem that led you to feel down and/or depressed. What did you need? How were you treated? Was it as you felt you needed to be treated?

3 What skills does a service provider need to be able to adopt a person-centred approach?

LINK IT UP

To remind yourself about care values, which are integral to a person-centred approach, go to Section B1 in Component 2.

CHECK MY LEARNING

1 What is meant by a person-centred approach?

2 What skills and qualities are needed to be able to adopt such an approach?

Recommended actions to improve health and wellbeing

GETTING STARTED

Reflect on your own health, thinking about what you could change to improve it and how you could go about tackling the task.

A health and wellbeing improvement plan is exactly what the name suggests: a plan to help an individual improve some aspect of their health and wellbeing.

ACTIVITY

1. In a group, discuss the first task of aiming to improve an individual's health and wellbeing. How could this task be tackled?
2. Recap on how an individual's health and wellbeing can be assessed.
3. Identify the features you think need to be included in a good health and wellbeing improvement plan.
4. Sketch out a few formats that include the features you have identified until you find one that your group feels is the best.

KEY TERMS

Goal is what you want to achieve in the long term.

Norm is something that is usual, typical or standard.

LINK IT UP

To remind yourself about the risks to health (for the improvement plans covered in this learning aim), go to Section A2 in Component 1 and Section B1 in Component 2.

Starting a health and wellbeing improvement plan

A good health and wellbeing improvement plan will start with a statement of the problem to be dealt with. There should be an overall **goal** or aim. This will be based on the assessment of a person's present health status through:

- the use of physical measures of health
- the factors that affect this.

The plan should have certain features, one of which is a set of recommended actions designed to improve health and wellbeing.

Recommended actions based on a person's physiological indicators

If you look at a person's health indicators and compare them with what is considered normal, you can tell if that person needs to improve one or more aspects of their health and wellbeing. The aim for that person is to improve their health to match the '**norms**'. Now take a look at these health indicators.

- A 22-year-old adult has a pulse rate during, or just after, exercise of 165 bpm. For their age, this should be between 119 bpm and 158 bpm. The bpm could indicate: a sedentary lifestyle, with little activity; an active lifestyle but overweight; or a sedentary lifestyle and overweight. Actions for this adult might be to reduce their pulse rate during or just after exercise to below 158 bpm; they could do this by becoming more active – for example, by going for a brisk walk every day, building up to running, or joining a gym/exercise class.
- A person with a reading of 160/93 mmHg has high blood pressure. This could be because they are overweight or stressed, they smoke and/or drink alcohol; they are inactive; or they do not get enough sleep. An assessment of their health would identify the key factors. Recommendations could then be made such as to stop smoking, to reduce alcohol consumption and go on a diet to lose weight.
- A 40-year-old woman is 1.45 m tall. Her peak flow is 350 L/min. Her 'norm' should be 450 L/min. If she is not asthmatic, this could be because she smokes. A recommended action would be to stop smoking.

- A person with a BMI of 37 is classed as severely obese. A recommended action might be to go on a diet and do more exercise to reduce their BMI until it falls below 24.9, which is in the healthy weight category.

Recommended actions based on a person's lifestyle indicators

Some people may need to improve their lifestyle to achieve good health and wellbeing. Recommended actions will help to bring improvements in lifestyle. Think about these examples.

- A recommended action for a person who smokes would be to stop smoking. The person could get some nicotine replacement patches or gum, or swap to e-cigarettes to start with.
- A recommended action for a person who consumes too much alcohol would be to reduce their consumption to the safe level of 14 units a week, spread out over a few days. They could perhaps have a soft drink between alcoholic drinks when at a party.
- A recommended action for an inactive 40-year-old adult would be a weekly target: of at least 150 minutes (2.5 hours) of moderate activity (such as cycling or fast walking); or 75 minutes vigorous aerobic activity (such as running); or a mix of moderate and vigorous aerobic activity each week. Strength exercises working all the major muscles should additionally be done 2 days or more each week.

DID YOU KNOW?

Vigorous activity of 1 minute provides the same health benefits as 2 minutes of moderate activity.

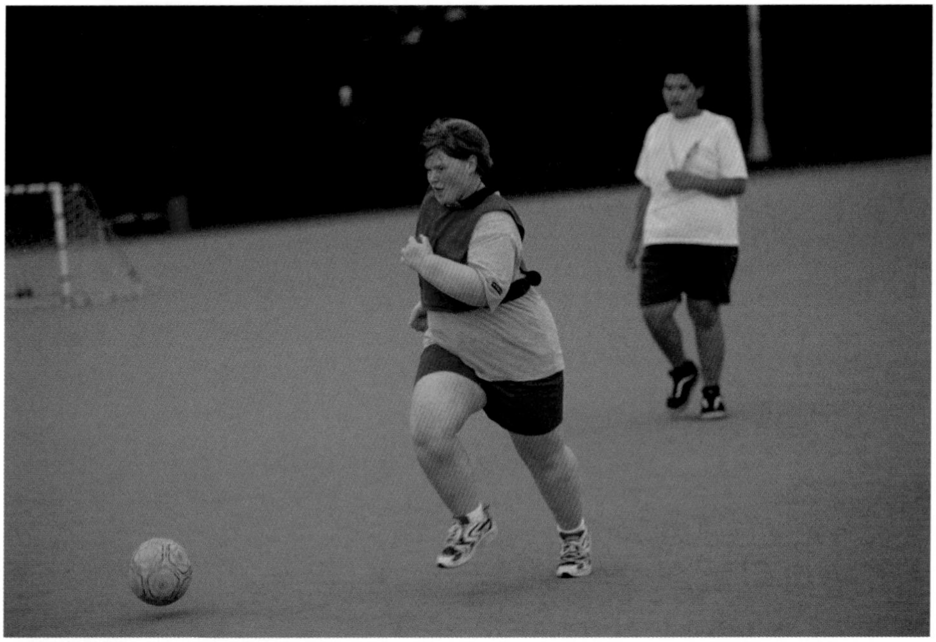

This person is taking recommended action for inactivity; what other types of exercise might they be doing?

CHECK MY LEARNING

What actions would you recommend to improve the health and wellbeing of an overweight, stressed asthmatic with a high BMI, low peak flow reading and a high blood pressure?

Short- and long-term targets

GETTING STARTED

In a small group, share a New Year's resolution (or other) you have made and either kept or failed. What made it easy to succeed or hard to achieve?

KEY TERMS

Targets are challenges to help you reach your goal.

Targets can motivate people. They can also be monitored. A mix of short- and long-term targets is a key feature of a good health and wellbeing improvement plan.

Creating targets

A plan needs both long- and short-term targets.

- A long-term target is generally 6 months or more. An example might be to lose 10 kg in that space of time. But that can seem a long time away and you might be tempted to put off actually getting started.
- A short-term target can be anything less than 6 months. An example might be to lose 1 kg in a week. This might seem achievable because it is not a major challenge.

Breaking down your final long-term goal into smaller steps seems less daunting and removes excuses for not getting started.

SMART targets

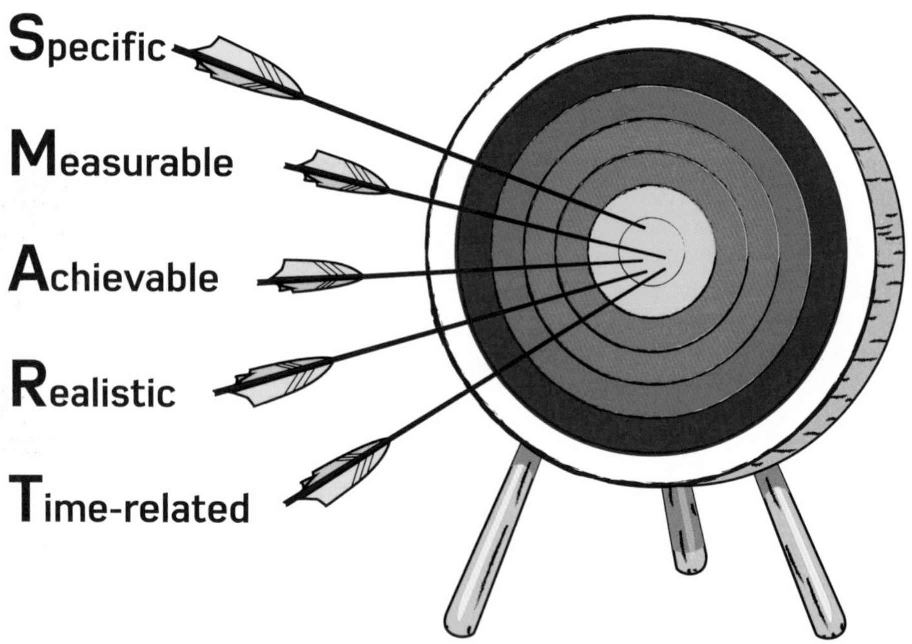

Figure 3.23: Targets should be SMART; try to memorise what that stands for

SMART is short for Specific, Measurable, Achievable, Realistic and Time-related. These five targets can be very useful in your health and wellbeing plans for others. If a target is not SMART it can give you an opportunity to make an excuse not to start the plan; see Table 3.8.

Table 3.8: SMART targets and what they mean

'SMART' word	The target
Specific	The target must be clearly stated. It should say exactly what you mean, such as to 'lose 2 kg in weight in a week'. The target should be clear and not open to any misunderstanding.
Measurable	A target of to 'lose weight' is too vague. A specific amount must be stated so you can prove you have met your target.
Achievable/attainable	If you are following a health and wellbeing improvement plan you must feel it is possible to achieve the target set. If you do not, you will probably give up before you have started. An achievable (reasonable) target is to 'lose 1 kg this week'; an unachievable target would be to 'lose 20 kg this week'.
Realistic	The target set must be realistic in that you must be able to physically do it. It is not realistic to expect a person who is older and not very fit to run for 30 minutes a day to help weight loss but it is realistic to ask the same of a fitter, younger person.
Time-related	The target must have a deadline, so that you know when you need to achieve the target by and progress can be assessed.

ACTIVITY

1 In a group, discuss the difference between a target and a goal. If you are not sure, check in a dictionary.
2 With a partner, write a blog saying why targets are easier to stick to if they are SMART.
3 Read or show your blog to the rest of the class.
4 Self-evaluate your blog and peer-evaluate the blogs of others in your class.

Monitoring targets

Targets need to be monitored. You can do this yourself by, for example, checking your weight at home each week if you are on a diet. Remember to keep a note of the date and your weight and add to this information each week. Alternatively, you could join a slimming club. Generally, someone else will weigh you each week and keep the details for you.

Reviewing targets

By setting SMART targets you can monitor progress regularly and amend your plan if necessary. For example, if you aim to lose 1 kg a week, but in fact you manage to lose more, your longer-term targets need adjusting.

Alternatively, if you are not successful straight away for any reason, it may be necessary to **review** and change your longer-term targets to reflect this. Someone who is overweight may start and stop many diets before they manage to make the necessary lifestyle changes to help them reach and stay at their goal weight.

KEY TERMS

Review involves assessing or inspecting something with the intention of making change if necessary.

CHECK MY LEARNING

1 What is meant by a SMART target?
2 Why is it necessary to monitor and review targets?

Sources of support

GETTING STARTED

Draw a mind map showing all the different people and groups of people who have given you support since starting secondary school. Remember to say what *kind* of support they gave you.

We all need help and support sometimes. A very important feature of health and wellbeing improvement plans is listing the forms of support that are available.

ACTIVITY

1 Pick one of the following types of support: informal; formal; voluntary or other (such as health promotion materials, alternative medicines, practical aids).
2 Prepare a six-slide PowerPoint® presentation on your type of support.
3 Show your PowerPoint® slides to the rest of the class.
4 Peer- and self-evaluate presentations.

Formal support

KEY TERMS

Formal support is given by a trained health and social care professional who is paid to provide support.

Formal support is provided by health and social care professionals. These are people who are trained and paid to give support. Take a look at the diagram to see what formal support can include.

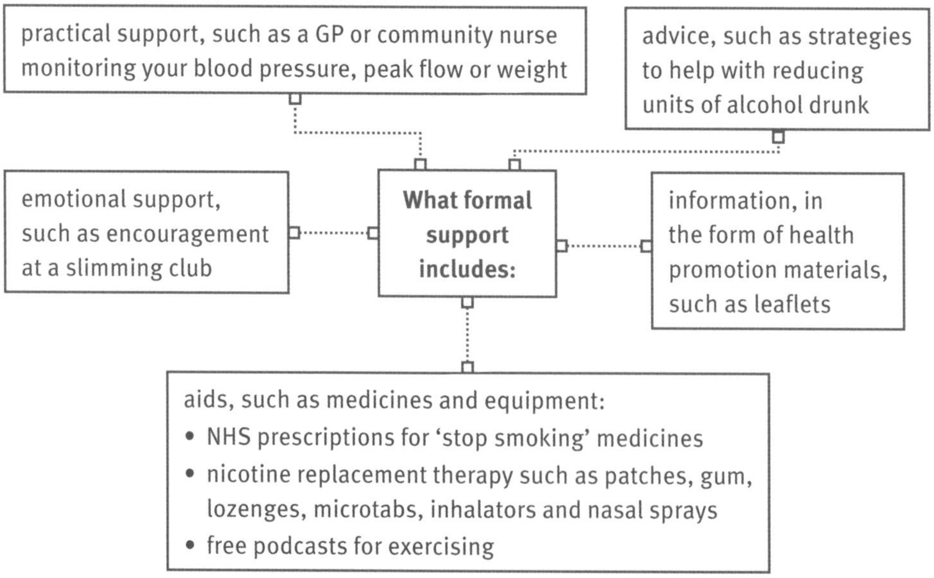

What formal support includes:
practical support, such as a GP or community nurse monitoring your blood pressure, peak flow or weight
advice, such as strategies to help with reducing units of alcohol drunk
emotional support, such as encouragement at a slimming club
information, in the form of health promotion materials, such as leaflets
aids, such as medicines and equipment:
• NHS prescriptions for 'stop smoking' medicines
• nicotine replacement therapy such as patches, gum, lozenges, microtabs, inhalators and nasal sprays
• free podcasts for exercising

Figure 3.24: Professionals can help in many ways

Informal support

KEY TERMS

Informal support often comes from friends and family who want to encourage you and are not paid.

Informal support is often provided by family and friends. They are not paid to help, but they do anyway. Now take a look at the diagram on the next page to see what informal support can include.

What informal support includes:

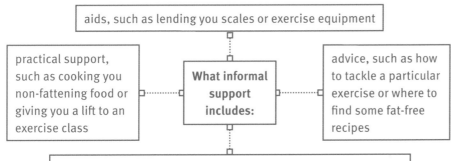

- aids, such as lending you scales or exercise equipment
- practical support, such as cooking you non-fattening food or giving you a lift to an exercise class
- advice, such as how to tackle a particular exercise or where to find some fat-free recipes
- emotional support, such as:
  - family encouragement if you have to go out for a run in the cold
  - a friend watching a film at home with you instead of going to a party with lots of food and alcohol
  - your family going on a diet at the same time as you

Figure 3.25: Family and friends are very important sources of support

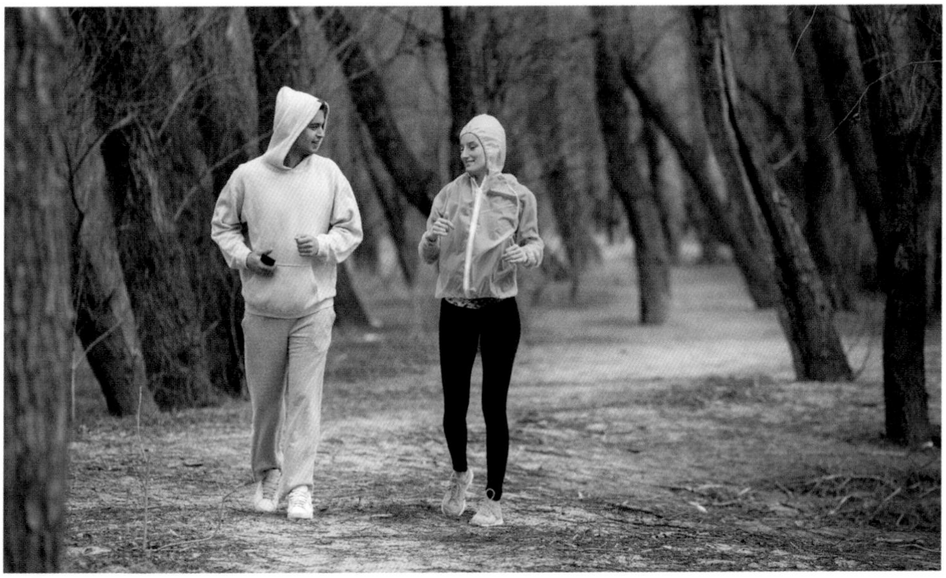

Support from friends and family can really help you to stay on target

Support in the voluntary sector

Voluntary organisations often run events which help you meet a target such as weight loss or improved activity levels, and some of them also raise money for the charity through the events

For example, the charity Cancer Research UK runs sponsored 'Race for Life' events throughout the UK. These provide:

- a good opportunity for exercising
- a feel-good factor, because you are raising money for charity at the same time.

Another example is Walking for Health, a voluntary group that supports others to improve activity rates and wellbeing through walking. Its volunteers lead groups of walkers (some of whom may be very inactive), helping them along the way.

There are also many self-help groups. One example might be a weight loss group where people can discuss aspects of weight loss such as nutrition, emotions and exercise, and also take part in exercise sessions.

CHECK MY LEARNING

1 Why is it important to identify sources of support (formal and informal) on a health and wellbeing improvement plan?

2 How can voluntary organisations such as charities be a source of support for a health and wellbeing improvement plan?

Potential obstacles to implementing plans

GETTING STARTED

In pairs, reflect on what obstacles you have faced when trying to stick to a plan to improve an aspect of your health and wellbeing – for example, diet, exercise or even a skin care routine.

LINK IT UP

To remind yourself about barriers to accessing help (which is covered in this and the rest of the lessons in this learning aim), go to Section A2 in Component 2.

A key factor in a successful health and wellbeing improvement plan is the willingness of the person to follow it. It is important that no obstacles are put in their way.

ACTIVITY

1 Pool your ideas from the starter activity.

2 On your own, explain why each of the factors shown in the diagram below needs to be considered when drawing up a health and wellbeing improvement plan. You also need to consider how that factor can become an obstacle to sticking to the plan, by giving an example for each.

3 In a group, share your examples for each factor. Now pick the one you all think best shows how each factor can become an obstacle to sticking to a health and wellbeing improvement plan.

Obstacles

The final important factor in designing a health and wellbeing improvement plan is to assess any difficulties a person might face when they implement the plan. What could stop them succeeding? How can you help them to overcome any obstacles they may face?

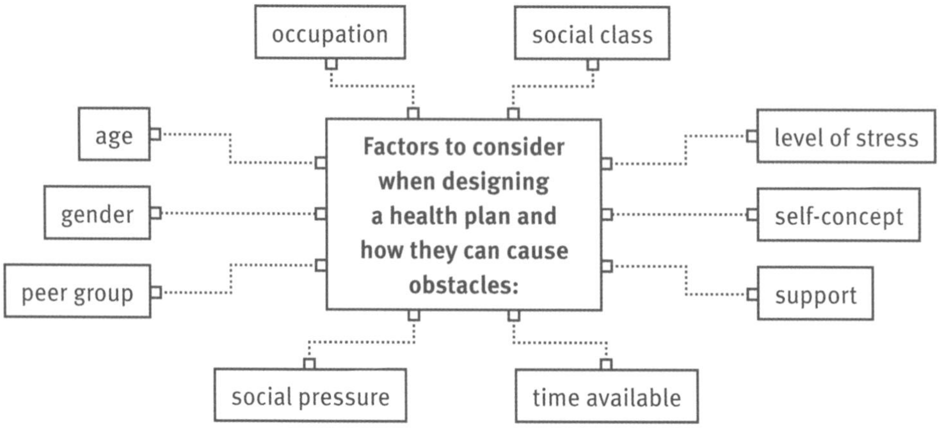

Figure 3.26: There can be many potential barriers to health improvements

DID YOU KNOW?

KISS is an acronym where each letter in the word stands for another word (Keep It Simple and Straightforward). Can you remember what SMART stands for? Acronyms are shorter to use. Always mention once what the acronym stands for.

A person is more likely to want to follow a plan and use the support identified if they have been involved in drawing it up. As a health practitioner, you would need to:

- assess the person's current state of health
- discuss the health issue to be tackled with the person, to build a relationship with them
- discuss different options to tackle the issue
- **K**eep **I**t **S**imple and **S**traightforward (the KISS rule); in other words, do not use lots of jargon (words that not everyone knows), acronyms or medical terms the person will not understand
- decide *together* which options should be followed; in other words, do it *with* the person, not *to* the person (person-centred approach)
- explain how they can access support

- make the plan as clear and straightforward to follow as possible
- make the plan look attractive so the person will not mind putting it in a place they can always see it (for example, a kitchen wall).

Take a look at Table 3.9, which is an example of a health and wellbeing improvement plan. Can you see where obstacles might occur? Could you make any improvements?

Table 3.9: An example of a health and wellbeing improvement plan

Problem: Unfit office worker. Lifestyle too sedentary, so needs to become more active				
Recommended actions	**Short-term SMART targets**	**Long-term SMART targets**	**Sources of support**	**How support will help**
Get 2.5 hours moderate exercise a week	• Go for a 30-minute walk on Mondays, Wednesdays and Fridays, and a 1-hour walk on Sundays for the first 4 weeks, in your lunch break if necessary. • Walk more briskly, so you walk further in the same time and on the same days for the next 4 weeks. • Cycle or jog instead of walking for at least the same time, getting faster each week.	• Go for at least a 30-minute run at least three times a week. • Walk at least 10,000 steps on the days you do not run.	• Ask a family member or friend to exercise or go with you • Fact sheet 4: Physical activity guidelines for adults (19–64 years) on www.gov.uk. • 'Couch to 5K' running app • 'Couch to 5K+' running podcasts when you get past 5k on www.nhs.uk	• Less likely to get bored or make an excuse not to go if with someone else • Gives examples of physical activity that meets the guidelines, so you can change what is suggested here for something else to give more variety. Also explains the benefits to spur you on • Shows you what to do; designed to get you running in just 9 weeks • Provides longer structured runs to help you continue to improve
Do strengthening exercises twice a week	Do exercises to work the legs, hips, back, abdomen, chest, shoulder and arms twice a week.	Do exercises to work the legs, hips, back, abdomen, chest, shoulder and arms at least three times a week.	NHS *Fitness Studio* exercise videos (www.nhs.uk)	These instructor-led videos are different lengths, and exercise different muscles, so you can find some that suit your needs.

CHECK MY LEARNING

1. Write an evaluation of the health plan shown.
2. Does it follow the KISS rule?
3. Are the actions clear and the targets SMART?
4. Are the sources of support helpful and explained well? What obstacles may the person face?

Emotional/psychological obstacles

GETTING STARTED

In a small group, discuss what is meant by the term 'emotional/psychological obstacle'. Give some examples.

KEY TERMS

Psychological relates to the mental and emotional state of a person.

Potential obstacles to implementing a health and wellbeing improvement plan are not just physical. Sometimes they can be emotional/**psychological**.

ACTIVITY

1 Each member of the class will be given a risk to physical health to consider (diet, drugs, smoking, alcohol or inactivity).
2 Write examples of how 'lack of motivation', 'low self-esteem' and 'acceptance of current state' can become emotional/psychological obstacles in following a plan to deal with the health risk. Give examples of how to overcome these obstacles.
3 Find others in the class working on the same risk. Form a group and compare.
4 In your group, produce an advice sheet for overcoming emotional/psychological obstacles to the health risk. Make this sheet informative and easy to read.
5 Print copies for the class.

Lack of motivation

It can be hard to get started on any task – including those on a health and wellbeing improvement plan. In fact, some people might find it easier not to start at all! They might also get bored once they *have* started. This is known as lack of motivation.

Figure 3.27: What ways can you think of to kick-start motivation?

For some people, a lack of motivation for their health and wellbeing improvement plan can be overcome by:

- reminding themselves of the benefits of sticking to their plan (for example, feeling fitter, having more energy, reducing health risks and feeling better about themselves)
- choosing activities they enjoy; they will be more likely to stick to something if they like what they are doing
- doing activities at a time when they feel most energetic
- having a variety of strategies (for example, on a fitness plan, swimming instead of walking, joining a gym or going hiking)
- building in rewards (for example, for every 7 kg of weight lost treat themselves to a new item of clothing).

Low self-esteem

Low self-esteem can affect almost every aspect of life – from what you think about yourself to the way you react to situations. For some people, low self-esteem could result in:

- negative thoughts about themselves and their abilities
- feeling less able to take on the challenges life presents – such as sticking with their health and wellbeing improvement plan
- giving up on challenges before they even begin.

But sticking with a plan, and making the effort to meet targets, can help to overcome obstacles and increase self-esteem. For example, a person on a fitness plan might feel great that they stuck with it (however hard it felt at first) because they have lost weight and feel fitter.

Acceptance of current state

Someone who accepts their current state of physical health, because they feel fine now, has probably convinced themselves they do not need to take any action. For example, they may have high blood pressure but not feel any different from normal. They may have a low peak flow reading but do not really notice any issues with their breathing. The same applies to lifestyle factors. A person who smokes or drinks too much alcohol, for example, may feel perfectly all right now and therefore not even consider giving up.

However, as you have already learned, an abnormal health indicator can lead to a number of conditions. These conditions may have serious consequences and could even be life-threatening.

CHECK MY LEARNING

1 Compare the different fact sheets and remind yourself of the three main categories of emotional/psychological obstacles.

2 Do you understand how each of them can be an emotional/psychological obstacle to implementing a health and wellbeing improvement plan?

LINK IT UP

To remind yourself about negative attitudes towards health and wellbeing, go to Section A1 in Component 1.

Time constraints

GETTING STARTED

Reflect on what commitments you have that might sometimes stop you having enough time for looking after your own physical needs.

We all have busy lives nowadays and some people struggle to fit everything in. These time constraints can often become an obstacle to implementing a health and wellbeing improvement plan.

Why time can be an obstacle

A common excuse when sticking to any plan is: 'I don't have enough time.' People may feel they have too many other commitments such as work and family. A good health and wellbeing improvement plan will help to present solutions to this obstacle.

Work/study commitments

Work or study can often be demanding and evenings can often be busy. These things can leave people feeling tired. They can also be used as an excuse not to stick to, for example, a plan to improve activity levels. But there are strategies that can help to overcome these obstacles, as the diagram shows.

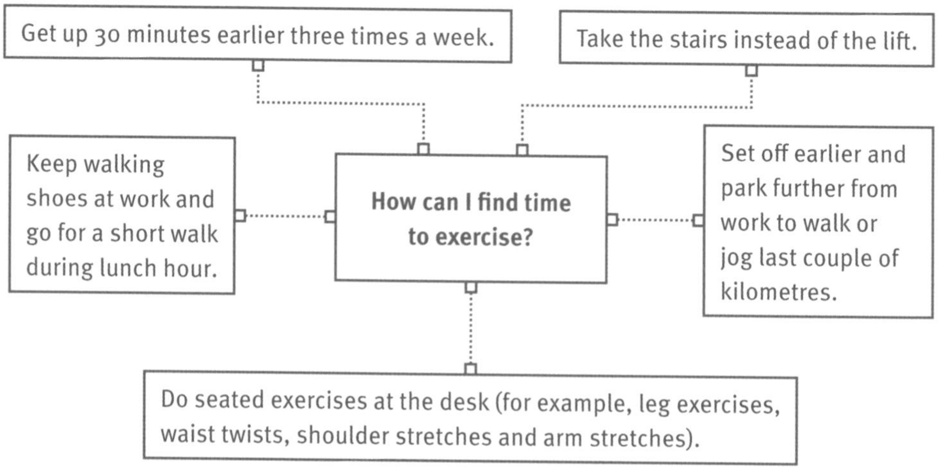

Get up 30 minutes earlier three times a week.
Take the stairs instead of the lift.
Keep walking shoes at work and go for a short walk during lunch hour.
How can I find time to exercise?
Set off earlier and park further from work to walk or jog last couple of kilometres.
Do seated exercises at the desk (for example, leg exercises, waist twists, shoulder stretches and arm stretches).

Figure 3.28: Suggestions for making more time to exercise

It is even possible to exercise while you are sitting at your desk!

Family commitments

Away from work, family commitments may take up a lot of time. There may be children who need to be taken to places, older relatives who may visit or family friends to socialise with. Trying to keep up a health and wellbeing improvement plan alongside so many other things could be achieved through advanced planning and involving the whole family, as the diagram shows. It is also important that the family supports the person doing the plan and understands how important it is that the person makes the recommended changes.

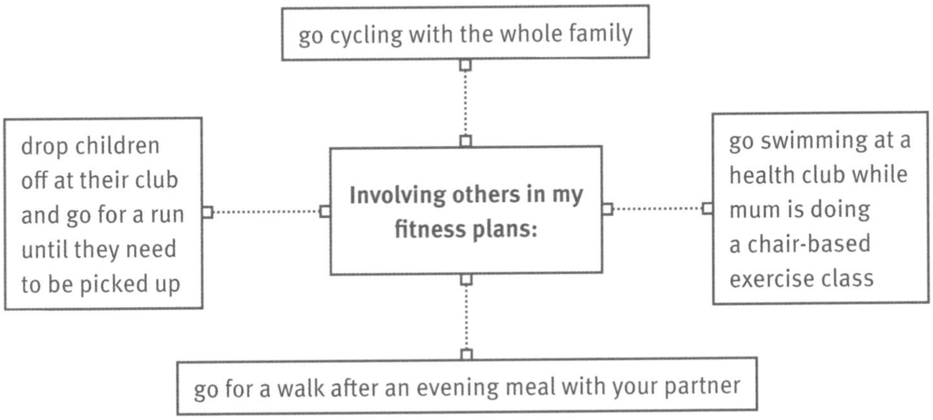

Figure 3.29: Suggestions for family-friendly exercise

ACTIVITY

1. Working in pairs, pick someone you know or a character from TV who is very busy with work and family commitments. Their lifestyle may create risks to their physical health.
2. Write a case study on this person/character.
3. One of you role plays the person/character while the other interviews them for a one-to-one chat show, on how time constraints are an obstacle to making lifestyle changes that could improve their health and wellbeing.
4. Show your interview to the rest of the class.
5. After each interview, suggest ways the time constraints can be overcome for the character.

DID YOU KNOW?

Many adults spend more than 7 hours a day sitting down at work, on transport or in their leisure time. Many adults aged 65 and over, spend 10 hours or more each day sitting or lying down.

CHECK MY LEARNING

1. Suggest three ways the potential obstacles to implementing a health and wellbeing improvement plan can be overcome for:
   - work commitments
   - family commitments.

Availability of resources

GETTING STARTED

In a small group, discuss how availability of resources can be an obstacle to sticking to a health and wellbeing improvement plan. Think of all the different risks to physical health.

Imagine devising a health and wellbeing improvement plan for someone who cannot afford or does not have what they need to do some of it. Not having enough money or the correct equipment might be an obstacle to achieving success.

Financial resources

When you design a health and wellbeing improvement plan, you need to think about the cost of each action, to avoid money becoming an obstacle to someone's health and wellbeing improvements. For example, if you are drawing up an exercise plan that includes a person joining a gym, you need to:

- consider if they can afford gym membership
- provide details of free alternatives.

It is also important to point out on the plan:

- how much things cost
- how to access funding to help.

For example, a number of aids that help people to stop smoking are available on prescription from the NHS. Depending on the financial circumstances of the person, this means they may spend a small amount or nothing at all. Those on a low income may be able to get help with NHS costs through the NHS Low Income Scheme.

The NHS website (www.nhs.uk/Livewell/fitness) has a section called 'Get fit for free'. You could direct someone on an exercise plan to this website and discuss the suggestions with them before adding them to their plan. Also, local authorities offer initiatives to encourage people to get fitter such as:

- free exercise classes or swimming sessions
- free weight advice and exercise classes for morbidly obese people.

You could find out the details of your local authority, check what initiatives they provide, then add them to the person's plan.

Check out the free resources to add to someone's fitness plan to help keep them motivated

Physical resources

Physical resources could mean equipment. An obstacle could occur if the person following the plan does not have access to the equipment they need. Look at the example below of someone who is on a diet: they need bathroom scales to weigh themselves and kitchen scales to weigh their food. You could make suggestions like these on their plan.

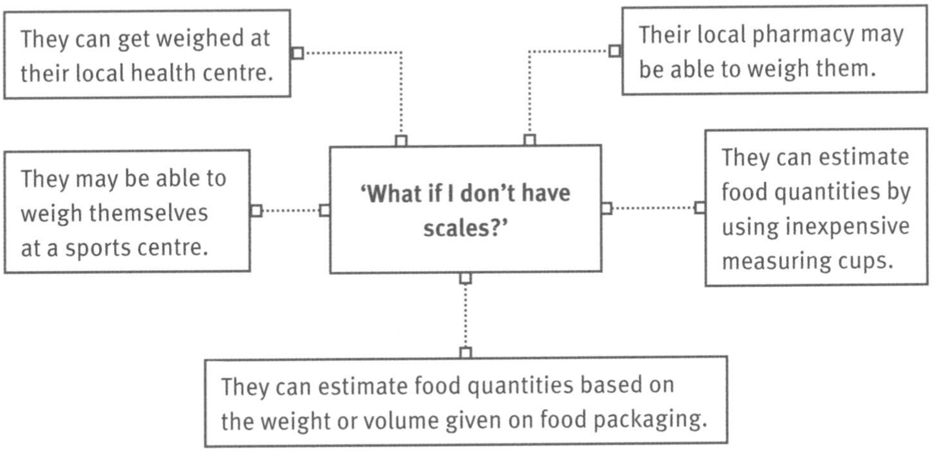

Figure 3.30: Think of ways you can get round an apparent problem

The NHS website suggests ways of accessing free equipment – for example, free running podcasts. Community websites such as Freegle, Freecycle.org® and SnaffleUp may also be useful resources for finding free equipment. It may be possible to find weights, skipping ropes, exercise balls and even exercise machines – all being given away by people who no longer need them.

Other ideas for free physical resources include:

- local authority outdoor gyms, tennis courts, football pitches and basketball hoops in parks around the area
- free gym taster sessions to check out the environment and range of options, before committing to membership
- a 'green gym', if there is one in your area, where people can volunteer to exercise by digging, planting and path clearing, which means they can be helping the environment while getting fitter.

DID YOU KNOW?

The Conservation Volunteers charity runs 'green gym' schemes across the country. To find out if there is one near you, check www.tcv.org.uk/greengyml/find-green-gym

ACTIVITY

1 Work in a small group to research and produce a presentation, in whichever form your group chooses, on the availability of resources in your local area to help a person stick to a health and wellbeing improvement plan based on a risk to physical health of your choice.

2 Deliver the presentation and give out handouts to other members of the class.

CHECK MY LEARNING

1 How can a lack of availability of resources be a potential obstacle to sticking to a health and wellbeing improvement plan?

2 How can such obstacles be overcome?

Unachievable targets

GETTING STARTED

In a small group, discuss how it makes you feel if you are given a big task to complete in a short amount of time.

Meeting targets can be encouraging. But if those targets are unachievable or unrealistic, then they are likely to become an obstacle to someone implementing a health and wellbeing improvement plan.

Unachievable for the individual

Why might an individual find their targets unachievable? Table 3.10 gives some reasons that should be considered before putting together a health and wellbeing improvement plan that will be realistic and achievable.

Table 3.10: Why targets might be unachievable

Reason	Examples of how to avoid the problem on a plan
Too ambitious	The individual may be very overweight and unfit. They may not have exercised for years. Instead of sending them to, e.g. an aerobics class, which they may not be able to finish, suggest a gentler class to begin with.
Not appropriate	• The individual may have many time commitments. Instead of suggesting daily 10 km runs or long swims, plan them in for twice a week. • The individual may be an older person who lives alone. Instead of suggesting they take a long walk alone, try to team them up with another person who can go with them. Ensure their exercise is age-appropriate – perhaps a class specifically for older people.
Lack of understanding	The individual may not understand what is expected of them because the instruction on the plan is either too vague or too technical/complicated. Make sure the language of the plan is very clear and very simple. Be aware that some people may have difficulties understanding the written word.
Not in the right frame of mind	An individual may be depressed, upset about something or just not emotionally ready to commit to a plan (perhaps they have other things that they feel will stand in their way). Discuss a new start date – one the individual feels happy with. It is better that the person is feeling determined and positive from the start.
Timing	Some people may find they have too much going on at certain times of the year – e.g. a lot of socialising around Christmas might make a weight loss programme that starts in early December difficult to carry on with, or dark cold mornings and evenings during the winter months can make a running programme difficult. Start a weight loss programme after special events and plan exercise that can be done inside or outside.
Fear of failure	An individual may make excuses because they are afraid of failing. Many people who fear failure often find doing new things very difficult – in case they do not do them well enough. Ensure the targets are very realistic and easily achievable to give the individual confidence.
Task is too big	An individual with several health concerns (e.g. is morbidly obese, leads a sedentary lifestyle, smokes and drinks too much alcohol) may feel that making any of the necessary changes is too big a task to tackle and will take years, so do not bother. Again, ensure the targets are realistic – encouraging the individual to look at permanent lifestyle changes rather than for a fixed period.

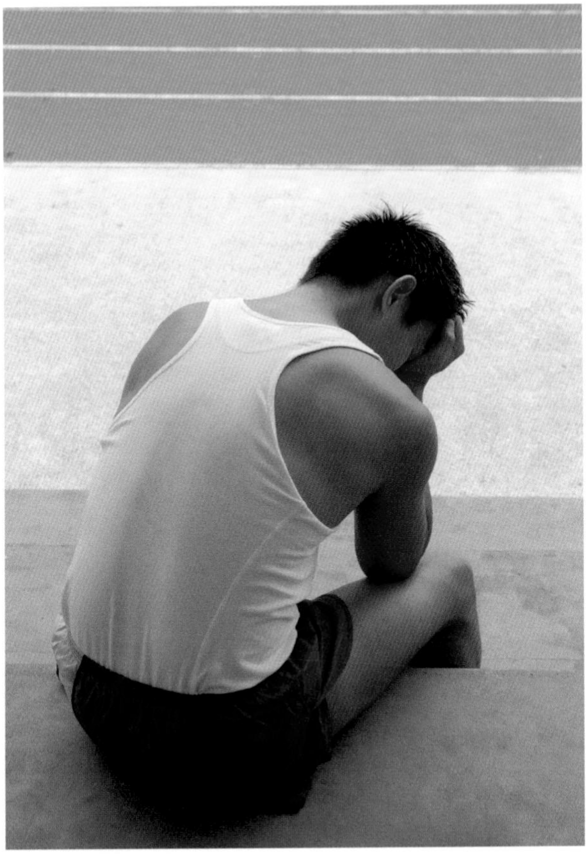

An unrealistic deadline for meeting health targets can be very stressful and off-putting

Unrealistic timescales

A person who feels their goals are unrealistic may already feel as though there is no point in trying. For example, if a person is given a health and wellbeing improvement plan with a goal of losing 20 kg in 4 weeks, they may not even attempt to start the plan. Some timescales need to be much longer to ensure success and give the individual confidence that their health and wellbeing improvement plan is working.

ACTIVITY

1 Write ten targets for any risk to physical health (e.g. obesity) – some of which are achievable and others that are not.
2 Swap with a partner, who will identify which targets are achievable and which are not.
3 Swap back and read what your partner has written.
4 Discuss with your partner whether you agree with them and why.

CHECK MY LEARNING

1 Give an example of a person not able to stick to a health and wellbeing improvement plan because:
- the targets are unachievable. Think of one not already given
- the timescales are unrealistic. Think of one not already used.

Lack of support

GETTING STARTED

With a partner, reflect on times when you have felt unsupported by either family members or friends. How did it make you feel?

We all need support sometimes – whether to take up something new or finish off something.

Lack of support as an obstacle

Lack of support could lead an individual following a health and wellbeing improvement plan to give it up. If no one is properly supporting the individual, they could feel there may be difficulties with, for example, keeping to a diet, stopping smoking and cutting down on alcohol.

Diet

Difficulties could occur if a person on a healthy eating plan is:

- surrounded by family and friends who enjoy 'ready' meals and takeaways
- fed by someone who is a good cook and gives generous helpings
- tempted by chocolates and biscuits bought for special occasions
- treated to regular meals out.

To overcome these obstacles, the individual will need to explain why they need to lose weight and why family support would be useful. To support the individual, a family could:

- join in with eating the same healthy, balanced diet as the individual
- hide away biscuits and treats
- go bowling, for example, rather than eating out
- pick healthy options from a takeaway menu that the whole family could share.

These kinds of support will help to keep the individual on track with their plan.

Smoking

How would you feel here if you were trying not to smoke?

If an individual is on a plan to stop smoking, they may find it difficult if friends and family continually offer them cigarettes. We all know that smoking is bad for us. But some people lack the willpower to give it up. So they may try to persuade the individual not to give up, because it makes them feel better about smoking.

Being offered cigarettes is a constant temptation and an obstacle. To overcome this potential obstacle the individual could:

- explain they *want* to give up to feel better and improve their health
- ask family and friends not to offer them cigarettes
- try to persuade family and friends to also give up cigarettes with them.

The individual may also need the support of aids (such as nicotine patches, special chewing gum and so on) to help them. If you were writing a 'quit smoking' plan for someone, you would research all the aids available and add them to the plan.

Alcohol consumption

An individual who is used to regular drinking with family and friends may find it hard to cut down or give up without their support. For example, it may be difficult to avoid pressure if:

- a family regularly drinks wine with meals
- friends centre a night out on drinking heavily at clubs and pubs.

The diagram shows how others could support someone on an alcohol-reduction plan.

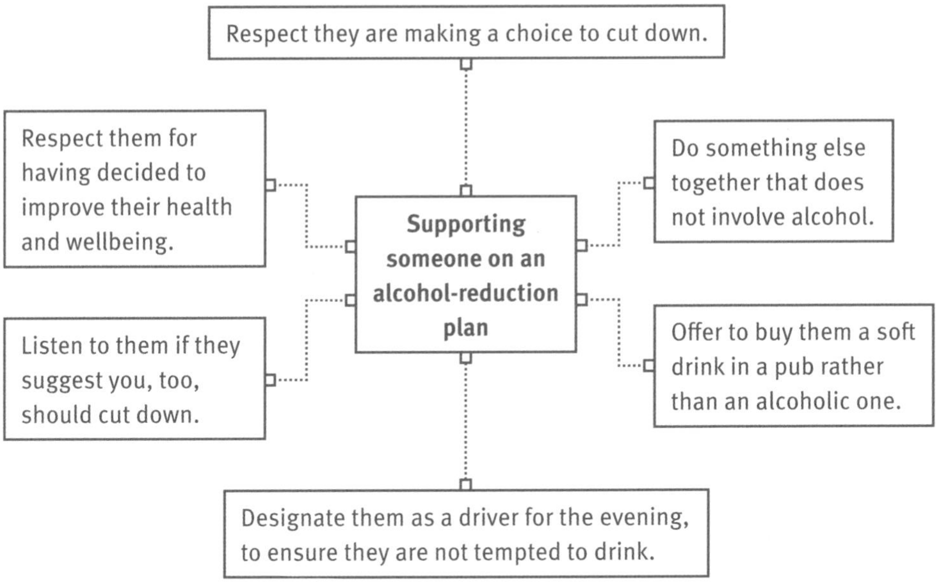
Respect they are making a choice to cut down.
Respect them for having decided to improve their health and wellbeing.
Do something else together that does not involve alcohol.
Supporting someone on an alcohol-reduction plan
Listen to them if they suggest you, too, should cut down.
Offer to buy them a soft drink in a pub rather than an alcoholic one.
Designate them as a driver for the evening, to ensure they are not tempted to drink.

Figure 3.31: Ways to support someone to cut their alcohol intake

ACTIVITY

1. With a partner, write down how having support would help an individual implement a health and wellbeing improvement plan to improve their poor personal hygiene and habits such as having unprotected sex after binge drinking.
2. Do a short piece of creative writing in a style of your choice to sum up the effect it has on you when family and friends do not support you.

CHECK MY LEARNING

Give three examples of how lack of support from family and friends can be an obstacle to a person wanting to follow a health and wellbeing improvement plan to improve the quality and length of their sleeping.

Ability/disability and addiction

GETTING STARTED

Work in a small group to identify factors specific to an individual that may form obstacles, other than those already covered in the last few lessons.

Sometimes there are factors specific to an individual that are potential obstacles to implementing a health and wellbeing improvement plan, such as ability/disability and addiction.

Ability

A person with learning difficulties may find it harder to understand, learn and remember new things. They may also find it hard to manage everyday tasks independently. If they need to follow a health and wellbeing improvement plan, the layout of the plan and the language used might be obstacles because they may not be able to understand what is being asked of them. So it is very important that sources of support are identified in the plan. It is also important that some of these sources are involved in implementing the plan because they can help the individual to:

- understand what they need to do
- learn how to make the required changes in their lives.

Family and friends can offer support. So can teachers if the individual is still at school, for instance, by ensuring they join in PE if following a fitness plan. If the individual attends a day care centre, staff at the centre need to be informed that the person is following a plan, for example, a weight reduction plan, so they can check what the person should be eating.

Disability

An individual with a physical disability may come across obstacles in their health and wellbeing improvement plan if the plans have not been carefully thought through. If you design a plan for someone who uses a wheelchair, for example, you should ensure that:

- any places the individual needs to visit are wheelchair accessible
- any exercise you advise should be wheelchair friendly.

Advising a person to join a local slimming club that does not have wheelchair access will not work. Nor will asking someone with limited mobility to join a self-help group in a building in the middle of town with no close parking.

A blind person may need their plan translated into Braille. They may need access to equipment labelled in Braille so they can follow their plan.

DID YOU KNOW?

Braille is raised 'writing' (like bumps) that blind people feel with their fingers and 'read' from left to right. A special typewriter is used to create Braille. Some computers have a Braille font.

Figure 3.32: Some people with sight problems may need plans and equipment labelled in Braille

Addiction

People become addicted to alcohol, nicotine and drugs because they like the way they make them feel, both physically and mentally. This creates a powerful desire to use these substances again. Sometimes, *not* using the substances results in withdrawal symptoms, which can be very unpleasant and even painful. Other addictions include eating.

Table 3.11 shows how addictions create obstacles to applying a health and wellbeing improvement plan.

Table 3.11 Examples of how an addiction creates obstacles

Plan type	Examples of obstacles and overcoming them
Weight reduction	Some people are compulsive eaters. Studies suggest it is the *act of eating* that is addictive rather than the food itself. Individuals need to be able to identify their triggers (things that make them want to eat), e.g. feeling fed up. Then they need to ask themselves: 'Am I really hungry?' These could be added to their plan as a reminder. They could also eat from smaller plates and give themselves non-food rewards for weight loss.
Stopping smoking	People who smoke regularly develop cravings for nicotine. Giving up nicotine can result in strong withdrawal symptoms. An individual giving up smoking should be made aware of any aids and medicines. They may also need to change their behaviour and lifestyle to avoid triggers. These are times that the individual links strongly with smoking, such as after food or in a social situation, so a plan needs to suggest something different to do during these times.
Stopping or reducing alcohol	An individual with an alcohol problem needs to admit they have a problem first before a plan can be successful. To overcome this obstacle, the plan should include visiting a GP for an open and honest assessment. The individual could then join a free local support group and go for alcohol counselling. The individual and plan should consider if alcohol should be reduced over a period of time. Stopping overnight could be harmful.

ACTIVITY

1. Think about people you know or a TV character affected by learning difficulties, a physical disability and/or an addiction. Write how this might be an obstacle to implementing a health and wellbeing improvement plan.
2. Pick one of these people/characters who you most admire and write a profile of them.
3. Add your profile to a wall display.
4. Be prepared to answer questions about your person.

CHECK MY LEARNING

Why does having (1) a disability and (2) an addiction make it harder to stick to a health and wellbeing improvement plan?

DID YOU KNOW?

About 2 million people in the UK are fighting an addiction of one kind or another.

LINK IT UP

To remind yourself about factors specific to an individual, go to Section A2 in Component 1 and Section B2 in Component 2.

Barriers to accessing identified services

GETTING STARTED

With a partner, talk about an occasion when you, or a family member, could not access a service you needed and how that made you feel.

An individual on a health and wellbeing improvement plan might find they are unable to access services that could be helpful. These barriers might create obstacles to their plans.

Barriers

Barriers to accessing services can include any of the following:

- physical
- psycholical
- financial
- cultural and language
- resources
- geographical.

Physical

Physical barriers to accessing services need to be thought about in any health and wellbeing improvement plan. Look at the diagram for accessing services in a building. Can you think of any other physical barriers?

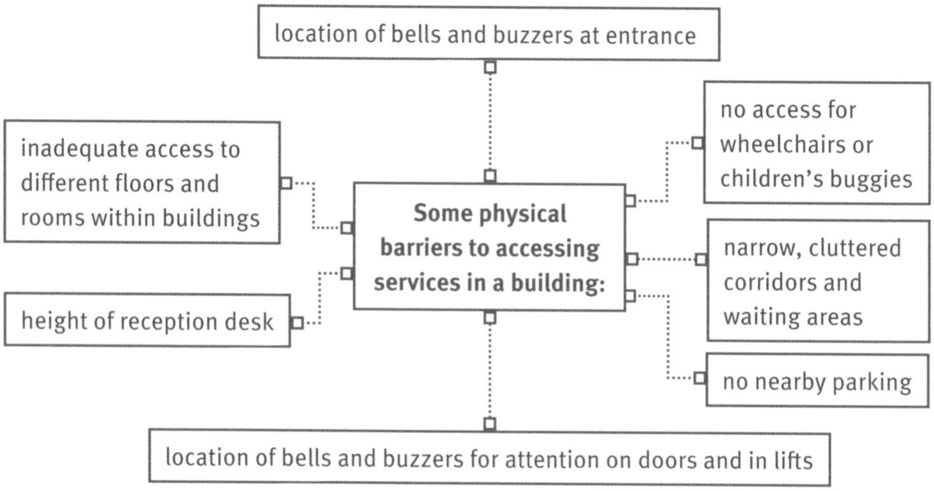

Figure 3.33: Bad design and layout will mean some people can't use the building

Physical barriers can be overcome by making adaptations such as:

- ramps through the main door
- lowering parts of the reception desks
- low buttons on doors or intercoms
- well-spaced seating
- wide automatic doors
- wide uncluttered corridors and disabled toilets.

Any transport provided should also be adapted.

Psychological

Psychological barriers to accessing services can happen when an individual may be too scared or worried to use a service, perhaps due to fear of contracting a superbug or losing their independence. Others may:

- be too proud to ask for help
- be embarrassed to be seen struggling
- be scared to find out what might be wrong with them
- feel there is a social **stigma** associated with some services such as mental health or weight loss.

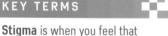

KEY TERMS

Stigma is when you feel that others disapprove of your circumstances and you have strong feelings of shame or embarrassment about something.

Information leaflets and other public information can help to overcome psychological barriers. So can offering help at places like pharmacists, which may seem less threatening than going to a health centre. Having someone go with the person can also help, as can having a private waiting room for those who have a problem they feel embarrassed about.

Financial

Financial barriers to accessing services can happen because of the charges and fees, which can exclude and put off those who do not have the money to pay for the services they need that are not provided on the NHS. These might include, for example, disability aids and prescriptions. Some services are means tested. This means an individual or family is examined to see whether they are eligible to receive benefits and free treatments.

Geographical

Geographical barriers to accessing services can happen due to where someone lives, for example:

- a rural area may not have many services or transport links
- individuals may be sent long distances to access a service.

Geographical barriers can be overcome by services such as hospital transport. Alternatively, travel to a hospital can sometimes be avoided by using health centres, pharmacists or helplines.

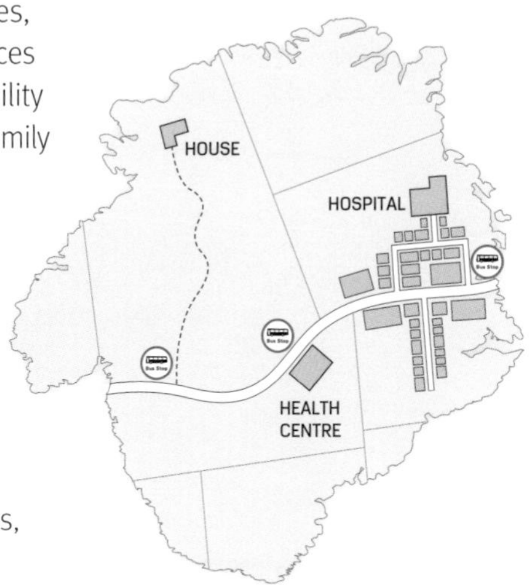

Figure 3.34: How could you overcome the barriers created by where someone lives?

Cultural and language

Language barriers to accessing services can happen when people speak a different language or do not understand the way things are expressed because of jargon, slang or dialect. Some individuals may not be used to female service providers because in their culture they are not used to dealing with women of a professional status.

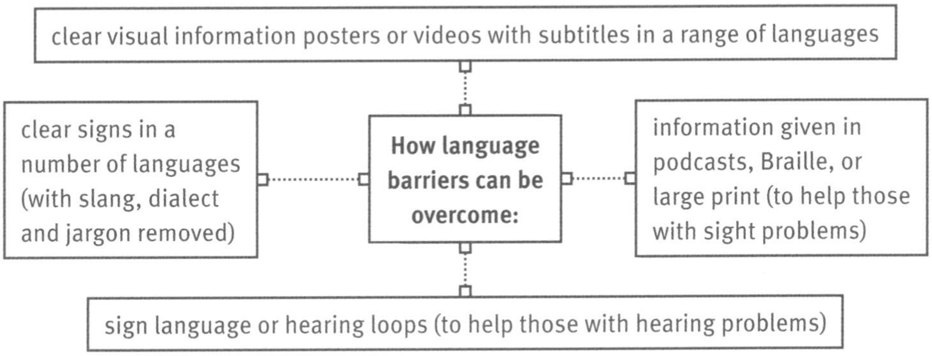

clear visual information posters or videos with subtitles in a range of languages
clear signs in a number of languages (with slang, dialect and jargon removed)
How language barriers can be overcome:
information given in podcasts, Braille, or large print (to help those with sight problems)
sign language or hearing loops (to help those with hearing problems)

Figure 3.35: Making communication accessible

Resources

Resource barriers can happen when there are staff shortages leading to, for example, a shortage of beds and too many people waiting long periods of time for an appointment.

ACTIVITY

1 Research local services that help individuals overcome obstacles they may face when implementing a health and wellbeing health improvement plan.

2 Draw a concept map based on barriers to accessing identified services, with branches for each type of barrier and strategies to overcome each type related to local identified services.

CHECK MY LEARNING

How can a person's culture or first language make them reluctant to access a service?

C: assessment practice

How you will be assessed

The final part of your externally set assessment involves Section B: Designing a health and wellbeing improvement plan, which consists of three activities.

- Activity 4 asks you to design a health and wellbeing improvement plan for the person in the case study covered in Section A (see pages 158–59 and pages 182–83), using the case study and the notes below.
- Activity 5 asks you to give a rationale for your plan, explaining how it takes into account the person's needs, wishes and circumstances.
- Activity 6 asks you to describe obstacles the person may face and suggest how these could be minimised.

CHECKPOINT

Strengthen

- What is meant by recommended action in a health and wellbeing improvement plan?
- What do you understand by the word 'rationale'?
- How can you identify the possible obstacles to the plan?

Challenge

- How can you make your explanation as to how the suggested support will help achieve the targets convincing?
- What do you need to do to make your explanation as to how the plan addresses needs, wishes and circumstances clear and comprehensive?
- How can you tell you have described the obstacles clearly with realistic suggestions for how these can be minimised?

ASSESSMENT ACTIVITY LEARNING AIM **C**

Before starting the practice assessment activity:

- look at the information about Susan from Activities 1, 2 and 3 (pages 158–59 and pages 182–83)
- study the notes below by the practice nurse.

Susan wants to:

- improve her mobility
- have more company
- lose weight
- reduce her drinking.

Susan does not want to:

- stop drinking completely
- give up chocolate completely.

Other information

Susan has tried to go for walks but finds it hard to get motivated to go on her own and does not like going up and down her steep driveway.

Activity 4

Design a health and wellbeing improvement plan for Susan. The plan should:

- describe three recommended actions
- set short- and long-term targets for each action
- suggest sources of support (formal and/or informal) and explain how these will help Susan achieve her targets.

Use three tables, each with these headings, to do this:

Recommended actions with short- and long-term targets	Sources of support and how these will help

(Total for Activity 4 = 12 marks)

Activity 5

Give a rationale for your plan that explains how it takes into account Susan's needs, wishes and circumstances.

(Total for Activity 5 = 10 marks)

Activity 6

Describe any obstacles Susan may face and suggest how these could be minimised.

(Total for Activity 6 = 8 marks)

TIPS

Read each part of the question carefully. If it asks you to describe three things, make sure your answer includes three points, not two!

TAKE IT FURTHER

Check that your health and wellbeing improvement plan clearly describes recommendations and gives sources of support to short- and long-term targets. Answers should include clear justifications for the plan on how it links to needs, wishes and circumstances and clearly describes obstacles with realistic suggestions to overcome them.

Glossary

Acute illness comes on quickly, is short-term and can be cured.
Adapt is to adjust to new conditions or circumstances.
Addiction is not having control of doing, taking or using something to the point where it could be harmful to you.
Arteries are blood vessels that carry blood away from the heart.
Bereavement is the process of coming to terms with the death of someone close.
Burnout is when a person becomes exhausted and stressed, usually due to excess pressure and frustration at work.
Cardiovascular system is the system that moves blood, nutrients and gases around our bodies. It is made up of the heart, blood and blood vessels; also known a circulatory system.
Characteristic is something that is typical of people at a particular life stage.
Chronic illness comes on gradually, is long-term (more than 3 months) and generally can be treated but not cured.
Classification involves grouping similar things into a category.
Collaboratively involves working well together.
Confidentiality is not passing on information or discussing a private conversation to anyone else.
Contentment is an emotional state when infants and children feel happy in their environment and with the way they are being cared for.
Development involves gaining new skills and abilities such as riding a bike.
Dignity is being respected and treated with care.
Domiciliary care is care and support given at home by a care worker to help a person with their daily life.
Empathy is being able to understand and share the feelings and views of another person.
Expected is a belief that something is likely to happen.
Formal support is given by a trained health and social care professional who is paid to provide support.
Gender role is the role and responsibilities determined by a person's gender.
Genetic inheritance is the genes a person inherits from their parents.
Goal is what you want to achieve in the long term.
Growth describes increased body size such as height, weight.
Identity is how you describe or define yourself.
Income is the money people receive from their work, savings, pension, benefits or investments.
Infancy begins from birth to 2 years.
Informal support often comes from friends and family who want to encourage you and are not paid.
Life circumstances impacts on day-to-day life and the choices you make.
Life events are expected or unexpected events that can affect development.
Life stages are distinct phases of life that each person passes through.
Lifestyle involves the choices made that affect health and development such as diet and exercise.
Long-term is 6 months or more.
Low self-esteem is when you do not feel good about yourself for any reason.
Material possessions are things owned by an individual.
Menopause is the ceasing of menstruation.
Monitor is to check progress over a period of time.
Neurological problems relate to the brain, spinal cord and nerves; for example a brain injury, stroke or multiple sclerosis.
Nicotine is a powerful, addictive drug found in tobacco.

Norm is something that is usual, typical or standard.
Person-centred approach is respecting and empowering individuals.
Physical events make changes to your body, physical health or mobility.
Physiological relates to how a person and their bodily parts function normally.
Physiotherapy involves massages, exercises and other treatments to help people gain physical health.
Pollution the act of introducing harmful substances or irritants that cause damage to living organisms into the environment.
Potential significance could develop into something important.
Professional describes a member of a profession who is trained and skilled in their area of work.
Psychological relates to the mental and emotional state of a person.
Relationship changes impact on informal and intimate relationships.
Respite care involves temporary care of an individual with ill health to provide relief for their parent(s) or usual carer.
Review involves assessing or inspecting something with the intention of making change if necessary.
Role model is someone a person admires and strives to be like.
Secondary care is specialist treatment or care such as psychiatry usually given in a hospital or clinic referred from a primary care service provider.
Self-esteem is how good or bad an individual feels about themselves and how much they value their abilities.
Self-image is how individuals see themselves or how they think others see them.
Self-respect is valuing yourself.
Sensory impairment is a weakness or difficulty that prevents a person from doing something.
Short-term is less than 6 months.
Social class is a broad group in society having the same social or economic status, most commonly upper, middle and lower class.
Stigma is when you feel that others disapprove of your circumstances and you have strong feelings of shame or embarrassment about something.
Targets are goals and aims.
Tertiary care is advanced specialist treatment or care given in hospital such as cancer treatment referred from a secondary care service provider.
Unexpected is not thought of as likely to happen.
Wealth is having lots of money and goods.

Index